Samuel Taylor Coleridge

Poetical and Dramatic Works

Vol. 1

Samuel Taylor Coleridge

Poetical and Dramatic Works
Vol. 1

ISBN/EAN: 9783337217839

Printed in Europe, USA, Canada, Australia, Japan

Cover: Foto ©Thomas Meinert / pixelio.de

More available books at **www.hansebooks.com**

THE POETICAL AND DRAMATIC WORKS OF SAMUEL TAYLOR COLERIDGE

FOUNDED ON THE AUTHOR'S LATEST EDITION OF 1834 WITH MANY ADDITIONAL PIECES NOW FIRST INCLUDED AND WITH A COLLECTION OF VARIOUS READINGS

IN FOUR VOLUMES

VOLUME ONE

London
MACMILLAN AND CO.
1880

CONTENTS.

JUVENILE POEMS:—   PAGE

Julia	3
Philedon	5
Anthem for the Children of Christ's Hospital	7
The Nose	9
To the Muse	10
Destruction of the Bastile	11
Music	13
Devonshire Roads	14
Inside the Coach	15
Monody on a Tea-Kettle	16
On Receiving an Account that his only Sister's death was inevitable	18
On seeing a Youth affectionately welcomed by a Sister	19
Pain	19
Life	20
Sonnet on quitting School for College	21
A Mathematical Poem	22
Introduction to a Greek Prize Ode on the Slave Trade	26
Time, Real and Imaginary: An Allegory	28
The Raven. A Christmas Tale	29
With Fielding's Amelia	31
Happiness	32
On Imitation	35
Progress of Vice	36

CONTENTS.

POEMS COLLECTED IN 1796-1797:— PAGE

Preface to Poems published in 1796	39
Preface to the Second Edition, published in 1797	43
Postscript to the Edition of 1797	45
Genevieve	47
Sonnet to the Autumnal Moon	47
Absence. A Farewell Ode on Quitting School for Jesus College, Cambridge	48
Songs of the Pixies	50
Monody on the Death of Chatterton	55
Lines on an Autumnal Evening	63
The Rose	68
The Kiss	69
To a Young Ass	70
The Sigh	72
Epitaph on an Infant	73
Lines written at the King's Arms, Ross	73
Lines to a Beautiful Spring in a Village	74
Lines on a Friend who died of a frenzy fever induced by calumnious reports	75
To a Young Lady, with a poem on the French Revolution	78
Imitated from the Welsh	80
To an Infant	80
Lines written at Shurton Bars	81
Lines to a Friend in answer to a melancholy letter	86
Religious Musings	88
To the Rev. W. J. H., while teaching a young lady some song-tunes on his flute	109
To a Friend, together with an Unfinished Poem	110
To the Nightingale	112
The Composition of a Kiss	113
Lines composed while climbing the left ascent of Brockley Coomb	114
Lines in the manner of Spenser	115
Imitated from Ossian	117
The Complaint of Ninathoma	118

CONTENTS.

POEMS COLLECTED IN 1796-1797 (*continued*) :— PAGE
   The Hour when we shall meet again . . . 119
   Written after a walk before supper . . . 120
   To Joseph Cottle 121
   The Silver Thimble 123

SONNETS :—
   Introduction to the Sonnets 129
   Sonnets on Eminent Characters :
      I. Stanhope 133
      II. Burke 134
      III. Priestley 134
      IV. La Fayette 135
      V. Kosciusko 136
      VI. Pitt 137
      VII. To the Rev. W. L. Bowles
         § First Version 138
         § Second Version 139
      VIII. Mrs. Siddons 140
      IX. To William Godwin 142
      X. To Robert Southey 143
      XI. To Richard Brinsley Sheridan . . . 144
      XII. Erskine 145
   Miscellaneous Sonnets :
      I. "Thou gentle look, that didst my soul beguile" 146
      II. To the River Otter 146
      III. "Sweet Mercy! how my very heart has bled" 147
      IV. "Pale roamer thro' the night, thou poor forlorn!" 148
      V. To the Author of *The Robbers* 148
      VI. Composed on a Journey homeward, the Author having received intelligence of the birth of a son 149
      VII. To a Friend who asked me how I felt when the Nurse presented my infant to me . . . 150
      VIII. "Thou bleedest, my poor heart, and thy distress" 151

CONTENTS.

POEMS COLLECTED IN 1796-1797 (*continued*) :—   PAGE

To an Unfortunate Woman, whom the Author had known in the days of her innocence . . 152
To a Friend, on his proposing to domesticate with the Author 153
On observing a Blossom on the first of February . 156
The Eolian Harp 157
Reflections on having left a place of retirement . 160
To the Rev. George Coleridge 163
Ode to the Departing Year 166

MISCELLANEOUS POEMS (1794-1797) :—

Melancholy, a Fragment 181
Parliamentary Oscillators 182
Imitation of Casimir 184
Fragment from an Unpublished Poem . . . 186
Count Rumford 186
On a late Connubial Rupture in High Life . . 187
The Destiny of Nations: A Vision . . . 188
Lines addressed to a young man of fortune who abandoned himself to an indolent and causeless melancholy 210
Sonnets of Nehemiah Higginbottom . . . 211
On the Christening of a Friend's Child . . 214
To a Primrose, the first seen in the season . . 216

APPENDIX :—

Translation of Coleridge's Greek Ode on Astronomy 219
Letter to the Monthly Magazine on his Monody on Chatterton 223
Note to "Lines on an Autumnal Evening" . . 224
Note to "The Silver Thimble" 224

MEMOIR

OF

SAMUEL TAYLOR COLERIDGE.

FROM 1760 to 1781, the pleasant little town of Ottery St. Mary in Devonshire had for its vicar the Rev. JOHN COLERIDGE, who was at the same time head-master of Henry VIII's Free Grammar-School, usually termed the King's School. Before his appointment to the School at Ottery, he had been head-master of the School at South Molton. He had assisted Dr. Kennicott in his Hebrew Bible, had published on his own account a Dissertation on part of the Book of Judges,* and some elementary Latin books for the use of his school, and was known beyond the narrow limits of his vicarage as a man of great learning and at the same time of great eccentricity. His profound erudition, combined with an equally profound ignorance and inexperience of the world and its usages, his primitive manners and guileless simplicity, made him a living realization of Parson Adams, with whom his illustrious son was wont in after life to compare him.† One of the learned Vicar's

<small>Coleridge's Father.</small>

---

* *Miscellaneous Dissertations arising from the* 17th *and* 18th *Chapters of the Book of Judges.* By the Rev. Mr. John Coleridge, Vicar of, and Schoolmaster at, Ottery St. Mary, Devon. London: Printed for the Author, 1768.

† De Quincey, in *Tait's Magazine*, Sept. 1834, p. 518; *The Life of Samuel Taylor Coleridge*, by *James Gillman*. Lond., William Pickering, 1838, p. 2.

elementary books on the Latin language made somewhat higher pretensions than a common school grammar. "In particular," says De Quincey, "an attempt is made to reform the theory of the cases; and it gives a pleasant specimen of the rustic scholar's *naïveté*, that he seriously proposes to banish such vexatious terms as the ablative; and, by way of simplifying the matter to tender minds, that we should call it, in all time to come, the *"quale-quare-quidditive"* case.* He used regularly to delight his village flock, on Sundays, with Hebrew quotations in his Sermons, which he always introduced as the "immediate language of the Holy Ghost." This proved unfortunate to his successor; he also was a learned man, and his parishioners admitted it, but generally with a sigh for past times and a sorrowful complaint that he was still

* *A Critical Latin Grammar, containing clear and distinct rules for boys just initiated; and Notes Explanatory of almost every antiquity and obscurity in the Language, for youth somewhat advanced in Latin Learning.* By John Coleridge, Vicar and Schoolmaster at Ottery St. Mary, Devon. London: Printed for the Author, 1772.

"The *Quale-quare-quidditive* Case is so called, because it denotes the manner of doing, *how,* the cause *why,* or the instrument *with which* the prior case effects its end."

The good Schoolmaster and Vicar also published:—

Sententiæ Excerptæ, explaining the Rules of Grammar, and the Various Signification of all the Prepositions, and

Government not originally proceeding from Human Agency, but Divine Institution, shewn in a Sermon preached at Ottery St. Mary, Devon, December 13, 1776, *on the Fast-Day, appointed by reason of our much-to-be-lamented American War, and published at the request of the hearers.* By John Coleridge, Vicar of, and Schoolmaster at Ottery St. Mary, Devon. London: Printed for the Author, 1777. 4to., pp. 15.

far below Parson Coleridge—for that *he* never gave them any "immediate language of the Holy Ghost:" Of the learned Vicar's absence of mind and short-sightedness his son used to relate a ludicrous instance. Dining in a large party, one day, the modest divine was suddenly shocked by perceiving some part, as he apprehended, of his own snowy shirt emerging from a part of his habiliments, which we shall suppose to have been his waistcoat. It was not that; but for decorum we shall so call it. The stray portion of his supposed tunic was admonished of its errors by a forcible thrust back into its proper home; but still another *limbus* persisted to emerge, or seemed to persist, and still another, until the learned gentleman absolutely perspired with the labour of re-establishing order. And after all, he saw with anguish, that some arrears of the snowy indecorum still remained to reduce into obedience. To this remnant of rebellion he was proceeding to apply himself when the mistress of the house, rising to lead away the ladies from the table, and all parties naturally rising with her, it became suddenly apparent to every eye that the worthy Orientalist had been most laboriously stowing away, into the capacious receptacles of his own habiliments, the snowy folds of a lady's gown, belonging to his next neighbour, and so voluminously, that a very small portion of it indeed remained for the lady's own use; the natural consequence of which was, of course, that the lady appeared inextricably yoked to the learned theologian, and could not in any way effect her release, until after certain operations on the Vicar's dress, and a continued refunding and rolling out of snowy mazes upon snowy mazes, in quantities which at length proved too much for the gravity of the company.

Stories of his absence of mind.

Inextinguishable laughter arose from all parties, except the erring and unhappy doctor, who, in dire perplexity, continued still refunding with all his might, until he had paid up the last arrears of his long debt, and thus put an end to a case of distress more memorable to himself and his parishioners than any "*qualequarc-quidditive*" case that probably had ever perplexed his learning.* On one occasion, having to breakfast with his bishop, he went, as was the practice of that day, into a barber's shop to have his head shaved, wigs being then in common use. Just as the operation was completed, the clock struck nine, the hour at which the bishop punctually breakfasted. Roused, as from a reverie, he instantly left the barber's shop, and in his haste forgetting his wig, appeared at the breakfast-table, where the bishop and his party had assembled. The bishop, well acquainted with his absent manners, courteously and playfully requested him to walk into an adjoining room, and give his opinion of a mirror which had arrived from London a few days previously, and which disclosed to his astonished guest the consequences of his haste and forgetfulness.† At another time, having to take a short journey on some professional business, which would detain him from home for three or four days, his good wife, in her care and watchfulness, had packed a few things in a small trunk, and gave them in charge to her husband with strong injunctions that he was to put on a clean shirt every day. On his return home, his wife went to search for his linen, when to her dismay, it was not in the trunk. A closer search, however, discovered

---

* De Quincey, *ubi suprâ*. This story is told somewhat differently by Mr. Gillman, pp. 4-5.

† Gillman, pp. 3-4.

that the Vicar had strictly obeyed her injunctions, and had put on daily a clean shirt, but had forgotten to remove the one underneath. This might have been the pleasantest and most portable mode of carrying half-a-dozen shirts in winter, but not so in the dog-days."*

Such was the father of SAMUEL TAYLOR COLERIDGE, who was born at Ottery St. Mary, on the 21st October, 1772, "about eleven o'clock in the forenoon," as the good Vicar, with rather a curious particularity, entered it in the register. Of his mother, the Vicar's second wife (whose maiden name was Ann Bowdon), a few words must also be said. She "seems to have been peculiarly fitted for the wife of a clergyman who had a large family and limited means. Her husband not possessing that knowledge usually termed worldly wisdom, she appeared to supply the place of the friend which such a man required in his wife. Though she had naturally a strong mind, and was industriously attentive to her household duties, and devoted to the care of her husband and family, she was, it seems, an uneducated woman." Possessing none of the most common female accomplishments of her day, she had neither love nor sympathy for the display of them in others. She disliked, as she would say, "your harpsichord ladies," and strongly tried to impress on her sons their little value, in their choice of wives. Though a very good woman, she was, like Martha, over careful in many things, very ambitious for the advancement of her sons in life, but wanting perhaps that flow of heart which her husband possessed so largely. †

<small>The poet's Mother.</small>

A valuable autobiographical note of Coleridge's, published by Mr. Gillman, may here be inserted.

* Gillman, p. 7.   † *Ib.* pp. 3, 6, 7.

"I was," says he, "the last child, the youngest child of ten by the same mother, that is to say, *John, William (who died in infancy), William, James, Edward, George, Luke, Ann, Francis, and myself, Samuel Taylor Coleridge, beneficially abridged Esteese (εστησε), i.e. S.T.C., and the thirteenth, taking in three sisters by my dear father's first wife,—Mary, afterwards Mrs. Bradley,—Sarah, who married a seaman

<small>Autobiographical Note on his Childhood.</small>

* (1) JOHN was a Captain in the East India Company's service; a successful officer, and a brave one. He died in India in 1786.

(2) WILLIAM went to Pembroke College, Oxford. Died a clergyman in 1780, just on the eve of his intended marriage. Against the title of the Vicar's Latin Grammar is printed:—
"A Proposal by William Coleridge, Son of the Author of this Grammar, for printing by subscription, price 5s. 6d., Greek Moral Sentences extracted from the purest Greek Authors, &c. The work will be revised by the Father." We do not know whether this announcement attracted sufficient encouragement to enable the book to appear.

(3) JAMES entered the army at the age of fifteen. Married a woman of fortune, one of the old Duke family of Otterton, in Devon. Father of Henry Nelson Coleridge, who married his cousin Sara, the poet's accomplished daughter, and of the late Mr. Justice Coleridge, and grandfather of the present Lord Coleridge of Ottery St. Mary.

(4) EDWARD, the wit of the family. Went like William to Pembroke College, and became a clergyman.

(5) GEORGE also went to Pembroke and took orders. Succeeded eventually to his father's School and Vicarage. Coleridge describes him as "a man of reflective mind and elegant talent. He possesses learning in a greater degree than any of the family, excepting myself. His manners are grave, and hued over with a tender sadness. In his moral character he approaches every way nearer to perfection than

and is lately dead, and Elizabeth, afterwards Mrs. Phillips—who alone was bred up with us after my birth, and whom alone of the three I was wont to think of as a sister, though not exactly, yet I did not know why, the same sort of sister as my sister Nancy. Being the youngest child, I possibly inherited the weakly state of health of my father, who died at the age of sixty-two, before I had reached my ninth year;

any man I ever yet knew. He is worth us all." (To Thomas Poole, March 1797.) To him Coleridge's volume of Juvenile Poems was dedicated in the second edition. *Vide infrà*, pp. 163-166.

(6) LUKE HERMAN was a surgeon, a severe student, and a good man. He died in 1790, leaving one child, a lovely boy, William Hart Coleridge, who became in 1824 Bishop of Barbadoes and the Leeward Islands, and afterwards Warden of St. Augustine's College, Canterbury.

(7) "My only sister, ANN, died at twenty-one, a little after my brother Luke :—

'Rest, gentle shade, and wait thy Maker's will;
Then rise unchanged, and be an angel still.'"

There are two poems referring to her early death (*Vide infrà*, pp. 18-19).

(8) FRANCIS-SYNDERCOMBE went out to India as a midshipman under Admiral Graves. He accidentally met his brother John on board ship abroad, who took him ashore and procured him a commission in the Company's army. He died in 1792, aged twenty-one, a lieutenant, in consequence of a fever brought on by excessive fatigue at and after the siege of Seringapatam and the storming of a hill fort, during all which his conduct had been so gallant that his commanding officer particularly noticed him. "All my brothers are remarkably handsome; but they were as inferior to Francis as I am to them. He went by the name of 'the handsome Coleridge.'" (S. T. C. to Thomas Poole.)

and from certain jealousies of old Molly, my brother Frank's dotingly fond nurse, (and if ever child by beauty and loveliness deserved to be doted on, my brother Francis was that child,) and by the infusions of her jealousy into my brother's mind, I was in earliest childhood huffed away from the enjoyments of muscular activity from play, to take refuge at my mother's side, on my little stool, to read my little book, and to listen to the talk of my elders. I was driven from life in motion, to life in thoughts and sensation. I never played except by myself, and then only acting over what I had been reading or fancying, or half one, half the other, with a stick cutting down weeds and nettles, as one of the seven champions of Christendom. Alas! I had all the simplicity, all the docility of the little child, but none of the child's habits. I never thought as a child, never had the language of a child. I forget whether it was in my fifth or sixth year, but I believe the latter, in consequence of some quarrel between me and my brother, in the first week in October, I ran away from fear of being whipped, and passed the whole night, a night of rain and storm, on the bleak side of a hill on the Otter, and was there found at daybreak, without the power of using my limbs, about six yards from the naked bank of the river.

"In my ninth year, about the same time, if not the very same time, i. e. Oct. 4th, my most dear, most revered father, died suddenly. O that I might so pass away, if like him, I were an Israelite without guile. The image of my father, my revered, kind, learned, simple-hearted father is a religion to me!"

Death of his father: Oct. 4, 1781.

Before he had attained his tenth year a presentation to Christ's Hospital was obtained for young Coleridge by Judge Buller, a former pupil of his father's. He was entered there on the 18th July, 1782. "Oh! what a change!" he continues, in the autobiographical note above quoted. "Depressed, moping, friendless, poor orphan, half-starved (at that time the portion of food to the Bluecoats was cruelly insufficient for those who had no friends to supply them)." To this early severance from his home and native place, there is a touching allusion in the Dedication of his Juvenile Poems to his brother George : {.margin: Entered at Christ's Hospital.}

> " Me from the spot where first I sprang to light
> Too soon transplanted, ere my soul had fix'd
> Its first domestic loves ; and hence through life
> Chasing chance-started friendships."*

Whatever deprivations and sufferings he had to undergo during his school-life at this period, and they seem to have been considerable (for Mr. Gillman dwells upon them with somewhat unpleasant particularity),† it is certain that he ere long began to distinguish himself among his school-mates. One of them with whom he maintained a life-long friendship, and who also was destined to become distinguished as an English writer, has left us in his own quaint and delightful style, a picture of Coleridge, as a Blue-coat boy :— {.margin: Charles Lamb.}

" Come back into memory, like as thou wert in the day-spring of thy fancies, with hope like a fiery column before thee—the dark pillar not yet turned—Samuel Taylor Coleridge—logician, metaphysician, bard !— How have I seen the casual passer through the cloisters

---

* *Vide infrà*, pp. 163, 164.
† *e. g.* pp., 16, 17, 18.

VOL. I.   b

stand still, entranced with admiration (while he weighed the disproportion between the *speech* and the *garb* of the young Mirandula), to hear thee unfold, in thy deep and sweet intonations, the mysteries of Iamblichus or Plotinus (for even in those years thou waxedst not pale at such philosophic draughts), or reciting Homer in his Greek, or Pindar—while the walls of the old Grey Friars re-echoed to the accents of the *inspired charity boy!*"*

Coleridge has himself informed us in his *Biographia Literaria* that he had translated the eight Hymns of Synesius from the Greek into English Anacreontics, before his fifteenth year. The severity and strict discipline of Bowyer the head master (of which several examples, as applied to Coleridge, are related by Mr. Gillman,†) was probably not in the main unsalutary. To Bowyer's powers as a teacher Coleridge has himself paid a high tribute.

As a natural consequence of the faculties and assiduity which he displayed, Coleridge was eventually chosen by his master as one of those destined for the University. "Against my will," says he, "I was chosen by my master as one of those destined for the university; and about this time my brother Luke, or 'the Doctor,' so called from his infancy, because being the seventh son, he had, from his infancy, been dedicated to the medical profession, came to town to walk the London Hospital under the care of Sir William Blizard. Mr. Saumarez, brother of the Admiral Lord Saumarez, was his intimate friend. Every Saturday I could make or obtain

_{Brother Luke.}

---

* *Christ's Hospital, London Magazine,* November 1820 (one of the Essays of Elia).

† pp. 20, 22, 24.

leave, to the London Hospital trudged I. O the bliss if I was permitted to hold the plaisters, or to attend the dressings. Thirty years afterwards, Mr. Saumarez retained the liveliest recollections of the extraordinary, enthusiastic blue-coat boy, and was exceedingly affected in identifying me with that boy. I became wild to be apprenticed to a surgeon. English, Latin, yea, Greek books of medicine read I incessantly. Blanchard's Latin Medical Dictionary I had nearly by heart. Briefly, it was a wild dream, which gradually blending with, gradually gave way to a rage for metaphysics, occasioned by the Essays on Liberty and Necessity in Cato's Letters, and more by theology.* S.T.C. studies medicine.

About this time he also became acquainted with a widow lady, "whose son," says he, " I, as upper boy, had protected, and who therefore looked up to me, and taught me what it was to have a mother. I loved her as such. She had three daughters, and of course I fell in love with the eldest. From this time to my nineteenth year, when I quitted school for Jesus, Cambridge, was the era of poetry and love." An early love.

Coleridge left Christ's Hospital on 7th September, 1790, and entered at Jesus College, Cambridge, on 5th February, 1791. In the summer of the same year he gained Sir William Browne's gold medal for a Greek Ode on the Slave Trade.‡ At Cambridge.

---

* Gillman, pp. 22, 23.   † *Ib*, p. 28.

‡ The Introduction to this Ode is printed in the present volume, *infrà*, pp. 26, 27; the remainder does not appear to be now extant.

The following account of Coleridge's University life has been given by a schoolfellow who followed him from Christ's Hospital to Cambridge in 1792 :—"He was very studious, but his reading was desultory and capricious. He took little exercise merely for the sake of exercise; but he was ready at any time to unbend his mind in conversation; and, for the sake of this, his room (the ground-floor room on the right hand of the staircase facing the great gate) was a constant rendezvous of conversation-loving friends; I will not call them loungers, for they did not call to kill time, but to enjoy it. What evenings have I spent in those rooms! What little suppers, or *sizings*, as they were called, have I enjoyed; when Æschylus, and Plato, and Thucydides were pushed aside, with a pile of lexicons, &c. to discuss the pamphlets of the day. Ever and anon a pamphlet issued from the pen of Burke. There was no need of having the book before us. Coleridge had read it in the morning, and in the evening he would repeat whole pages verbatim. Frend's trial was then in progress. Pamphlets swarmed from the press. Coleridge had read them all; and in the evening, with our negus, we had them *viva voce* gloriously."*

[margin: C. V. Le Grice.]

In 1793 Coleridge wrote a Greek Ode on Astronomy, but was unsuccessful in obtaining the prize. † The original is not now known to exist; but a translation of it into English verse, made by Robert Southey eight years

[margin: Greek Ode on Astronomy.]

* *Gentleman's Magazine*, December 1834.

† "The finest Greek Poem I ever wrote lost the prize, and that which gained it was contemptible."
    S. T. C. *to Joseph Cottle*, Stowey, 1797.

afterwards, will be found in the Appendix to the present volume.* He passed the long vacation this year at his native place, and it was during this visit that he produced the *Songs of the Pixies*.† He returned to Cambridge in October; and in the following month, in chagrin at his disappointment in a love-affair,‡ or as others say in a fit of dejection and despondency, caused by some debts not amounting to a hundred pounds, Coleridge suddenly left his College and went up to London. *Quits college suddenly.* This gave rise to one of the most singular adventures in his early life, which has been related in many different ways, but of the substantial facts of which there can be no doubt whatever. Coming as

* pp. 219-222.   † pp. 50-55.

‡ Some affair of this kind is obscurely but pathetically enough hinted at in the course of a letter addressed to his college-friend Masters (July 22, 1794), during the tour in Wales already alluded to:—"It had entirely escaped my memory that Wrexham was the residence of a Miss E. Evans, a young lady with whom in happier days I had been in habits of fraternal correspondence.... As I was standing at the window of the inn, she passed by, and with her, to my utter astonishment, her sister, Mary Evans, *quam afflictim et perdite amabam*,—yea even to anguish. They both started, and gave a short cry, almost a faint shriek; I sickened, and well nigh fainted, but instantly retired. Had I appeared to recognise her, my fortitude would not have supported me :—

Vivit, sed mihi non vivit—nova forte marita.
Ah, dolor! alterius nunc a cervice pependit.
Vos, malefida valete accensæ insomnia mentis,
Littora amata valete; vale, ah! formosa Maria.

(Biographical Supplement to *Biographia Literaria*, vol. ii, p. 340.)

might have been expected in a few days to the end of his slender resources, and apprehensive of being cast adrift and reduced to want in the great wilderness of London, he chanced to observe a recruiting advertisement, applied to the serjeant, was marched down to Reading, and regularly enlisted as a private in the 15th Light Dragoons on the 3rd December 1793, under the name of "Silas Titus Comberback."

Enlists as a dragoon.

"Being at a loss when suddenly asked my name," he writes, "I answered *Comberback;* and verily my habits were so little equestrian, that my horse I doubt not was of that opinion." Coleridge continued four months as a light dragoon; of his misadventures during that time; of his clumsiness in riding and grooming his horse; and of the causes which eventually led to his discovery and discharge, various versions exist:* his superior officer by an accident

---

* Mr. Gillman tells the story with ridiculous circumstantiality (pp. 57-62); as does also poor Mr. Bowles, in the following letter to the *Times* which appeared only a few days after Coleridge's death; and in which the reverend writer is pleased to inform us that what in his opinion is "by far the most correct, sublime, chaste and beautiful of Coleridge's poems (*Religious Musings*), was written *non inter sylvas academi*, but in the tap-room at Reading."

THE LATE MR. COLERIDGE A COMMON SOLDIER

(*Times :* August 13, 1834).

"I am perhaps the only person now living who can explain all the circumstances from Mr. Coleridge's own mouth, with whom I became acquainted after a Sonnet addressed to me in his Poems; moreover, being intimate from our school-days and at Oxford with that very officer in his regiment who alone detected his education, and the chance recognition of an acquaintance in the street eventually led to his friends being communicated with: the upshot was that he obtained his discharge (not at Reading but) at Hounslow on the 10th April, 1794, and returned again to Cambridge.

Is discharged and returns to Cambridge.

procured his discharge, from whom also I heard the facts after Coleridge became known as a poet.

"The regiment was the 15th Elliot's Light Dragoons: the officer was Nathaniel Ogle, eldest son of Dr. Newton Ogle, Dean of Winchester; I believe he was then Captain of Coleridge's troop. Going into the stables at Reading, he remarked written on the white wall, under one of the saddles, in large pencil characters:—

"'*Eheu! quam infortunii miserrimum est fuisse felicem!*'

"Being struck with the circumstance, and himself a scholar, Captain Ogle inquired of a soldier whether he knew to whom the saddle belonged. 'Please your honour, to Comberback,' answered the dragoon. 'Comberback!' said his captain, 'send him to me.' Comberback presented himself, with the inside of his hand in front of his cap. His officer mildly said, 'Comberback, did you write the Latin sentence which I have just read under your saddle?' [Comberback confessing, the Captain replied] 'Then, my lad, you are not what you appear to be. I shall speak to the commanding officer and you may depend on my speaking as a friend.' The commanding officer, I think, was General Churchill. When he enlisted he was asked his name. He hesitated, but saw the name Camberback over a shop door near Westminster-bridge, and instantly said his name was "Comberback." Comberback was examined, and it was found out that having left Jesus College, Cambridge, and being in London without resources, he had enlisted in this regiment. He was soon discharged,—not from his democratical feelings, for whatever those feelings

In the following June, at the commencement of the Long Vacation, Coleridge went to Oxford on a visit to an old school-fellow, where an accidental introduction to Robert Southey, then an undergraduate of Balliol, laid the foundations of a friendship destined largely to influence their future lives. In July he left Oxford, and with two or three acquaintances made a pedestrian tour in Wales. It was on this occasion that the *Lines on the Man of Ross* * were composed.

Introduction to Southey.

Walking tour in Wales.

In the course of the ensuing August, Coleridge, having returned from his excursion in Wales, came to Bristol; and Southey, who was then at Bath, having gone over to meet him, introduced him to Robert Lovell, through whom, it appears, they both at this time became known to Mr. Cottle the bookseller; and here, also, Coleridge first became acquainted with his future wife, Sarah Fricker, the eldest of five sisters, one of whom, Mary, was married to Robert Lovell, a third, Edith, having been engaged for some time to Southey. They were the

might be, as a soldier he was remarkably orderly and obedient, though he could not rub down his own horse. He was discharged from respect to his friends and his station. His friends having been informed of his situation, a chaise was soon at the door of the Bear Inn, Reading, and the Officers of the 15th cordially shaking his hands, particularly the officer who had been the means of his discharge, he drove off, not without a tear in his eye, whilst his old companions of the tap-room gave him three hearty cheers as the wheels rapidly rolled away along the Bath road to London and Cambridge. WILLIAM L. BOWLES.
"To the Editor of *The Times*."

* pp. 73, 74.

daughters of Stephen Fricker, who had carried on a large manufactory of sugar-pans or moulds at Westbury, near Bristol, and, who having fallen into difficulties, in consequence of the stoppage of trade by the American war, had lately died, leaving his widow and six children wholly unprovided for. "Never," says De Quincey, "was there a baser insinuation, viler in the motive, or more ignoble in the manner, than that passage in '*Don Juan*,' where, by way of vengeance on Southey, Lord Byron described both him and Coleridge as having married two 'milliners from Bath.' . . . The whole sting of the libel was a pure falsehood of Lord Byron's. Bath was not the native city, nor at any time the residence of the ladies in question, but Bristol. As to the other word "milliners," that is not worth inquiring about. Whether they, or any one of their family, ever did exercise this profession, I do not know: they were at all events too young, when removed by marriage from Bristol, to have been much tainted by the worldly feelings which may beset such a mode of life. But what is more to the purpose . . . the whole family of four or five sisters had maintained an irreproachable character, though naturally exposed by their personal attractions to some peril and the malevolence of envy." *

The Fricker sisters.

It was during this visit to Bath that the tragedy entitled *The Fall of Robespierre* was written.†

From Bath, after a brief visit to London, Coleridge returned for the last time, in September, as a student,

---

* *Tait's Magazine*, Sept. 1834.

† The circumstances of its composition are related more fully in a quotation from a letter of Southey's, printed in Vol. iii. p. 2.

to Cambridge, full of the new scheme of Pantisocracy and emigration to the Susquehana, in which Southey, Lovell, Favell, Burnett, Robert Allen, Le Grice and others, with Southey's mother and all the Frickers, were to join him. After being talked about, and forming the subject of many plans, letters and conversations, this wild and extravagant project was in the course of about a year abandoned, as might have been expected.

Pantisocracy.

Michaelmas Term of 1794 was the last which Coleridge kept in Cambridge. We find him spending the vacation following in London, mainly with Charles Lamb. At this period his series of "Sonnets on Eminent Characters" and a few other pieces, appeared from time to time in the *Morning Chronicle*. Lamb refers in his letters to their meetings during this season at the "Cat and Salutation."

Coleridge and Lamb at the Salutation.

Poems in the Morning Chronicle.

The lines "to a Friend, together with an unfinished Poem," dated December 1794,* were addressed to Lamb before the dark shadow had fallen over his life: they refer to Mary Lamb also, and to her brother's affectionate tendance at her sick-bed, and Coleridge alludes also to the early loss of his own only sister, a few years before.

In the beginning of 1795 Coleridge returned with Southey to Bristol. During the spring and summer of this year he devoted himself to the delivery of public lectures in that city. Of these the first four (or the substance of them), delivered in the month of February, were shortly afterwards printed in a pamphlet form.†

Lectures at Bristol.

---

* *Vide infrà*, pp. 110-112.
† 1. *A Moral and Political Lecture, delivered at Bristol.* By

In a copy of the *Conciones ad Populum*, on reperusing it far on in later life at Highgate, Coleridge wrote the following remarks, in defence of his substantial political consistency throughout the whole of his career as an author :—" Except the two or three pages involving the doctrine of philosophical necessity and Unitarianism, I see little or nothing in these outbursts of my youthful zeal to retract, and with the exception of some flame-coloured epithets applied to persons, as to Mr. Pitt and others, or rather to personifications (for such they really were to me), as little to regret. *Qualis ab initio* ἐστήση (S. T. C).

In June and July Coleridge gave a course of six lectures, presenting a comparative view of the Civil War under Charles I. and the French Revolution. The tone throughout them all was vehemently hostile to the policy of the great Minister of that day; but it was equally opposed to the spirit and maxims of Jacobinism.

Another course of six Lectures followed "On Revealed Religion, its corruptions, and its political views." The Prospectus states that " these Lectures are intended Second course of Lectures.

S. T. Coleridge, of Jesus College, Cambridge. Bristol: Printed by George Routh, in Corn-Street, (price sixpence), pp. 19: substantially the same as the Introductory Address in the *Conciones*. Noticed in the *Critical Review* of April 1795.

2. *Conciones ad Populum, or Addresses to the People.* By S. T. Coleridge, 1795, pp. 69. The Preface is dated Clevedon, November 16, 1795. Then follows "A Letter from Liberty to her dear friend Famine." § Introductory Address, dated February 1795. § On the Present War, same date.

3. *The Plot Discovered; or An Address to the People, against Ministerial Treason.* By S. T. Coleridge. Bristol, 1795, pp. 52.

for two classes of men, Christians and Infidels; to the former, that they may be able to give a reason for the hope that is in them;—to the latter, that they may not determine against Christianity from arguments applicable to its corruptions only." Nothing remains of these Addresses, nor of two detached Lectures or Sermons on the Slave Trade and the Hair Powder Tax, which were delivered in the interval between the two principal courses.

It has been stated by one of his biographers,* that during an excursion into Somersetshire in the summer of this year, Coleridge first met Wordsworth at the house of a Mr. Pinney, and Mr. Gillman † had seen (he says) a letter of this period from Wordsworth to a brother of Charles Mathews the elder, who was at that time educating for the bar, in which Wordsworth wrote: "To-morrow I am going to Bristol to see those two extraordinary young men, Southey and Coleridge." If Wordsworth and Coleridge actually met once or twice at so early a period, which for reasons one and another I take leave to doubt,‡ it is certain that they did not become intimate until two years later.

Supposed first meeting with Wordsworth.

On the 4th October, 1795, Samuel Taylor Coleridge was married at St. Mary Redcliffe Church, Bristol, to Sarah (or as he always insisted on spelling it, Sara §) Fricker, and went to reside in

Marriage.

---

* Henry Nelson Coleridge, in the Biographical Supplement to *Biographia Literaria* (vol. ii. p. 346).

† *Life of Coleridge*, p. 74.   ‡ See Note *infrà*, p. 82.

§ "My love to Sara, if so it must be . . . . however, as it is the casting out of a *spiritus asper*, which is an *evil spirit*—for the omen's sake, Amen!"—*Southey to Coleridge*, Bristol, Aug. 4, 1802.

a cottage at Clevedon on the Bristol Channel, which is described in two of his early poems.* "The cottage," says kind Mr. Cottle, who visited the newly-married pair a few days afterwards, "possessed everything that heart could desire. The situation also was peculiarly eligible. It was in the extremity, not in the centre of the village. It had the benefit of being but one story high; the rent was only five pounds per annum, and the taxes nought. There was also a small garden with several pretty flowers; and the "tallest rose-tree" failed not to be pointed out, which "peeped at the chamber window." I observed, however, that the parlour, from my perverted taste, looked rather awkward, in being only whitewashed, and the same effected in rather the olden time; to remedy which fanciful inconvenience, on my return to Bristol, I sent an honest upholsterer down to this retired and happy abode, with a few pieces of sprightly paper, to tarnish the half immaculate sitting-room walls.... The cottage at Clevedon had walls and doors and windows; but furniture only such as became a philosopher."†

Cottage at Clevedon.

Means were now wanting, however, to keep love warm even in a cottage, and Coleridge was determined to be up and doing. He had taken of late to preaching occasionally in Unitarian pulpits; and he had vague projects for establishing a school. The latter scheme never came to any maturity, and was ap-

* *The Eolian Harp*, infrà, p. 157; *Reflections on having left a place of retirement*, p. 160.

† *Early Recollections chiefly relating to the late Samuel Taylor Coleridge during his long residence in Bristol*, by Joseph Cottle, Lond. 1837, vol. i. pp. 58-60.

parently abandoned. But in the early part of 1796 Coleridge issued the Prospectus of a small newspaper-magazine, to be published every eight days and to be entitled *The Watchman*. He made a canvassing tour in the midland counties, to obtain subscribers, preaching also in the various towns through which he passed; and though his applications were in some cases met with rebuffs*—with boorish incivility or bovine obtuse-

<small>Starts *The Watchman*.</small>

---

* "I set off on a tour to the north, from Bristol to Sheffield, for the purpose of procuring customers, preaching by the way in most of the great towns, as a hireless volunteer, in a blue coat and white waistcoat, that not a rag of the woman of Babylon might be seen on me; for I was at that time, though a Trinitarian (*i. e. ad normam Platonis*) in philosophy, yet a zealous Unitarian in religion... My campaign commenced at Birmingham, and my first attack was on a rigid Calvinist, a tallow-chandler by trade. He was a tall dingy man, in whom length was so predominant over breadth, that he might almost have been borrowed for a foundry poker. O that face! a face κατ' ἔμφασιν! I have it before me at this moment. The lank, black, twine-like hair, pingui-nitescent, cut in a straight line, along the black stubble of his thin gunpowder eyebrows, that looked like a scorched aftermath from a last week's shaving. His coat-collar behind in perfect unison, both of colour and lustre, with the coarse yet glib cordage that I suppose he called his hair, and which with a bend inward at the nape of the neck, (the only approach to flexure in his whole figure) slunk in behind his waistcoat; while the countenance lank, dark, very hard, and with strong perpendicular furrows, gave me a dim notion of some one looking at me through a used gridiron, all soot, grease, and iron!... A person to whom one of my letters of recommendation had been addressed, was my introducer. It was a new event in my life, my first stroke in the new business I had

ness—he returned after several weeks' absence not in
undertaken of an author; yea, and of an author trading on his
own account. My companion after some imperfect sentences,
and a multitude of hums and hahs, abandoned the cause to his
client; and I commenced an harangue of half an hour to
Phileleutheros, the tallow-chandler, varying my notes through
the whole gamut of eloquence, from the ratiocinative to the
declamatory, and, in the latter, from the pathetic to the indignant.... My taper man of lights listened with perseverant and
praiseworthy patience, though (as I was afterwards told, in
complaining of certain gales that were not altogether ambrosial) it was a melting-day with him. "And what, sir!" he
said, after a short pause, "might the cost be?" "Only FOUR-
PENCE," (O! how I felt the anti-climax, the abysmal bathos of
that FOURPENCE!) "*only fourpence, sir, each number, to be published on every eighth day.*" "That comes to a deal of money at
the end of a year. And how much did you say there was to be
for the money?" "Thirty-two pages, sir, large octavo, closely
printed." "Thirty and two pages? Bless me, why except
what I does in a family way on the Sabbath, that's more than
I ever reads, sir! all the year round. I am as great a one as
any man in Brummagem, sir, for liberty and truth, and all
them sort of things, but as to this, (no offence, I hope, sir!) I
must beg to be excused."...

" From this rememberable tour I returned with nearly a
thousand names on the subscription list of the 'Watchman;'
yet more than half convinced that prudence dictated the abandonment of the scheme. But for this very reason I persevered in
it; for I was at that period of my life so completely hag-
ridden by the fear of being influenced by selfish motives, that
to know a mode of conduct to be the dictate of *prudence*, was
a sort of presumptive proof to my feelings that the contrary
was the dictate of *duty*. Accordingly I commenced the
work, which was announced in London by long bills in letters
larger than had ever been seen before, and which eclipsed the
glories even of the lottery puffs. But, alas! the publication of

the main unsuccessful. During this tour, it may be the very first number was delayed beyond the day announced for its appearance. In the second number, an essay against fast days, with a most censurable application of a text from Isaiah,* for its motto, lost me near five hundred of my subscribers at one blow. In the two following numbers I made enemies of all my Jacobin and democratic patrons; for, disgusted by their infidelity and their adoption of French morals, and French philosophy, and, perhaps, thinking that charity ought to begin nearest home, instead of abusing the government and the aristocrats chiefly or entirely, as had been expected of me, I levelled my attacks at '*modern patriotism*,'. and even ventured to declare my belief, that whatever the motives of ministers might have been for the sedition (or as it was then the fashion to call them the *gagging*) bills, yet the bills themselves would produce an effect to be desired by all the true friends of freedom, as far as they should contribute to deter men from openly declaiming on subjects, the principles of which they had never bottomed, and from 'pleading *to* the poor and ignorant, instead of pleading *for* them.' At the same time I avowed my conviction, that national education, and a concurring spread of the gospel were the indispensable condition of any true political amelioration. Thus, by the time the seventh number was published, I had the mortification of seeing the preceding numbers exposed in sundry old iron shops for a penny a piece. At the tenth number I dropped the work, and I should have been inevitably thrown into jail by my printer, if the money had not been paid for me by a man by no means affluent, a dear friend who attached himself to me from my first arrival at Bristol, who has continued my friend with a fidelity unconquered by time, or even by my own apparent neglect; a friend from whom I never received an advice that was not wise, or a remonstrance that was not gentle and affectionate.... Of the unsaleable nature

---

* " Wherefore my bowels shall sound like an harp." ISAIAH XVI. 11.

remarked, he wrote, while near Sheffield, the lines "On observing a blossom on the first of February."*

The first number of *The Watchman* appeared on March 1, and the tenth and last on May 14, 1796. The venture proved a pecuniary loss both to the Editor and to his friend Cottle, who had helped him by supplying the paper and otherwise. The money in many cases was not forthcoming from the agents in London and other places, and was frequently not paid by private subscribers.

In the meantime, early in April, a more promising venture, viz. Coleridge's first volume of Poems, had appeared at Bristol † under the auspices of his friend Cottle,‡ who had generously given the author thirty guineas for the copy-

First Volume of Poems.

---

of my writings I had an amusing memento one morning from our servant girl. For happening to rise at an earlier hour than usual, I observed her putting an extravagant quantity of paper into the grate in order to light the fire, and mildly checked her for her wastefulness; "La, Sir!" (replied poor Nanny) "why, it is only WATCHMEN!" (*Biographia Literaria*, Lond. 1817, Vol. 1. pp. 168-178.)

* *infrà*, p. 56.

† *Poems on various Subjects, by S. T. Coleridge, late of Jesus College, Cambridge.* [Motto from STAT. *Silv.* liv. iv. 4.] London: printed for G. G. and J. Robinsons, and J. Cottle, bookseller, Bristol, 1796, pp. xvi. 188 (and two leaves of Errata and Advertisements).

‡ Joseph Cottle was a bookseller and publisher in Bristol from 1791 to 1798: he retired from business in the latter year shortly after the publication of *Lyrical Ballads*, the joint production of Coleridge and Wordsworth.

right, and advanced him the money as his occasions required. In this volume were printed three or four sonnets of Charles Lamb's. "The effusions signed C. L.," says Coleridge, at the end of the Preface, "were written by Mr. Charles Lamb, of the India House—independently of the signature their superior merit would have sufficiently distinguished them."

The Contents of this volume were as follows (the page being indicated after each piece at which it appears in the present edition) :—

Page in orig. ed.		Page in present edition.
1	Monody on the Death of Chatterton	55
12	To the Rev. W. J. H., while teaching a young lady some song-tunes on his flute	109
15	Songs of the Pixies	50
26	Lines written at the King's Arms, Ross, formerly the house of the "Man of Ross"	73
28	Lines to a Beautiful Spring in a village	74
31	Epitaph on an Infant	73
32	Lines on a Friend who died of a frenzy fever induced by calumnious reports	75
36	To a Young Lady with a Poem on the French Revolution	78
40	Absence. A Farewell Ode	48

EFFUSIONS.

45	I. "My heart has thank'd thee, Bowles, for those soft strains"	139
46	II. "As late I lay in Slumber's shadowy vale"	134
47	III. "Not always should the tear's ambrosial dew"	137
48	IV. "Tho' roused by that dark Vizir Riot rude"	134

Page in orig. ed.			Page in present edition.
49	V.	"When British Freedom for an happier land"	145
50	VI.	"It was some spirit, Sheridan, that breathed"	144
51	VII.	"As when a child on some long winter's night"*	140
52	VIII.	"O what a loud and fearful shriek was there"	136
53	IX.	"As when far off the warbled strains are heard"	135
54	X.	"Not, Stanhope! with the Patriot's doubtful name"	133
55	XI.	"Was it some sweet device of faeryland"	(C. L.)†
56	XII.	"Methinks how dainty sweet it were, reclined"	(C. L.)
57	XIII.	Written at Midnight, by the seaside, after a voyage	(C. L.)‡

* Signed C. L., but retained in the edition of 1803, from which Lamb's other contributions were eliminated. *Vide in loco.*

† This Sonnet of Lamb's was much altered by Coleridge, not to the satisfaction of the former. In the edition of 1797 it was restored by Lamb's wish to its original form, as he wrote it. "The wand of Merlin," he writes to Coleridge (Jan. 10, 1797), "looks so like Mr. Merlin, the ingenious successor of the immortal Merlin, now living in good health and spirits, and flourishing in magical reputation in Oxford Street," &c.

‡ Coleridge altered the last two lines thus :—
 "How Reason reel'd! What gloomy transports rose!
 Till the rude dashings rock'd them to repose."
Lamb writes (June 11, 1796) that "these are good lines, but

Page in orig. ed.			Page in present edition.
59	XIV.	"Thou gentle look, that didst my soul beguile"	146
60	XV.	"Pale Roamer thro' the night, thou poor forlorn!" . . .	148
61	XVI.	"Sweet Mercy! how my very heart has bled"	147
62	XVII.	"Maid of my love! sweet Genevieve"	47
63	XVIII.	To the Autumnal Moon . . .	47
64	XIX.	"Thou bleedest, my poor heart, and thy distress"	151
65	XX.	To the Author of *The Robbers* . .	148
66	XXI.	Composed while climbing the left ascent of Brockley Coomb, in the County of Somerset, May 1795 .	114
68	XXII.	To a Friend, together with an unfinished Poem	110
71	XXIII.	To the Nightingale	112
73	XXIV.	In the Manner of Spenser . .	115
77	XXV.	To Domestic Peace * (Vol. III. p. 14)	
78	XXVI.	On a Kiss	113
80	XXVII.	"As late each flower that sweetest blows"	68
82	XXVIII.	"One kiss, dear maid! I said and sigh'd"	69

must spoil the whole with me who know it is only a fiction of yours, and that the 'rude dashings' did in fact not 'rock me to repose.'" Two rows of asterisks replaced these lines in the edition of 1797; the reader will find Lamb's own lines in his collected Works.

* In its original position, as a Song in the First Act of *The Fall of Robespierre*.

Page in orig. ed.			Page in present edition.
84	XXIX.	Imitated from Ossian	117
86	XXX.	Complaint of Ninathoma	118
88	XXXI.	From the Welsh	80
89	XXXII.	The Sigh	72
91	XXXIII.	To a Young Ass	70
94	XXXIV.	To an Infant	80
96	XXXV.	Written at Clevedon	157
101	XXXVI.	Written in Early Youth	63

EPISTLES.

111	I.	Written at Shurton Bars.	81
119	II.	To a Friend in answer to a melancholy Letter	86
122	III.	Written after a Walk	120
125	IV.	To the Author of Poems published in Bristol	121
129	V.	From a Young Lady *	123
139		Religious Musings	88

Inconveniences connected with his residence at Clevedon, not at first taken into the calculation, had compelled Coleridge to forsake with reluctance his rose-bound cottage, and to take up his abode at Bristol. *Quits Clevedon.* During his journey to the North, to collect subscribers for *The Watchman*, an accident had introduced him at Birmingham to Charles Lloyd, the eldest son of the eminent banker of that town. The admiration excited in Lloyd by Coleridge's genius and eloquence resulted in an ardent desire to domesticate himself permanently with a man

---

* A portion of this Epistle was probably written by Mrs. Coleridge. But *vide infrà*, p. 224.

whose conversation was to him a revelation from Heaven. The preliminaries having been settled, and the parents of Lloyd having given their consent to the arrangement, Coleridge went to Birmingham on Saturday, September 17, to have an interview with Lloyd's father.* Here, on the following Tuesday morning, he was surprised by a letter from the medical attendant informing him of the birth of a son on the previous day, Monday, 19th September, 1796. The child was named after the metaphy-sician whose writings Coleridge at this time prized so highly, David Hartley.† His feelings on receiving the intelligence and on first beholding the infant are recorded in three Sonnets, two of which appeared in the Second Edition of his Poems. He hastened home, and Charles Lloyd returned with him, and remained with him, first at Bristol and afterwards at Stowey, until the close of 1797.‡

Birth of his son Hartley.

---

* See the lines "to C. Lloyd on his proposing to domesticate with the Author," printed in the Second Edition of Coleridge's Poems, 1797 (p. 153 of the present volume).

† "Hartley's name was given him in honour of the metaphysician, David Hartley; and had he been baptized in his infancy, he would have borne both names. His baptism did not, in fact, take place till within the period of his distinct remembrance. The three surviving children, Hartley, Derwent and Sara, were all brought to the sacred font together, in the parish church of Crosthwaite, near Keswick." *Memoir of Hartley Coleridge. By his Brother.* (Prefixed to Hartley Coleridge's Poems. Moxon, 1851,) pp. xxii-xxiv.

‡ Vol. i. pp. 149, 150; and Vol. ii. p. 369, of the present edition.

The *Ode to the Departing Year* was composed on the 24th, 25th and 26th December, 1796, at the request of Mr. Flower, the editor of *The Cambridge Intelligencer*, in which paper it originally appeared on the last day of the year. It was immediately afterwards published in a separate form, as a thin quarto pamphlet,* accompanied by some *Lines addressed to a Young Man of Fortune who abandoned himself to an indolent and causeless Melancholy* † (most likely his new friend Charles Lloyd), and preceded by a long Dedication in prose to Thomas Poole, of Nether Stowey.

Ode to the Departing Year.

To Nether Stowey, accompanied by Lloyd, he removed early in the year 1797, in order to become a neighbour of his friend Poole, who had placed a cottage there at his disposal. From this new and delightful abode, where he passed the happiest and on the whole the most fruitful year of his life, the Dedicatory Lines to his brother George, prefixed to the second edition of his Poems, are dated. In this second edition nineteen pieces of the former publication were discarded, and twelve new pieces added. Several of these have been already enumerated : here follows a complete list of them :—

Removes to Nether Stowey.

Second Edition of Poems.

---

* *Ode on the Departing Year*, by S. T. Coleridge. Bristol: Printed by N. Biggs, and sold by J. Parsons, Paternoster-row, London, 1796, 4to pp. 16.

† *Vide infrà*, p. 210.

NEW PIECES IN THE EDITION OF 1797.

Page in present edition.

1. Dedication 163
2. Ode to the New Year * 166
3. Sonnet. To the River Otter . . . 146
4. Sonnet. On the birth of a son . . . 149
5. Sonnet. On first seeing my infant . . 150
6. On leaving a place of residence . . . 160
7. On an Unfortunate Woman 152
8. On observing a Blossom 156
9. The Hour when we shall meet again . . 119
10. Lines to C. Lloyd 153
11. Sonnet. "The piteous sobs that choke the virgin's breath" 217
12. On the Christening of a Friend's Child . 214

There were also added a new Preface and a Prose Introduction to the Sonnets. The volume was accompanied by some poems of Charles Lloyd, and by an enlarged collection of Sonnets and other Pieces by Lamb.†

---

* *sic* in the Contents of the original edition.

† *Poems by S. T. Coleridge, Second Edition. To which are now added Poems by* CHARLES LAMB *and* CHARLES LLOYD.

"*Duplex nobis vinculum, et amicitiæ et similium junctarumque Camœnarum; quod utinam neque mors solvat, neque temporis longinquitas!*"

      Groscoll. Epist. ad Car. Utenhov. et Ptol. Lux. Tast.

Printed by N. Biggs for J. Cottle, Bristol, and Messrs. Robinsons, London, 1797, pp. xx. 278.

The motto from Groscollias, Coleridge afterwards told Cottle, was all a hoax: not meeting with a suitable motto, he invented one, and with references purposely obscure. (*Cottle*, i. 294.)

In June 1797, about the time when the new volume was published, Charles Lamb and his sister came on a visit to Coleridge at his cottage at Stowey. On the morning of their arrival, Coleridge met with an accident which disabled him from walking during the whole of their stay. One evening, when they had left him for a few hours, he composed the poem, "This Lime-tree Bower my Prison,"* in which he refers to his old friend, while watching him in fancy with his sister, winding and ascending the hills at a short distance, himself detained as if a prisoner.

This brief visit of Lamb's had been preceded by a still more important event, not only prolific in its immediate consequences, but destined in its issues to affect more or less the whole of Coleridge's future life. In the summer of 1797 Coleridge and Wordsworth, if they did not actually meet for the first time, first became familiarly acquainted with each other at Racedown in Dorsetshire. Wordsworth was in his twenty-eighth and Coleridge in his twenty-fifth year, in the spring-tide of his creative faculty. *[sidenote: Coleridge and Wordsworth at Racedown.]*

The first impression made by the appearance of Coleridge, is thus described by Miss Wordsworth in a letter to a friend who had left Racedown early in 1797 :—

"You had a great loss in not seeing Coleridge. He is a wonderful man. His conversation teems with soul, mind, and spirit. Then he is so benevolent, so good-tempered and cheerful, and, like William, interests himself so much about every little trifle. At first I thought him very plain, that is, for about three

---

* See Vol. II. p. 206.

minutes: he is pale, thin, has a wide mouth, thick lips, and not very good teeth, longish, loose-growing, half-curling, rough black hair. But, if you hear him speak for five minutes, you think no more of them. His eye is large and full, and not very dark, but grey—such an eye as would receive from a heavy soul the dullest expression; but it speaks every emotion of his animated mind: it has more of 'the poet's eye in a fine frenzy rolling' than I ever witnessed. He has fine dark eyebrows, and an overhanging forehead."*

Coleridge had come over on a visit to Wordsworth from Nether-Stowey, where he had been engaged in writing the tragedy of *Osorio*, at the request of Sheridan. Wordsworth was also occupied with a tragedy, *The Borderers*, which was completed in the following November, offered to the managers of Covent Garden Theatre, and summarily rejected by them, and which only saw the light forty-five years afterwards.

Osorio.

Charles Lamb writes to Coleridge (June 13th, 1797):—"Lloyd tells me that Sheridan put you upon writing your tragedy. I hope you are only Coleridge-izing when you talk of finishing it in a few days. Shakespeare was a more modest man; but you best know your own power."

During the time of the visit above-mentioned, Miss Wordsworth writes from Racedown to a friend:—"After tea he (Coleridge) repeated to us two acts and a half of his tragedy, *Osorio*." Coleridge writing at the time of this visit to his friend Cottle (June, 1797) says:—"He (Wordsworth) admires my tragedy, which gives me great hopes."

* *Memoirs of Wordsworth* (Lond. 1851), vol. i. pp. 98, 99.

In a letter received by Cottle from Coleridge soon after, he says :—I shall now stick close to my tragedy (called *Osorio*), and when I have finished it, shall walk to Shaftesbury to spend a few days with Bowles." This letter, as usual, has no date, but a letter from Wordsworth determines approximately the time when Coleridge had nearly completed his play. Wordsworth says, under date September 13, 1797 :—" Coleridge is gone over to Bowles with his tragedy, which he has finished to the middle of the fifth Act. He set off a week ago."*

In the meantime, Wordsworth himself was hard at work on *The Borderers*. Both the poets, however, were doomed to witness the disappointment of their hopes.

"William's play," says Miss Wordsworth (20th November, 1797), "is finished, and sent to the managers of the Covent Garden Theatre. We have not the faintest expectation that it will be accepted." On 21st December she writes :—"We have been in London : our business was the play; and the play is rejected. It was sent to one of the principal actors at Covent Garden, who expressed great approbation, and advised William strongly to go to London to make certain alterations." " Coleridge's play," she adds, "is also rejected;" and for this she expresses great sorrow and disappointment.

In the following year (1798), two scenes from *Osorio*, under the titles of *The Dungeon* and *The Foster-Mother's Tale*, were published, together with other pieces

---

* *Early Recollections, chiefly relating to the late Samuel Taylor Coleridge.* By Joseph Cottle. Lond., 1837. Vol. i. pp. 234, 235.

by Coleridge, in the volume of *Lyrical Ballads* which he produced conjointly with Wordsworth. Here, with the omission of some of the opening lines of the latter scene, they continued to appear in the successive editions of 1800, 1802, and 1805.

"The manuscript of *Osorio*," says Mr. Gillman, "had been sent to Sheridan, who did not even acknowledge the receipt of the letter which accompanied the drama; he, however, observed to a friend that he had received a play from Coleridge, but there was one extraordinary line in the Cave Scene, *drip, drip*, which he could not understand: 'in short,' said he, 'it is all dripping.' This was the only notice he took of the play; but the comment was at length repeated to the author through the medium of a third party." * We shall hear more of this play later on.

His *Annus Mirabilis*. We have said that the period of Coleridge's residence at Nether Stowey (1797-1798) was preeminently fruitful in the development of his poetical genius. Not only Osorio, but nearly all the chief works by which his name will live as a poet, were planned or produced during those two fortunate years of his life. Among these were The Ancient Mariner, the first part of Christabel, Kubla Khan, The Three Graves, The Wanderings of Cain, the Ode on France, Frost at Midnight, The Nightingale, and the Circassian Love-Chant.

From Racedown Wordsworth shortly afterwards removed to Alfoxden, and thus became a near neighbour of Coleridge.

In January 1798, Coleridge was induced to entertain the idea of taking charge of a Unitarian congregation

---

* Gillman's *Life of Coleridge* (Pickering, 1838), p. 265.

at Shrewsbury. He was luckily induced to abandon that project by the opportune liberality of his friends the Wedgwoods, who offered him an annuity of £150 on condition of his retiring from the ministry, and devoting himself entirely to the study of poetry and philosophy. This Shrewsbury episode is so graphically related by William Hazlitt * that we cannot do better than quote his account of it :—

"My father was a Dissenting Minister at Wem, in Shropshire; and in the year 1798 Mr. Coleridge came to Shrewsbury, to succeed Mr. Rowe in the spiritual charge of a Unitarian congregation there. He did not come till late on the Saturday afternoon before he was to preach; and Mr. Rowe, who himself went down to the coach in a state of anxiety and expectation, to look for the arrival of his successor, could find no one at all answering the description but a round-faced man in a short black coat (like a shooting-jacket) which hardly seemed to have been made for him, but who appeared to be talking at a great rate to his fellow-passengers. Mr. Rowe had scarcely returned to give an account of his disappointment, when the round-faced man in black entered, and dissipated all doubts on the subject by beginning to talk. He did not cease while he stayed; nor has he since, that I know of. He held the good town of Shrewsbury in delightful suspense for three weeks that he remained there, 'fluttering the *proud Salopians* like an eagle in a dove-cote;' and the Welsh mountains that skirt the horizon with their tempestuous confusion, agree to have heard no such mystic sounds since the days of

[margin: Hazlitt's account of S. T. C. at Shrewsbury]

* *The Liberal*, 1822, vol. ii. pp. 23-46. § *My first Acquaintance with Poets.*

'High-born Hoel's harp or soft Llewellyn's lay!'

"My father lived ten miles from Shrewsbury, and was in the habit of exchanging visits with Mr. Rowe. Coleridge had agreed to come over to see my father, according to the courtesy of the country, as Mr. Rowe's probable successor; but in the meantime I had gone to hear him preach the Sunday after his arrival. A poet and a philosopher getting up into a Unitarian pulpit to preach the Gospel, was a romance in these degenerate days, a sort of revival of the primitive spirit of Christianity, which was not to be resisted.

"It was in January, 1798, that I rose one morning before day-light, to walk ten miles in the mud, and went to hear this celebrated person preach. Never, the longest day I have to live, shall I have such another walk as this cold, raw, comfortless one, in the winter of the year 1798. When I got there, the organ was playing the 100th psalm, and, when it was done, Mr. Coleridge rose and gave out his text, 'And he went up into the mountain to pray, HIMSELF, ALONE.' As he gave out this text, his voice 'rose like a steam of rich distilled perfumes,' and when he came to the two last words, which he pronounced loud, deep, and distinct, it seemed to me, who was then young, as if the sounds had echoed from the bottom of the human heart, and as if that prayer might have floated in solemn silence through the universe. The idea of St. John came into mind, 'of one crying in the wilderness, who had his loins girt about, and whose food was locusts and wild honey.' The preacher then launched into his subject, like an eagle dallying with the wind. The sermon was upon peace and war; upon church and state—not their alliance, but their separation—on the spirit of the world and the spirit of Christianity, not as the same, but as opposed to one another. He talked of those who had 'inscribed the cross of Christ on banners dripping with human gore.' He made a poetical and pastoral excursion,—and to shew the fatal effects of war, drew a striking contrast between the simple shepherd boy, driving his team afield, or sitting under the hawthorn, piping to his flock, 'as though he should never be old,' and the same poor country-lad, crimped, kidnapped, brought into town, made drunk at an alehouse, turned into a wretched drummer-boy, with his hair sticking on end with powder and pomatum, a long cue at his back, and tricked out in the loathsome finery of the profession of blood.

"On the Tuesday following, the half-inspired speaker came. I was called down into the room where he was, and went half-hoping, half-afraid. He received me very graciously, and I listened for a long time without uttering a word. I did not suffer in his opinion by my silence. 'For those two hours,' he afterwards was pleased to say, 'he was conversing with W. H.'s forehead!' His appearance was different from what I had anticipated from seeing him before. At a distance, and in the dim light of the chapel, there was to me a strange wildness in his aspect, a dusky obscurity, and I thought him pitted with the small-pox. His complexion was at that time clear, and even bright. His forehead was broad and high, light as if built of ivory, with large projecting eyebrows, and his eyes rolling beneath them like a sea with darkened lustre. 'A certain tender bloom his face o'erspread,' a purple tinge as we see it in the pale thoughtful complexions of the Spanish portrait-painters, Murillo and Velasquez. His mouth was gross, voluptuous, open, eloquent; his chin good-humoured and round; but his nose, the rudder of the face, the index of the will, was small, feeble—nothing like what he has done. It might seem that the genius of his face as from a height surveyed and projected him (with sufficient capacity and huge aspiration) into the world unknown of thought and imagination, with nothing to support or guide his veering purpose, as if Columbus had launched his adventurous course for the New World in a scallop, without oars or compass. Coleridge in his person was rather above the common size, inclining to the corpulent. His hair was then black and glossy as the raven's, and fell in smooth masses over his forehead.

"It was curious to observe the contrast between him and my father, who was a veteran in the cause, and then declining into the vale of years. No two individuals were ever more unlike than were the host and his guest. A poet was to my father a sort of nondescript: yet whatever added grace to the Unitarian cause was to him welcome. He could hardly have been more surprised or pleased, if our visitor had worn wings. Indeed his thoughts had wings; and as the silken sounds rustled round our little wainscoted parlour, my father threw back his spectacles over his forehead, his white hairs mixing with its sanguine hue; and a smile of delight beamed across his rugged cordial face, to think that Truth had found a new ally in Fancy! Besides Coleridge seemed to take considerable notice of me, and that of itself was enough. He talked very familiarly, but agreeably, and glanced over a variety of subjects. At dinner-time he grew more animated, and dilated in a very edifying manner on Mary Wolstonecraft and

Mackintosh. The last, he said, he considered as a clever scholastic man—a master of the topics,—or as the ready warehouseman of letters, who knew exactly where to lay his hand on what he wanted, though the goods were not his own. He thought him no match for Burke, either in style or matter. Burke was a metaphysician, Mackintosh a mere logician. Burke was an orator (almost a poet) who reasoned in figures, because he had an eye for Nature: Mackintosh, on the other hand, was a rhetorician, who had only an eye to common-places. On this I ventured to say that I had always entertained a great opinion of Burke, and that (as far as I could find) the speaking of him with contempt might be made the test of a vulgar democratical mind. This was the first observation I ever made to Coleridge, and he said it was a very just and striking one. I remember the leg of Welsh mutton and the turnips on the table that day had the finest flavour imaginable. Coleridge added that Mackintosh and Tom Wedgwood (of whom, however, he spoke highly) had expressed a very indifferent opinion of his friend Wordsworth, on which he remarked to them—'He strides on so far before you, that he dwindles in the distance!' Godwin had once boasted to him of having carried on an argument with Mackintosh for three hours with dubious success; Coleridge told him—'If there had been a man of genius in the room, he would have settled the question in five minutes.' He asked me if I had ever seen Mary Wolstonecraft, and I said, I had once for a few moments, and that she seemed to me to turn off Godwin's objections to something she advanced with quite a playful, easy air. He replied, that 'this was only one instance of the ascendancy which people of imagination exercised over those of mere intellect.'

He did not rate Godwin very high* (this was caprice or prejudice, real or affected); but he had a great idea of Mrs. Wolstonecraft's powers of conversation, none at all of her talent for book-making. We talked a little about Holcroft. He had been asked if he was not much struck *with* him, and he said, he thought himself in more danger of being struck *by* him. I complained that he would not let me get on at all, for he required a definition of even the commonest word, exclaiming, 'What do you mean by a *sensation*, Sir? What do you mean by an *idea?*' This, Coleridge said, was barricadoing the road to truth:—it was setting up a turnpike-gate at every step we took. I forget a great number of things, many more than I remember; but the day passed off pleasantly, and the next morning Coleridge was to return to Shrewsbury. When I came down to breakfast, I found that he had just received a letter from his friend, T. Wedgwood, making him an offer of £150 a-year if he chose to waive his present pursuit, and devote himself entirely to the study of poetry and philosophy. Coleridge seemed to make up his mind to close with this proposal in the act of tying on one of his shoes. It threw an additional damp on his departure. It took the wayward enthusiast quite from us to cast him into Deva's winding vales, or by the shores of old romance. Instead of living at ten miles distance, of being the pastor of a Dissenting congregation at Shrewsbury, he was henceforth to inhabit

---

* He complained in particular of the presumption of his attempting to establish the future immortality of man, "without" (as he said) "knowing what Death was or what Life was"—and the tone in which he pronounced these two words seemed to convey a complete image of both.

the Hill of Parnassus, to be a Shepherd on the Delectable Mountains. Alas! I knew not the way thither, and felt very little gratitude for Mr. Wedgwood's bounty. I was presently relieved from this dilemma; for Coleridge, asking for a pen and ink, and going to a table to write something on a bit of card, advanced towards me with undulating step, and giving me the precious document, said that that was his address, *Mr. Coleridge, Nether Stowey, Somersetshire;* and that he should be glad to see me there in a few weeks' time, and, if I chose, would come half-way to meet me. I was not less surprised than the shepherd-boy (this simile is to be found in Cassandra) when he sees a thunder-bolt fall close at his feet. I stammered out my acknowledgments and acceptance of this offer (I thought Mr. Wedgwood's annuity a trifle to it) as well as I could; and this mighty business being settled, the poet-preacher took leave, and I accompanied him six miles on the road. It was a fine morning in the middle of winter, and he talked the whole way. The scholar in Chaucer is described as going

——' sounding on his way.'

So Coleridge went on his. In digressing, in dilating, in passing from subject to subject, he appeared to me to float in air, to slide on ice. He told me in confidence, going along, that he should have preached two sermons before he accepted the situation at Shrewsbury, one on Infant Baptism, the other on the Lord's Supper, shewing that he could not administer either, which would have effectually disqualified him for the object in view. I observed that he continually crossed me on the way by shifting from one side of the foot-path to the other. This struck me as an odd movement; but I did not at that time connect it with any instability of purpose or involuntary change of principle, as I have done since. He seemed unable to keep on in a straight line. He spoke slightingly of Hume (whose Essay on Miracles he said was stolen from an objection started in one of South's Sermons —*Credat Judæus Apella!*). I was not very much pleased at this account of Hume, for I had just been reading, with infinite relish, that completest of all metaphysical choke-pears his *Treatise on Human Nature*, to which the *Essays*, in point of scholastic subtlety and close reasoning, are mere elegant trifling, light summer-reading. Coleridge even denied the excellence of Hume's general style, which I think betrayed a want of taste or candour. He however made me amends by the manner in which he spoke of Berkeley. He dwelt particularly on his *Essay on Vision* as a masterpiece of analytical reasoning. So it undoubtedly is. He was exceedingly angry with Dr. Johnson for striking the stone with his foot, in allusion to this author's Theory of Matter and Spirit, and saying, 'Thus I confute him, sir.' Coleridge drew a parallel (I don't know how he brought about the connexion) between Bishop Berkeley and Tom Paine. He said the one was an instance of a subtle, the other of an acute mind, than which no two things could be more distinct. The one was a shop-boy's quality, the other the characteristic of a philosopher. He considered Bishop Butler as a true philosopher, a profound and conscientious thinker, a genuine reader of nature and of his own mind. He did not speak of his *Analogy*, but of his *Sermons at the Rolls' Chapel*, of which I had never heard. Coleridge somehow always contrived to prefer the *unknown* to the *known*. In this instance he was right. The *Analogy* is a tissue of sophistry.

of wire-drawn, theological special-pleading; the *Sermons* (with the Preface to them) are in a fine vein of deep, matured reflection, a candid appeal to our observation of human nature, without pedantry and without bias. I told Coleridge I had written a few remarks, and was sometimes foolish enough to believe that I had made a discovery on the same subject (the *Natural Disinterestedness of the Human Mind*)—and I tried to explain my view of it to Coleridge, who listened with great willingness, but I did not succeed in making myself understood. If I had the quaint Muse of Sir Philip Sidney to assist me, I would write a *Sonnet to the Road between Wem and Shrewsbury*, and immortalise every step of it by some fond enigmatical conceit. I would swear that the very milestones had ears, and that Harmer-hill stooped with all its pines, to listen to a poet, as he passed! I remember but one other topic of discourse in this walk. He mentioned Paley, praised the naturalness and clearness of his style, but condemned his sentiments, thought him a mere time-serving casuist, and said that 'the fact of his work on Moral and Political Philosophy being made a text-book in our Universities was a disgrace to the national character.' We parted at the six-mile stone; and I returned homeward pensive but much pleased. I had met with unexpected notice from a person, whom I believed to have been prejudiced against me. 'Kind and affable to me had been his condescension, and should be honoured ever with suitable regard.' He was the first poet I had known, and he certainly answered to that inspired name. I had heard a great deal of his powers of conversation, and was not disappointed. In fact, I never met with any thing at all like them, either before or since. I could easily credit the accounts which were circulated of his holding forth to a large party of ladies and gentlemen, an evening or two before, on the Berkeleian Theory, when he made the whole material universe look like a transparency of fine words."

Of his subsequent visit to Coleridge at Nether Stowey Hazlitt has given the following picturesque account :—

"I arrived, and was well received. The country about Nether Stowey is beautiful, green and hilly, and near the sea-shore. In the afternoon, Coleridge took me over to Alfoxden, a romantic old family-mansion of the St. Aubins, where Wordsworth lived. It was then in the possession of a friend of the poet's, who gave him the free use of it. Wordsworth himself was from home, but his sister kept house, and set before us a frugal repast; and we had free access to her brother's poems, the *Lyrical Ballads*, which were still in manuscript, I dipped into a few of these with great satisfaction, and with the faith of a novice. I slept that night in an old room with blue hangings, and covered with the round-faced family-portraits of the age of George I. and II. and from the wooded declivity of the adjoining park that overlooked my window, at the dawn of day, could

———' hear the loud stag speak.'

"That morning, as soon as breakfast was over, we strolled out into the park, and seating ourselves on the trunk of an old ash-tree that stretched along the ground, Coleridge read aloud, with a sonorous and musical voice, the ballad of *Betty Foy*. I was not critically or sceptically inclined. I saw touches of truth and nature, and took the rest for granted. But in the *Thorn*, the *Mad Mother*, and the *Complaint of a Poor Indian Woman,* I felt that deeper power and pathos which have been since acknowledged as the characteristics of this author; and the sense of a new style and a new spirit in poetry came over me. It had to me something of the effect that arises from the turning up of the fresh soil, or of the first welcome breath of Spring.

"Coleridge and myself walked back to Stowey that evening, and his voice sounded high

'Of Providence, foreknowledge, will, and fate,
Fix'd fate, free-will, foreknowledge absolute,'

as we passed through echoing grove, by fairy stream or waterfall, gleaming in the summer moonlight! He lamented that Wordsworth was not prone enough to belief in the traditional superstitions of the place, and that there was a something corporeal, a *matter-of-fact-ness,* a clinging to the palpable, or often to the petty, in his poetry, in consequence. His genius was not a spirit that descended to him through the air; it sprung out of the ground like a flower, or unfolded itself from a green spray, on which the gold-finch sang. He said, however (if I remember right), that this objection must be confined to his descriptive pieces, that his philosophic poetry had a grand and comprehensive spirit in it, so that his soul seemed to inhabit the universe like a palace, and to discover truth by intuition, rather than by deduction. The next day Wordsworth arrived from Bristol at Coleridge's cottage. He answered in some degree to his friend's description of him, but was more gaunt and Don Quixote-like. He was quaintly dressed (according to the *costume* of that unconstrained period) in a brown fustian jacket and striped pantaloons.

"We went over to Alfoxden again the day following, and Wordsworth read us the story of Peter Bell in the open air. There is a *chaunt* in the recitation both of Coleridge and Wordsworth, which acts as a spell upon the hearer, and disarms the judgment. Perhaps they have deceived themselves by making habitual use of this ambiguous accompaniment. Coleridge's manner is more full, animated, and varied; Wordsworth's more equable, sustained, and internal. The one might be termed more *dramatic*, the other more *lyrical*. Coleridge has told me that he himself liked to compose in walking over uneven ground, or breaking through the straggling branches of a copsewood; whereas Wordsworth always composed walking up and down a straight gravel-walk, or in some spot where the continuity of his verse met with no collateral interruption. Returning that same evening, I got into a metaphysical argument with Wordsworth, while Coleridge was explaining the different notes of the nightingale to his sister, in which we neither of us succeeded in making ourselves perfectly clear and intelligible. Thus I passed three weeks at Nether Stowey and in the neighbourhood, generally devoting the afternoons to a delightful chat in an arbour made of bark by the poet's friend Tom Poole, sitting under two fine elm-trees, and listening to the bees humming round us, while we quaffed our *flip*. It was agreed, among other things, that we should make a jaunt down the Bristol-Channel, as far as Linton. We set off together on foot, Coleridge, John Chester, and I. This Chester was a native of Nether Stowey, one of those who were attracted to Coleridge's discourse as flies are to honey, or bees in swarming-time to the sound of a brass pan. He had on a brown cloth coat, boots, and corduroy breeches, was low in stature, bow-legged, had a drag in his walk like a drover, which he assisted by a hazel switch, and kept on a sort of trot by the side of Coleridge, like a running footman by a state coach, that he might not lose a syllable or sound that fell from Coleridge's lips. He told me his private opinion that Coleridge was a wonderful man. He scarcely opened his lips, much less offered an opinion the whole way: yet of the three, had I to choose during that journey, I would be John Chester. He afterwards followed Coleridge into Germany. We passed Dunster on our right, a small town between the brow of a hill and the sea. We had a long day's march—(our feet kept time to the echoes of Coleridge's tongue)—through Minehead and by the Blue Anchor, and on to Linton, which we did not reach till near midnight, and where we had some difficulty in making a lodgment. The view in coming along had been splendid. We walked for miles and miles on dark brown heaths overlooking the Channel, with the Welsh hills beyond, and at times descended into little sheltered valleys close by the sea-side, with a smuggler's face scowling by us, and then had to ascend conical hills with a path winding up through a coppice to a barren top, like a monk's shaven crown, from one of which I pointed out to Coleridge's notice the bare masts of a vessel on the very edge of the horizon and within the red-orbed disk of the setting sun, like his own spectre-ship in the *Ancient Mariner*. At Linton the character of the sea-coast becomes more marked and rugged. There is a place called the *Valley of Rocks* (I suspect this was only the poetical name for it) bedded among precipices overhanging the sea, with rocky caverns beneath, into which the waves dash, and where the sea-gull for ever wheels its screaming flight. On the tops of these are huge stones thrown transverse, as if an earthquake had tossed them there, and behind these is a fretwork of perpendicular rocks, something like the *Giant's Causeway*. A thunder-storm came on while we were at the inn, and Coleridge was running out bareheaded to enjoy the commotion of the elements in the *Valley of Rocks*, but as if in spite, the clouds only muttered a few angry sounds, and let fall a few refreshing drops. Coleridge told me that he and Wordsworth were to have made this place the scene of a prose tale, which was to have been in the manner of, but far superior to, the *Death of Abel*, but they had relinquished the design.* In the morning of the second day, we breakfasted luxuriously in an old-fashioned parlour, on tea, toast, eggs, and honey, in the very sight of the bee-hives from which it had been taken, and a garden full of thyme and wild flowers that had produced it. On this occasion Coleridge spoke of Virgil's Georgics, but not well. I do not think he had much feeling for the classical or elegant. It was in this room that we found a little worn-out copy of the *Seasons*, lying in a window-seat, on which Coleridge exclaimed, '*That* is true fame!' He said Thomson was a great poet, rather than a good one; his style was as meretricious as his thoughts were natural. He spoke of Cowper as the best modern poet. He said the *Lyrical Ballads* were an experiment about to be tried by him and Wordsworth, to see how far the public taste would endure poetry written in a more natural and simple style than had hitherto been attempted; totally discarding the artifices of poetical diction, and making use only of such words as had probably been common in the most ordinary language since the days of Henry II. Some comparison was introduced between Shakespeare and Milton. He said 'he hardly

---

* This refers to *The Wanderings of Cain*.—ED.

knew which to prefer. Shakespeare seemed to him a mere stripling in the art; he was as tall and as strong, with infinitely more activity than Milton, but he never appeared to have come to man's estate; or if he had, he would not have been a man, but a monster.' He spoke with contempt of Gray, and with intolerance of Pope. He did not like the versification of the latter. He observed that 'the ears of these couplet-writers might be charged with having short memories, that could not retain the harmony of whole passages.' He thought little of Junius as a writer; he had a dislike of Dr. Johnson; and a much higher opinion of Burke as an orator and politician, than of Fox or Pitt. He however thought him very inferior in richness of style and imagery to some of our elder prose-writers, particularly Jeremy Taylor. In short, he was profound and discriminating with respect to those authors whom he liked, and where he gave his judgment fair play; capricious, perverse, and prejudiced in his antipathies and distastes. We loitered on the 'ribbed sea-sands,' in such talk as this, a whole morning, and I recollect met with a curious sea-weed, of which John Chester told us the country-name! A fisherman gave Coleridge an account of a boy that had been drowned the day before, and that they had tried to save him at the risk of their own lives. He said 'he did not know how it was that they ventured, but, sir, we have a *nature* towards one another.' This expression, Coleridge remarked to me, was a fine illustration of that theory of disinterestedness which I (in common with Butler) had adopted. I broached to him an argument of mine to prove that *likeness* was not mere association of ideas. I said that the mark in the sand put one in mind of a man's foot, not because it was part of a former impression of a man's foot (for it was quite new) but because it was like the shape of a man's foot. He assented to the justness of this distinction and John Chester listened; not from any interest in the subject, but because he was astonished that I should be able to suggest anything to Coleridge that he did not already know. We returned on the third morning, and Coleridge remarked the silent cottage-smoke curling up the valleys where, a few evenings before, we had seen the lights gleaming through the dark.

"In a day or two after we arrived at Stowey, we set out, I on my return home, and he for Germany. It was a Sunday morning, and he was to preach that day for Dr. Toulmin of Taunton. I asked him if he had prepared any thing for the occasion? He said he had not even thought of the text, but should as soon as we parted. I did not go to hear him,—this was a fault,—but we met in the evening at Bridgewater. The next day we had a long walk to Bristol, and sat down, I recollect, by a well-side on the road, to cool ourselves and satisfy our thirst, when Coleridge repeated to me some descriptive lines from his tragedy of Remorse; which I must say became his mouth and that occasion better than they, some years after, did Mr. Elliston's and the Drury-lane boards."

On returning to Nether Stowey, after his abandonment of the ministry, Coleridge again devoted himself to the Muses. A singular vehicle he found during the next four or five years for conveying some of his finest verse to the world. Hitherto his connexion with the periodical press had been exiguous and unimportant. It had been confined to some early productions contributed to the *Morning Chronicle*, and to a few occasional verses printed in the *Cambridge Intelligencer*, in one of the Bristol newspapers, and in the *Monthly*

MEMOIR OF COLERIDGE. lxi

Magazine. But on a visit to London in the later days of 1797, shortly before he went to Shrewsbury, Coleridge was introduced to Mr. Daniel Stuart, the editor and proprietor of the *Morning Post,* and thus commenced his long and important connexion with that newspaper, a connexion which forms one of the important epochs of his life. At a stipulated annual payment Coleridge was engaged by Stuart to contribute an occasional copy of verses. He sent five or six important pieces in 1798, before his departure for Germany, viz., {margin: The Morning Post.}

January 8. Fire, Famine, and Slaughter.
March 10.* The Raven.
April 13. Lewti, or Circassian's Love-Chant.
April 16. The Recantation : An Ode.†
July 30. The Mad Ox.

Here at Nether-Stowey, May 10, 1798, was born his second son, whom he named after another great philosopher, Berkeley. This child was destined to be taken from him in early infancy. He died while his father was in Germany, February 10, 1799. {margin: Birth and death of Berkeley Coleridge.}

Berkeley, it appears, was an infant of a noble and

---

* Perhaps also *The Old Man of the Alps,* March 8 (See vol. ii., p. 355).

† This magnificent Ode, now better known as the Ode on France, and acknowledged to be one of Coleridge's master-pieces, appeared shortly afterwards in a thin quarto pamphlet together with two other pieces under the following title:—

Fears in Solitude, written in 1798, *during the alarm of an invasion. To which are added France, an Ode, and Frost at Midnight.* By S. T. Coleridge. London: printed for J. Johnson, in St. Paul's Church-yard. 1798. 4to., pp. iv. 23.

lovely style of beauty, his large, soft eyes of a "London smoke" colour, exquisite complexion, regular features and goodly size. His father was very proud of him, and one day, when he saw a neighbour approaching his little cottage at Stowey, snatched him away from the nurse half-dressed, and with a broad smile of pride and delight, presented him to be admired, saying, "This is my second son." Yet when the answer was, "Well, this is something like a child!" he felt affronted on behalf of his little darling Hartley. Berkeley was of a taller make than any of the three children who survived.

In the autumn of 1798 the famous volume of *Lyrical Ballads*, the joint production of Wordsworth and Coleridge, was published by Joseph Cottle, at Bristol, and *Lyrical Ballads.* fell almost still-born from the press.* To this volume Coleridge contributed *The Ancient Mariner, The Nightingale,* and two scenes from the rejected Tragedy of *Osorio,* viz. *The Dungeon,* and *The Foster-Mother's Tale.*

The liberality of his friends the Wedgwoods now enabled Coleridge to carry out a cherished scheme of finishing his education at the great German universities.

On the 16th of September, 1798, he sailed from Great Yarmouth to Hamburg, in company with Wordsworth and his sister, in his way to Germany. Full and interesting notices of this important episode of Coleridge's life may be found in "Satyrane's Letters" printed in *The Friend* and in the *Early Years and Late Recollections* of his fellow-student, Dr. Carlyon, which we have had

Student-life in Germany.

---

* Cottle retired from business shortly afterwards, and disposed of the remaining copies to a London bookseller of the name of Arch.

occasion to quote once or twice elsewhere in the course of these volumes.

Coleridge returned to England after an absence of fourteen months, and arrived in London the 27th November, 1799.

His first literary occupation was the translation of Schiller's Wallenstein, which he completed in six weeks, in a lodging in Buckingham street, in the Strand; it was printed and published in 1800. The manuscript was purchased by Longman's house under the condition that the English Version and the original were to be published at the same time. Coleridge truly prophesied its fate, for when translating it, he said it would fall dead from the press, and indeed but few of the copies were sold;—his advice to the publishers, whom he had forewarned of this failure, was to reserve the unsold copies, and wait till it might become fashionable. They however parted with it as waste paper, though sixteen years afterwards, on the publication of *Christabel*, it was eagerly sought for, and the few remaining copies doubled their price.*

Translation of Wallenstein.

While still in Germany, Coleridge had renewed his

---

* The rarity of the book a few years later, before it was reprinted, is evident from the fact that Mr. Carlyle, when publishing his Life of Schiller in 1824, could not obtain access to a copy. "Mr. Coleridge's translation," he writes (*London Magazine*, August, 1824), "is as a whole unknown to us; but judging from many large specimens, we should pronounce it to be the best, indeed the only sufferable translation from the German with which our literature has yet been enriched." It was not reprinted until 1828, when it formed the third volume of the first Collected Edition of Coleridge's Poetical and Dramatic Works, published by the late William Pickering.

intermitted connexion with the *Morning Post* by sending over some poetical pieces, one of which seems to have created a profound sensation on its first appearance. His contributions of this period, and that immediately succeeding his return to England, were as follows :—

1799.

Aug. 24.   The British Stripling's War-Song.
Aug. 27.   Names. (Song from Lessing.)
Sept. 6.   The Devil's Thoughts.*
Sept. 7.   Epigram.
Sept. 17.   Lines written in the Album at Elbingerode.
Sept. 23.   Epigram.
Sept. 24.   Lines composed in a Concert-Room.
Nov. 14.   Epigram.
Nov. 16.   Epigram.
Dec. 9.   To a Young Lady on her first appearance after illness.
Dec. 21.   Introduction to the Tale of the Dark Ladie.
Dec. 24.   Ode to Georgiana, Duchess of Devonshire.
Dec. 25.   A Christmas Carol.

In the summer of 1800, Coleridge left London, and repaired to Keswick, in Cumberland, in the heart of the then beautiful and retired Lake District, in which his friend Wordsworth had already sought and found a home at Grasmere, in Westmoreland, some fifteen miles distant. At Keswick the second part of *Christabel* was written during this year; but Coleridge never proceeded any farther in

Settlement at Keswick.

---

* When this humorous piece first appeared in the *Morning Post*, according to the Editor of that Journal, it made so great a sensation that several hundred sheets extra were sold by them, as the paper was in request for days and weeks afterwards.

it, and the Fragment of it was not published till sixteen years afterwards. Even then he had not given up all thoughts of completing it, as is evident from the Preface; but the idea, if never actually abandoned, was never destined to be carried out. In later life he observed: "The reason of my not finishing *Christabel* is not that I don't know how to do it—for I have, as I always had, the whole plan entire from beginning to end in my mind; but I fear I could not carry on with equal success the execution of the idea, an extremely subtle and difficult one." *

"The following relation," says Mr. Gillman, "was to have occupied a third and fourth canto, and to have closed the tale. Over the mountains, the Bard, as directed by Sir Leoline, hastes with his disciple; but in consequence of one of those inundations supposed to be common to this country, the spot only where the castle once stood is discovered—the edifice itself being washed away. *Proposed plot of the unwritten portion of Christabel.* He determines to return. Geraldine being acquainted with all that is passing, like the Weird Sisters in Macbeth, vanishes. Re-appearing, however, she waits the return of the Bard, exciting in the mean time, by her wily arts, all the anger she could rouse in the Baron's breast, as well as that jealousy of which he is described to have been susceptible. The old Bard and the youth at length arrive, and therefore she can no longer personate the character of Geraldine, the daughter of Lord Roland de Vaux, but changes her appearance to that of the accepted though absent lover of *Christabel*. Next ensues a courtship most distressing to *Christabel*,

---

* *Table-Talk of S. T. Coleridge*, Lond. 1835, vol. ii. pp. 221, 222 (under date July 6, 1833); see also Gillman, p. 281.

who feels—she knows not why—great disgust for her once favoured knight. This coldness is very painful to the Baron, who has no more conception than herself of the supernatural transformation. She at last yields to her father's entreaties, and consents to approach the altar with this hated suitor. The real lover returning, enters at this moment, and produces the ring which she had once given him in sign of her betrothment. Thus defeated, the supernatural being Geraldine disappears. As predicted, the castle bell tolls, the mother's voice is heard, and to the exceeding great joy of the parties, the rightful marriage takes place, after which follows a reconciliation and explanation between the father and daughter.

"Lamb, who visited us soon after Coleridge's death, and not long before his own, talking of the *Christabel*, observed, 'I was very angry with Coleridge, when I first heard that he had written a second canto, and that he intended to finish it; but when I read the beautiful apostrophe to the two friends, it calmed me.' He was one of those who strongly recommended Coleridge to leave as a fragment what he had so beautifully begun."*

In this year, or about the Christmas of 1799, Coleridge commenced his long and brilliant series of political articles in the *Morning Post*; of verse the little that he contributed was of a satirical kind, and amounted only to three pieces.

1800.

Jan. 10.   Talleyrand to Lord Grenville: a Metrical Epistle.
Jan. 24.   Epigram.
Dec. 4.   The Two Round Spaces.

* Gillman, pp. 301-303.

In this year appeared a second and enlarged edition of the *Lyrical Ballads*, with the famous Preface in which Wordsworth explained his theories and principles of poetry. This edition contained all Coleridge's former contributions, with the addition of a poem entitled *Love*, the substance of the *Introduction to the Tale of the Dark Ladie*, originally printed in the *Morning Post*, in the previous year.* The majority of Coleridge's other poetical contributions of 1798-9 to the *Morning Post* appeared, together with a few pieces never before printed, in the second volume of Southey's *Annual Anthology*, published at Bristol in 1800.

NEW PIECES IN THE SECOND VOLUME OF
"THE ANNUAL ANTHOLOGY."

	Page in Vol. ii. of the present edn.
Seventeen Epigrams	162-166
Lines to W. L., Esq., while he sang a song to Purcell's Music	181
To an Unfortunate Woman at the Theatre	181
Something Childish, but very Natural. Written in Germany	190
Home-Sick. Written in Germany	191

* In this enlarged edition of *Lyrical Ballads* the poem of *The Ancient Mariner* re-appeared in a considerably altered form—many stanzas being entirely rescinded, a few added, and some remodelled. The *Lyrical Ballads* passed into a third edition in 1802, and a fourth in 1805, after which *The Ancient Mariner* was not again published till it re-appeared in the *Sibylline Leaves* in 1817. In collecting his Minor Poems in 1815, Wordsworth discarded the compositions of his colleague, as Coleridge had himself discarded those of Lamb and Lloyd in the third edition of his Juvenile Poems, published in 1803.

	Page in Vol. ii. of the present edition.
This Lime-Tree Bower my Prison	. . . 206
*To a Friend who had declared his intention of writing no more poetry	 222

In the summer of 1800 the beautiful, accomplished and unfortunate Mary Robinson (once celebrated under the *sobriquet* of 'Perdita,') visited the Lake District, and resided chiefly at Keswick. Here she naturally became acquainted with Coleridge, who had just settled there, and who seems to have been much fascinated by her person, talents, and amiable manners. The impression made by Coleridge's wonderful verse and wonderful talk on poor Perdita seems to have been an equally strong one. She addressed to him some lines full of enthusiastic admiration; and on the birth of his son Derwent, which took place at Keswick† September 14, 1800,

'Perdita' Robinson.

Birth of Derwent Coleridge.

---

* Cottle (i. 244) seems to imply that these lines originally appeared in a Bristol newspaper in 1796. The other pieces may have first seen the light in a similar way, but with the exception of a few of the Epigrams, I have not traced any of them to an earlier source than this second volume of *The Annual Anthology*. There is nothing of Coleridge's in the first volume.

† "It was in the autumn of the year 1800," says the Rev. Derwent Coleridge, "shortly before my own birth, that my father came with my mother and brother to reside in that land of lakes and mountains with which a supposed school of poetry came to be associated. A large house, in a most beautiful situation, in the vale of Derwentwater, on the bank of the river Greta, and about a mile from the lake, since better known under its name of Greta Hall, as the residence

she honoured the occasion with an ode,* in which she invoked the hills and lakes and streams to be gracious to the infant, and to foster and develop in him the gifts and genius of his father. Coleridge missed this gracious lady of the soft blue eye and sweet song, when she departed from the district, and in November of the same year, a few weeks only, as it happened, before the soft blue eyes were closed for ever in death, he addressed to her some exquisite verses, which have until now never appeared in any edition of his Poems.†

The following description of the house he was then inhabiting at Keswick, was written by Coleridge to Southey, who himself afterwards came to inhabit it until his death :—

" Our house stands on a low hill, the whole front of which is one field and an enormous garden, nine-tenths of which is a nursery garden. Behind the house is an orchard, and a small wood on a steep slope, at the foot of which flows the river Greta, which winds round and catches the evening lights in the front of the house. In front we have a giant's camp—an encamped army of tent-like mountains, which by an inverted arch gives a view of

Greta Hall.

of Robert Southey, was then in building by a Mr. Jackson. An arrangement was made by which this house when completed was to have been divided between my father and his landlord. As it turned out, the portion then completed was shared by them in common, the other portion, and eventually the whole (my father's health obliging him to quit Keswick as a place of permanent residence) being occupied by Southey, who came to reside with my father in 1803."

* Both these pieces appear in her Collected Poems. Lond. 1806, vol. i. p. 221, *sqq.*

† See vol. ii. pp. 158-160.

another vale. On our right the lovely vale and the wedge-shaped lake of Bassenthwaite; and on our left Derwentwater and Lodore full in view, and the fantastic mountains of Borrowdale. Behind us the massy Skiddaw, smooth, green, high, with two chasms and a tent-like ridge in the larger. A fairer scene you have not seen in all your wanderings."*

This letter, as well as another of later date, contained a most gloomy account of his own health.

During the later part of the year 1801 Coleridge contributed the following pieces of verse to the columns of *The Morning Post* :—

Sept. 15. Ode after bathing in the sea.
Sept. 18. Song to be sung by the lovers of all the noble liquors comprised under the name of Ale.
Sept. 22. Epitaph on a Bad Man.
Sept. 25. Drinking versus Thinking.
Sept. 26. The Devil Outwitted.
Dec. 1. The Wills of the Wisp. A Sapphic.
Dec. 4. Tranquillity: An Ode.
Dec. 16. To a Critic.

In 1802 the poetical contributions of Coleridge to the *Morning Post* were very rich and varied, and included the magnificent Ode, entitled *Dejection*. If, therefore, we seem to catch in Wordsworth's sublime *Intimations of Immortality from Recollections of Childhood* the same key-note of thought, and some of the same subtle harmonies, it must be remembered that

---

* *S. T. C. to Robert Southey:* Greta Hall, Keswick, April 13, 1801.

MEMOIR OF COLERIDGE. lxxi

Coleridge's Ode can claim not only priority of composition, but priority of publication.*

POEMS BY S. T. C. IN THE MORNING POST, 1802.

Sept. 6. The Picture, or the Lover's Resolution.
Sept. 11. Chamouni, the Hour before Sunrise.
Sept. 17. The Keepsake.
Sept. 23. Original Epigrams.
Sept. 24. Inscription on a Jutting Stone over a Spring.
Sept. 27. A Hint to Premiers and First Consuls.
Sept. 27. Westphalian Song.
Oct. 4. Dejection: an Ode.
Oct. 2. ⎫
Oct. 9. ⎬ Original Epigrams.
Oct. 11. ⎭
Oct. 16. The Language of Birds.
Oct. 19. The Day-Dream. From an Emigrant to his Absent Wife.

His political articles of the same period were also numerous and important. After the autumn of this year, however, Coleridge ceased to contribute to the paper either verse or prose; and in August 1803, Stuart sold the proprietorship of it.

In the summer of 1802 Charles Lamb, in company with his sister, visited the lakes, and spent three weeks with Coleridge at Keswick. Wordsworth was not in the lake-country during Lamb's visit.

"I set out with Mary to Keswick," he writes,

---

* Wordsworth's Ode originally appeared in his collection of Poems published in 1807, and seems from the date attached to it to have been commenced in 1803 and finished in 1806.

"without giving Coleridge any notice. He received us with all the hospitality in the world, and gave up his time to show us all the wonders of the country. He dwells upon a small hill by the side of Keswick, in a comfortable house, quite enveloped on all sides by a net of mountains: great floundering bears and monsters they seemed, all couchant and asleep. We got in in the evening, travelling in a post-chaise from Penrith, in the midst of a gorgeous sunset, which transmuted all the mountains into colours, purple, &c. &c. We entered Coleridge's comfortable study just in the dusk, when the mountains were all dark with clouds upon their heads. Glorious creatures, I never shall forget ye, how ye lay about that night, like an intrenchment: gone to bed, as it seemed, for the night, but promising that ye were to be seen in the morning. Coleridge had got a blazing fire in his study, which is a large, antique, ill-shaped room, with an old-fashioned organ, never played upon, big enough for a church, shelves of scattered folios, an Eolian harp, and an old sofa, half bed, &c. And all looking out upon the last fading view of Skiddaw, and his broad-breasted brethren: what a night! Here we stayed three full weeks."*

<small>Lamb at Keswick.</small>

In November and during the greater part of December 1802 Coleridge was absent on a tour in Wales with his friend Thomas Wedgwood. On the eve of his return, his fourth child and only daughter, Sara, was born at Greta Hall, Keswick, December 21, 1802. Her father reached home again apparently the day after her birth.

<small>Birth of Sara Coleridge.</small>

---

* Lamb to Manning: Sept. 24, 1802.

A pretty word-picture of the three children, partly from the father's, and partly from the daughter's pen, finds a fit place here :—

Coleridge wrote thus of Hartley and of Sara in a letter to Mr. Poole (1803) :—

"Hartley is what he always was, a strange, strange boy, 'exquisitely wild,' an utter visionary; like the moon among thin clouds he moves in a circle of light of his own making. He alone is a light of his own. Of all human beings I never saw one so utterly naked of self. He has no vanity, no pride, no resentments; and, though very passionate, I never yet saw him angry with anybody. He is, though seven years old, the merest child you can conceive; and yet Southey says he keeps him in perpetual wonderment; his thoughts are so truly his own. His dispositions are very sweet, a great lover of truth, and of the finest moral nicety of feelings; and yet always dreaming ... If God preserve his life for me, it will be interesting to know what he will become; for it is not only my opinion, or the opinion of two or of three, but all who have been with him talk of him as a thing that cannot be forgotten ......

A pretty child-picture.

"My meek little Sara is a remarkably interesting baby, with the finest possible skin, and large blue eyes; and she smiles as if she were basking in a sunshine as mild as moonlight of her own quiet happiness."

There is an allusion in the Memoir of Sara Coleridge * to her brother Derwent's sweet childhood. "I have often heard from mamma what a fine, fair, broad-chested little fellow he was at two years old, and

---

* *Memoir and Letters of Sara Coleridge.* Edited by her Daughter. Lond. 1873, vol. i. pp. 3, 4, 6, 7.

how he got the name of Stumpy Canary when he wore a yellow frock, which made him look like one of these feathery bundles in colour and form. I fancy I see him now as my mother's description brought him before me, racing from kitchen to parlour, and from parlour to kitchen, just putting in his head at the door, with roguish smile, to catch notice, then off again, shaking his little sides with laughter. Charles Lamb and his sister, who paid a visit of three weeks to S. T. C. in the summer of 1802, were charmed with the little fellow, and much struck with the quickness of eye and of memory that he displayed in naming the subjects of prints in books which he was acquainted with. 'Pi-pos, Pot-pos,' were his names for the *striped* or *spotted opossum*, and these he would utter with a nonchalant air, as much as to say, 'Of course I know it all as pat as possible.' Lamb calls him *'Pi-pos'* in letters to Greta Hall, after his visit to the lakes." *

<small>Third Edition of Poems.</small> In 1803, a new edition of Coleridge's Juvenile Poems,† of which Longmans had purchased the copyright from Cottle, when the latter retired from business, was decided upon by the London firm. In this edition Coleridge

---

* In letters to Coleridge of Oct. 11 and 23, 1802, Lamb alludes to "Pi-pos." Talfourd says this was "a nickname of endearment for little *Hartley* Coleridge."—ED.

† POEMS, by S. T. COLERIDGE.
    Felix curarum, cui non Heliconia cordi
    Serta, nec imbelles Parnassi e vertice laurus !
    Sed viget ingenium, et magnos accinctus in usus
    Fert animus quascunque vices.—Nos tristia vitæ
    Solamur cantu.   *Stat. Silv.* Lib. iv. 4.
Third Edition. London : Printed by N. Biggs, Crane-court, Fleet-street, for T. N. Longman and O. Rees, Paternoster-row, 1803, pp. xi. 202.

could now have had little interest, either pecuniary or paternal. Indeed, he was so indifferent as to its fate that he allowed his friend Charles Lamb to see it through the press, giving him, without much demur, what seems to have almost been *carte blanche* as to selection and omission of pieces, alteration of lines, &c. Lamb's own productions, and those of Lloyd, ceased to appear in this edition: it contained, however, none of the magnificent productions of the maturity and manhood of Coleridge's genius, and indeed contained no entire new piece of his of any kind or period whatever. Nevertheless the edition is interesting for the sake of its various readings; the fine taste of Lamb having frequently extorted from Coleridge a delicate and happy revision, as in the last two lines of the fourth Miscellaneous Sonnet,* and in the last two lines of the Sonnet to Bowles.†

In the summer of this year (1803), Coleridge was induced to join Wordsworth and his sister in a tour in Scotland, where Coleridge had never before set foot. They left Keswick on Monday morning,

---

* See p. 148 *infra*, note.

† Second version, p. 139 *infra*. It must be borne in mind that the majority of these Juvenile Poems did not re-appear again until 1828, when Coleridge's Poetical Works were first collected (very few of them being included in the collection published in 1817 under the title of *Sibylline Leaves*). When they did so re-appear, the text was in most of the cases alluded to above restored to the original reading, possibly from deliberate preference; but more probably from want of access to a copy of the third edition, and absolute or partial forgetfulness of the improvements made in it. My reasons for this supposition will be better understood by referring to a note in the Appendix to vol. ii. p. 379.

lxxvi   MEMOIR OF COLERIDGE.

<small>Tour in Scotland.</small> August 15, but Coleridge's health appears to have been shattered, and his spirits heavily depressed from the outset; and after a fortnight he was compelled to leave them, a little after they had passed Loch Lomond, and to make the best of his way to Edinburgh.

Miss Wordsworth writes (Monday, Aug. 29) :—"It rained heavily this morning, and having heard so much of the long rains since we came into Scotland, as well as before, we had no hope that it would be over in less than three weeks at the least, so poor Coleridge being very unwell, determined to send his clothes to Edinburgh, and make the best of his way thither, being afraid to face much wet weather in an open carriage." *

At this period Coleridge had already become a prey to oft-recurring mental and physical misery, from indulgence in opium. <small>Opium-eating.</small> He took it at first for assuagement of pain, and delighting in the soothing elation it produced, repeated the dose again and again, till the habit became confirmed. He rapidly became its slave. Won by its temporary effects on body and mind, and regarding not the ever-recurring Nemesis of the morrow, he succumbed more and more to terrible excess, and living for years in an alternate state of diseased exaltation and suicidal depression, wrecked on it the hopes of his life. Under the influence of watchful care, his doses of the pernicious drug were abridged in later years; but furtively and openly, he was an opium-taker to the end.

The following autobiographical note (written in April 1826) refers to this painful subject :—"I wrote a

* *Recollections of a Tour made in Scotland in* 1803, by Dorothy Wordsworth. Edinburgh, 1874, p. 117.

few stanzas * three and twenty years ago, soon after my eyes had been opened to the true nature of the habit into which I had been ignorantly deluded by the seeming magic effects of opium, in the sudden removal of a supposed rheumatic affection, attended with swellings in my knees, and palpitations of the heart, and pains all over me, by which I had been bed-ridden for nearly six months. Unhappily, among my neighbour's and landlord's † books were a large parcel of medical reviews and magazines. I had always a fondness (a common case, but most mischievous turn with reading men who are at all dyspeptic) for dabbling in medical writings; and in one of these reviews I met a case, which I fancied very like my own, on which a cure had been effected by the Kendal Black Drop. In an evil hour I procured it:— it worked miracles—the swellings disappeared, the pains vanished; I was all alive, and all around me being as ignorant as myself, nothing could exceed my triumph. I talked of nothing else, prescribed the newly-discovered panacea for all complaints, and carried a bottle about with me, not to lose any opportunity of administering 'instant relief and speedy cure' to all complainers, stranger or friend, gentle or simple. Need I say that my own apparent convalescence was of no long continuance; but what then?— the remedy was at hand and infallible. Alas! it is with a bitter smile, a laugh of gall and bitterness, that I recall this period of unsuspecting delusion, and how I first became aware of the Maelstrom, the fatal whirl-

* The stanzas alluded to are probably those entitled *The Visionary Hope*, first published in *Sibylline Leaves*, 1817 (Vol. ii. p. 259 of the present edition).

† Mr. Jackson, of Keswick.

pool, to which I was drawing just when the current was already beyond my strength to stem. The state of my mind is truly portrayed in the following effusion, for God knows! that from that moment I was the victim of pain and terror, nor had I at any time taken the flattering poison as a stimulus, or for any craving after pleasurable sensations."

In 1804 Coleridge's rheumatic sufferings augmented, and he determined to try the effects of a thorough and protracted change of climate.

Visit to Malta.

Leaving his wife and children under the care of Southey at Keswick, he took his passage in the 'Speedwell' for Malta, having accepted an invitation from his friend Mr., afterwards Sir, John Stoddart, who was then residing there as Judge of the Island. At four o'clock on Friday afternoon, April 18, 1804, the 'Speedwell' dropped anchor in the harbour of Malta; and here, as events proved, Coleridge was destined to remain for nearly eighteen months. Soon after landing he was introduced to Sir Alexander Ball, the Governor of the Island, whose Secretary being absent, Coleridge officiated for some months in that capacity. Sir Alexander Ball became greatly attached to Coleridge, who a few years afterwards drew his character in a masterly manner in the *Friend*. "There was found in Coleridge," says Mr. Gillman, "what at that time was so much required—an able diplomatic writer in this department of correspondence. The dignities of the office he never attempted to support: he was greatly annoyed at what he thought its unnecessary parade, and he petitioned Sir Alexander to release him from this annoyance. There can be no doubt that to a person accustomed to public business his occupation might appear light, and even agree-

Sir Alexander Ball.

able; but his health, which was the object of this change, not being benefited, and the duties of the employment greater than he was equal to, made it for him an arduous one. In one of the journals which he kept during this period, he speaks of having been for months past "incessantly employed in official tasks, subscribing, examining, administering oaths, auditing, &c."

The simplicity of Coleridge's manners, and entire absence of all show of business-like habits, amongst men chiefly mercantile, made him an object of curiosity, and gave rise to the relation of many whimsical stories about him. *S. T. C. at Malta.* But his kindness and benevolence lent a charm to his behaviour and manners, in whatever he was engaged. From the state of his own lungs, invalid-like, he was in the habit of attending much to those about him, and particularly those who had been sent to Malta for pulmonary disease. He frequently observed how much the invalid, at first landing, was relieved by the climate and the stimulus of change; but when the novelty, arising from that change, had ceased, the monotonous sameness of the blue sky, accompanied by the summer heat of the climate, acted powerfully as a sedative, ending in speedy dissolution,—even more speedy than in a colder climate. The effects on Coleridge seemed to run parallel to this. At first he remarked that he was relieved, but afterwards speaks of his limbs "as lifeless tools," and of the violent pains in his bowels, which neither opium, ether, nor peppermint, separately or combined, could relieve. The news from home, meantime, was not of a nature to cheer him. His accomplished and affectionate friend and munificent benefactor, Thomas Wedgwood, died suddenly on July 10,

1805. Mrs. Coleridge writes to Josiah Wedgwood from Keswick, Oct. 13, 1805:—"It will, I fear, prove a dreadful shock to Coleridge on his landing, for I have not written him an account of it, knowing how much mischief things of that nature occasion him. He kept his bed for a fortnight after being suddenly told of the fate of his friend Captain John Wordsworth ... He is only waiting the arrival of Mr. Chapman, the former Secretary, to resign his office to him. He says Sir A. B. behaves so well to him, and with so much kindness, that he should be sorry to occasion him any inconvenience."*

At last the long-expected Secretary did arrive to relieve him; and Coleridge, glad to be released from an occupation which however honourable and lucrative, was burdensome to him from its discordance with his habits and tastes, left Malta September 27, 1805.

Still officially employed, he took Sicily on his way to Rome. It seems that he had contracted for corn so ably in Sicily, that he had been requested to go to the Morea to *handle* and contract for bullocks. There is no evidence that Coleridge visited the Morea, but he spent some time in Naples and Rome. While in Rome, he was actively employed in visiting the great works of art, statues, pictures, buildings, palaces, &c., &c., observations on which he minuted down for publication. Here he became acquainted with the eminent literary men at that time collected there, and here the American painter Allston painted his portrait. Here he met Tieck and other illustrious Germans, to one of whom he was mainly

S. T. C. at Rome.

---

* See *A Group of Englishmen* (1795-1815), *being Records of the younger Wedgwoods and their friends*, &c., by Eliza Meteyard. Lond. Longmans, 1871, pp. 303, 304.

indebted for his safety, otherwise he might have terminated his career in the Temple at Paris: for to Bonaparte, through one of his industrious emissaries, Coleridge had become obnoxious, in consequence of an article written by him in the *Morning Post*. This salutary warning he obtained from the brother of the celebrated traveller, Humboldt, of whom he had inquired, whether he could pass through Switzerland and Germany, and return by that route to England. Humboldt then informed Coleridge that having passed through Paris on his journey to Rome, he had learnt that he, Coleridge, was a marked man, and unsafe: when within the reach of Bonaparte he advised him to be more than usually circumspect, and do all in his power to remain unknown.* Rather unexpectedly, he had a visit early one morning from a noble Benedictine, with a passport signed by the Pope, in order to facilitate his departure. He left him a carriage, and an admonition for instant flight, which was promptly obeyed by Coleridge. Hastening to Leghorn, he discovered an American vessel ready to sail for England, on board of which he embarked. On the voyage she was chased by a French vessel, which so alarmed the American that he compelled Coleridge to throw his

* The order for Coleridge's arrest had already been sent from Paris, but his escape was so contrived by the good old Pope as to defeat the intended indulgence of the tyrant's vindictive appetite, which would have " preyed equally on a Duc D'Enghien, and a contributor to a public journal." In consequence of Mr. Fox having asserted in the House of Commons that the rupture of the Truce of Amiens had its origin in certain essays written in the *Morning Post*, which were soon known to have been Coleridge's, and that he was at Rome within reach, the ire of Bonaparte was immediately excited.

papers overboard, and thus, to his great regret, were lost the fruits of his literary labours in Rome.

After an absence of two years and a half, Coleridge arrived again in England, in August, 1806. De Quincey considered that Coleridge's visit to the Mediterranean was an unfortunate chapter in his life, as he there confirmed and cherished his habit of taking opium in large quantities.

During Coleridge's absence at Malta, Wordsworth had completed the Autobiographical Poem on the Growth of his Individual Mind,* which had been commenced as far back as 1799. The poem is addressed to Coleridge throughout, and towards its close Wordsworth, in alluding to the earlier period of their intercourse, speaks of

<small>Wordsworth's Autobiographical Poem.</small>

> "That summer, under whose indulgent skies
> Upon smooth Quantock's airy ridge we roved
> Uncheck'd, or loiter'd 'mid her sylvan combs,
> Thou in bewitching words, with happy heart,
> Didst chaunt the vision of that Ancient Man,
> The bright-eyed Mariner, and rueful woes
> Didst utter of the Lady Christabel."

The profound impression which its recitation made upon Coleridge on his return to the Lake District is recorded in some majestic and melancholy lines of blank verse.† His own far different lot, with high hopes unfulfilled and lofty purposes shattered by

---

* Afterwards entitled *The Prelude, or Growth of a Poet's Mind, an Autobiographical Poem*. It remained in manuscript until after the author's death in 1850.

† First printed in *Sibylline Leaves*, 1817. (Vol. ii. pp. 224-228 of the present edition.)

weakness of will and failure of moral courage, cried out like the avenging voice of an awakened conscience, stung with remorse, and he exclaimed in bitterness and agony of soul :—

> "Ah ! as I listen'd with a heart forlorn,
> The pulses of my being beat anew :
> And even as life returns upon the drown'd,
> Life's joy rekindling roused a throng of pains.
> Keen pangs of Love, awakening as a babe
> Turbulent, with an outcry in the heart ;
> And fears self-will'd, that shunn'd the eye of hope ;
> And hope that scarce would know itself from fear ;
> Sense of past youth, and manhood come in vain,
> And genius given, and knowledge won in vain ;
> And all which I had cull'd in wood-walks wild,
> And all which patient toil had rear'd, and all
> Commune with thee had open'd out—but flowers
> Strew'd on my corse, and borne upon my bier,
> In the same coffin, for the selfsame grave ! "

The next few months were apparently spent partly in London, and partly at Grasmere and Keswick. When in London, Stuart, who had now become proprietor of *The Courier*, gave Coleridge apartments at the office of that newspaper, to save expense. That Coleridge acknowledged this obligation, and also occasional advances of money, by general assistance in and contributions to the paper, can hardly be doubted : indeed Stuart's assertion * that Coleridge did not

---

* The *Gentleman's Magazine*, of May, June and August 1838 contains Letters and Anecdotes of Coleridge, chiefly relating to his connexion with the *Morning Post* and the *Courier*, communicated by Daniel Stuart. Coleridge's assertion that he had employed the prime and manhood of his intellect

write a line for *The Courier* till the autumn of 1809—if meant to be taken absolutely and *au pied de la lettre*—is easily and at once disproved; for the beautiful poem *To Two Sisters* * is undoubtedly Coleridge's, and it undoubtedly appeared in *The Courier* in December 1807.

In the summer of 1807 Coleridge was visiting in the West of England, together with his family, amongst old Somersetshire friends. In a letter from Thomas Poole to Josiah Wedgwood, preserved amongst the Mayer MS., we get another pleasant little glimpse of the three children, and a sad enough reference to Coleridge himself :—

"Hartley is exactly like his father. Derwent is also much like him, but is stronger bodied, and more of the common of the world in him. The little girl is a sweet little animated fairy, that looks like her mother's family with her cap on, but like her father with her cap off. . . . . Coleridge educates the boys and he is beginning with Greek, in which I think he is very right. He is forming a Grammar and Lexicon from Greek at once into English, for their use, and, I trust, for publication . . . . He has been with me for these three weeks, with Mrs. Coleridge and his children. . . I admire him and pity him more than ever. His

in writing for these two newspapers, is treated by Stuart as a wilful and unwarrantable exaggeration. That Coleridge's private conviction on this matter coincided with his public statement, is evident from some doggerel lines which he scribbled in an old book, which were certainly not intended for publication, and in which he therefore could not be posturing or attitudinizing as a martyr. In these he identifies his individuality, should any one question it, as "The Morning Post's and Courier's S. T. C." (See vol. ii. p. 367.)

* Vol. ii. pp. 233-235 of the present edition.

information is much extended, the *great* qualities of his mind heightened and better disciplined; but alas! his health is weaker, and his great failing, procrastination, or the incapability of acting agreeably to his wish and will, much increased." ..... *Thos. Poole to Josiah Wedgwood* (June 27 1807).

It was at this period that Thomas De Quincey, then a student at Oxford, after long ardently desiring an introduction to Coleridge, at last succeeded * (August 1807) in effecting his object. Coleridge was at that time at Bridgewater, passing a day or two with Mr. Chubb, at whose house his wife and children were. Here De Quincey followed him, after vainly seeking him at Nether Stowey. He gives the following description of Coleridge's personal appearance :— [De Quincey and S. T. C.]

"In height he might seem to be about five feet eight (he was, in reality, about an inch and a half taller, but his figure was of an order which drowns the height); his person was broad and full, and tended even to corpulence; his complexion was fair, though not what painters technically style fair, because it was associated with black hair; his eyes were large and soft in their expression; and it was from the peculiar appearance of haze or dreaminess which mixed with their light that I recognised my object. This was Coleridge."

Later in the same year, at Bristol, De Quincey, who was then in circumstances of affluence, had the enthusiasm to present to Coleridge, under the guise of an unknown admirer of his genius, and through the medium of Cottle, the munificent sum of £300. After some hesitation the poet accepted it: whether the source of the gift ever transpired is uncertain.

* Late in July or early in August.

Early in 1808 (February to May) Coleridge gave a series of Lectures at the Royal Institution, and again he had apartments in the *Courier* office. In these he already propounded those views on Shakespeare which he was afterwards accused of borrowing from Schlegel, but which Schlegel had not then promulgated. De Quincey attended this Course of Lectures, which he says were irregularly delivered, and were frequently slovenly and unworthy of Coleridge's genius.

<small>Lectures in 1808.</small>

In 1809 he settled his residence again in the Lake District, as the guest of Wordsworth, at Grasmere, and De Quincey, who had taken a lease of the cottage formerly occupied by Wordsworth (who had removed to a larger house, three quarters of a mile distant, called Allan Bank), was now the permanent neighbour of both, and saw Coleridge daily.

At Grasmere Coleridge projected his periodical publication entitled *The Friend*. In this work, which was mainly written by himself, appeared many of his finest prose essays. He occasionally, however, received assistance from other writers. Professor Wilson contributed the letter signed "Mathetes," Wordsworth contributed the reply to it, containing Advice to the Young, and signed M.M., as also the Essay on Epitaphs, with some translations from Chiabrera, several political Sonnets, and a passage from *The Prelude*. The only poetical pieces of Coleridge which appeared for the first time in *The Friend* were

<small>The *Friend*.</small>

   A Tombless Epitaph.*
   The Three Graves.†

* Vol. ii. pp. 204-206 of the present edition.
† *Ib.* pp. 238-254.

The former poem appears to have been suggested by his friend Wordsworth's employment upon Chiabrera, of one of whose Epitaphs it is an imitation. The latter had been written in the old Quantock days, and had remained, like *Christabel*, in manuscript.

The Friend was printed on stamped paper, by a printer of the name of Brown, at Penrith. The first number appeared on Thursday, June 1st, 1809, and the twenty-seventh and last on March 15th, 1810.* Though a work of far greater power and originality, as a commercial speculation, it shared the same fate as *The Watchman*. This was partly due to the unpopularity of the subjects treated of, and partly to the inconvenient mode of publication. The issue of *Fors Clavigera* in our time from Orpington is as nothing to it, for we live in an age of railways and halfpenny postage: moreover Mr. Ruskin, more provident than Coleridge, has been wise enough to receive his subscriptions in advance. Many of Coleridge's subscribers never paid at all; and in the later remodelled edition of *The Friend* issued nine years afterwards there is an amusing notification that outstanding subscriptions may be sent to the Author at Highgate. Whether any 'conscience-money' ever reached Coleridge in this way, we cannot say.

Shortly after the cessation of *The Friend*, Coleridge left the Lake District (never to return to it)† in company with Mr. Basil Montagu, at whose house he remained for some time domesticated. He had already

---

* In 1812 some of the unsold and unstamped copies were issued as a volume by Gale and Curtis of Paternoster-row.

† He alludes to this change twelve years afterwards, in a letter to Allsop, as one of the 'four griping and grasping sorrows' of his life.

commenced, in the autumn of 1809, while *The Friend* was still in existence, and he continued with occasional intermissions for several years, his long and brilliant series of political articles in *The Courier*.

From Mr. Montagu's house Coleridge removed to Hammersmith ('No. 7, Portland-place'), where he resided with an amiable and common friend of his and Southey's—a Mr. John Morgan, with whom they had formed an intimacy in the old Bristol days. Whilst here he delivered a course of Lectures at the London Philosophical Society, Crane Court, Fleet Street. The prospectus was as follows :—

<small>Course of Lectures 1811-1812.</small> "Mr. Coleridge will commence, on Monday, November 18, a Course of Lectures on Shakespeare and Milton, in illustration of the principles of Poetry, and their application, as grounds of criticism, to the most popular works of later English Poets, those of the living included. After an Introductory Lecture on False Criticism (especially in Poetry), and on its causes; two-thirds of the remaining course will be assigned, 1st, to a philosophical analysis and explanation of all the principal characters of our great dramatist, as Othello, Falstaff, Richard the Third, Iago, Hamlet, &c.; and 2nd, to a critical comparison of Shakespeare, in respect of diction, imagery, management of the passions, judgment in the construction of his dramas, in short, of all that belongs to him as a poet, and as a dramatic poet, with his contemporaries or immediate successors, Jonson, Beaumont and Fletcher, Ford, Massinger, &c., in the endeavour to determine what of Shakespeare's merits and defects are common to him, with other writers of the same age, and what remain peculiar to his own genius.

"The course will extend to fifteen lectures, which

MEMOIR OF COLERIDGE.   lxxxix

will be given on Monday and Thursday evenings successively."*

Two snatches of verse, undoubtedly by Coleridge, appeared this year in *The Courier*.

1811.

Aug. 30. The Virgin's Cradle-Hymn.†
Sept. 21. Mutual Passion. Altered and modernized from an old Poet.‡

and as these, so far as I am aware, close the series of his known and ascertained poetical con- Poems tributions to the *Post* and the *Courier*, it in *The* may be as well to mention that in both *Courier*. these papers, and especially in the latter, there may yet lie buried other poems by Coleridge, which we at present want sufficient internal or external evidence to identify.

A letter written by Wordsworth to Lady Beaumont (Nov. 20, 1811) contains the following passage :—

"In the *Courier* of Saturday [Nov. 16, 1811] is a little poem upon the 'The Comet,' which consists of five stanzas in the measure of the Faery Doubtful Queene. Though with several defects, Poems. some feeble and constrained expressions, it has great merit, and is far superior to the run, not merely of newspaper, but of modern poetry

---

* Seven of these fifteen Lectures, from shorthand notes taken at the time, and with an Introduction containing many interesting particulars relating to Coleridge, were published by Mr. Payne Collier in 1856.

† Vol. ii. pp. 230-231 of the present edition.

‡ *Ib.* pp. 236-237. Both these pieces were included in the collection of *Sibylline Leaves*, 1817.

in general. I half suspect it to be Coleridge's,* for though it is, in parts, inferior to him, I know no other writer of the day who can do so well." I have myself noted half-a-dozen pieces in *The Courier* of 1807 and the two following years (*Mary*, April 3; *How d'y'do and Goodbye*, April 25; *To a Lady who threatened to make the Author an April Fool*, June 12; *Arabian Song*, June 26, 1807; *On recovery from Sickness*, March 3, 1808; *A Recipe to make a Kiss*, Nov. 27, 1809), any or all of which may be his, though none of them (like the poem which appeared in the same newspaper later in that year and which we know to be his by the double evidence of its subscription † and its partial republication in the *Sibylline* Ἐστησε. *Leaves*) bear any form of his well-known and favourite Greek signature, sufficient in itself to authenticate any poem of those early years of the century, wherever it occurs.

In 1812 Coleridge contributed a number of short axioms and reflections in prose (all marked in the Contents with an asterisk) to the two volumes of his friend Southey's *Omniana*.‡ These have been reprinted in his *Literary Remains*.

A rare piece of good fortune now awaited Coleridge. His tragedy, remodelled and with an altered title, was

---

* It should be observed that the poem is signed "C." The aggregate internal and external evidence did not, however, seem to us sufficient to warrant its insertion, even in the Appendix.

† The lines "to Two Sisters" (*Courier*, Dec. 10, 1807) bore the signature of "Siesti."

‡ *Omniana, or Horæ Otiosiores*. London: Printed for Longman, Hurst, Rees, Orme and Brown, Paternoster-row, 1812.

destined, after a lapse of fifteen years, to be performed with brilliant success at the very theatre where it had before been so ignominiously rejected. This happy result was owing mainly to the good offices of Lord Byron, whose interest at the newly-rebuilt house secured its acceptance. The generous aid so opportunely extended by the noble poet to his less fortunate brother is one of the pleasantest episodes in the history of the much-maligned author of *Childe Harold.* It might fairly be considered to condone the boyish banter of the *English Bards,* and even the badinage of *Don Juan,* which De Quincey has perhaps taken too much *au sérieux.* _{Remorse performed at Drury Lane.}

The tragedy was performed for the first time, under the title of *Remorse,* at Drury Lane Theatre on Saturday, January 23, 1813. The Prologue was written by Charles Lamb, and the Epilogue by the author himself. The success was immediate and decisive, and the play had a run of twenty nights.

The success of the play does not however seem to have greatly exhilarated the poet himself. His fatal bondage to opium had by this time gone nigh to ruin him, physically and mentally; and it had now reached its worst stage. The Preface and Epilogue bear too sad and evident traces of the almost total eclipse during this period of his magnificent powers.

On Feb. 14, 1813, Coleridge wrote thus to his friend Poole :—" The receipt of your heart-engendered lines was sweeter than an unexpected strain of sweetest music ;—or in humbler phrase, it was the only pleasurable sensation which the success of the *Remorse* has given me. No grocer's apprentice, after his first month's permitted riot, was ever sicker of figs and raisins than I of _{S. T. C. to Thos. Poole.}

hearing about the *Remorse*. The endless rat-a-tat-tat at our black-and-blue bruised door, and my three master fiends, proof-sheets, letters,—and worse than these—invitations to large dinners, which I cannot refuse without offence and imputation of pride (&c.), oppress me so that my spirits quite sink under it. I have never seen the play since the first night. It has been a good thing for the theatre. They will get eight or ten thousand pounds by it, and I shall get more than by all my literary labours put together; nay, thrice as much."

<small>Lectures at Bristol in 1814.</small> In the earlier part of 1814, Coleridge paid a long visit to Bristol, and delivered a course of Lectures there, which, however, appear to have been very sparsely attended. His early friend Cottle, who had not seen him since 1807, and then for a short time only, was much shocked by Coleridge's utter prostration, of which he now first ascertained the cause.* He addressed to him a letter of remonstrance, not very delicately worded; and with still less delicacy, he lingers in his book of *Recollections* with somewhat prolix and unnecessary minuteness over the details of this painful period of Coleridge's life. All his kindness and goodwill to Coleridge cannot excuse his blundering exhortations and his still more grievous violation of friendship after Cole-

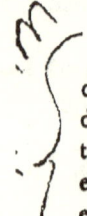

* "In 1814 S. T. C. had been long, very long, in the habit of taking from two quarts of laudanum a week to a pint a day; and on one occasion he had been known to take in the twenty-four hours a whole quart of laudanum! The serious expenditure of money resulting from this habit was the least evil, though very great, and must have absorbed all the produce of his writings and lectures, and the liberalities of his friends."—COTTLE.

ridge's death, under the specious plea of giving "a warning to others."

In an unpublished letter dated "Bristol, July 16, 1814," * Coleridge alludes to a complaint in one of his legs. "In head and vigour of mind I am not amiss, in disposition to activity much improved, but subject at times to strange relapses; for instance, all last Sunday I was thoroughly be-*belzebubbed*." <small>Unpublished letter.</small>

The same letter contains an interesting reference to Southey's *Joan of Arc*, and his own contribution to it:—

"I looked over the five first Books of the 1st (quarto) edition of *Joan of Arc* yesterday, in order to mark the lines written by me. I was really astonished—1, at the school-boy wretched allegoric machinery—2, at the transmogrification of the fanatic Virago, into a modern Novel-pawing proselyte of the Age of Reason, a Tom Paine in Petticoats, but so lovely! and in love more dear! ' *On her rubied cheek hung pity's crystal gem* '—3, at the utter want of all rhythm in the verse, the monotony and dead plumb down of the pauses, and of the absence of all bone, muscle, and sinew in the single lines."

Coleridge left Bristol in August 1814. "A general impression," says Cottle, " prevailed on the minds of his friends that it was a desperate case, that paralyzed all their efforts : that to assist Coleridge with money, which under favourable circumstances would have been most promptly advanced, would now only enlarge his capacity to obtain the opium which was consuming

---

* Formerly in the possession of the Publisher of the present volumes.

him. We merely knew that Coleridge had retired with his friend Mr. John Morgan, to a small house, at Calne, in Wiltshire." From this place he writes to Cottle, March 7, 1815 :—
"You will wish to know something of myself. In health I am not worse than when at Bristol I was best, yet fluctuating, yet unhappy, in circumstances poor indeed! I have collected my scattered and my manuscript poems, sufficient to make one volume. Enough I have to make another. But till the latter is finished, I cannot, without great loss of character, publish the former, on account of the arrangement, besides the necessity of correction. For instance, I earnestly wish to begin the volumes with what has never been seen by any, however few, such as a series of Odes on the different sentences of the Lord's Prayer,* and more than all this, to finish my greater work on 'Christianity considered as philosophy, and as the only philosophy.'" He then solicits of Cottle a loan of forty pounds on the security of his manuscripts; which Cottle declined, but sent him some smaller temporary relief. Finally he mentions a project for taking a house and receiving pupils to board and instruct, which Cottle (somewhat strangely, we think) seems to consider the crowning degradation and ignominy of all.

Again the good offices of Lord Byron were interposed to aid Coleridge. Besides presenting him with

---

* At the end of the first volume of *Biographia Literaria* Coleridge speaks of "the Critical Essay on the uses of the Supernatural in Poetry, and the principles that regulate its introduction, which the reader will find prefixed to the poem of 'The Ancient Mariner,'"—another scheme *meditated* at this period, but never accomplished.

MEMOIR OF COLERIDGE.

a hundred pounds, he writes to him from Piccadilly, March 13, 1815, urging him to make a second attempt:—"In Kean there is an actor worthy of expressing the thoughts of the characters which you have every power of embodying, and I cannot but regret that the part of 'Ordonio' was disposed of before his appearance at Drury Lane. We have had nothing to be mentioned in the same breath with *Remorse* for very many years, and I should think that the reception of that play was sufficient to encourage the highest hopes of author and audience." Coleridge did make the attempt; but unfortunately by that time his noble brother-poet had left England for ever; and Coleridge's second play *Zapolya*, though otherwise successful, was not destined to be produced on the stage. One other good office Lord Byron performed for Coleridge before his departure. He introduced him to Mr. Murray, the great publisher, who in 1816 brought out at last the marvellous poem that had so long lain in manuscript. *Christabel* was an immediate success; and ran through three editions in the same year.

Lord Byron to Coleridge.

Shortly before its publication Coleridge had at last found a friendly asylum, and hope of recovery, in the house of one whose name no lover of genius and excellence can ever think of without respect. On the representation of an eminent physician, and after a personal interview with Coleridge, Mr. James Gillman, a surgeon of Highgate, consented to receive the poet into his home, and to undertake and accomplish his gradual cure. Hither Coleridge came, 'bringing in his hand the proof-sheets of *Christabel*,' on the evening of Monday, April 15, 1816, and here he remained till death. On the

S. T. C. settles at Highgate.

previous Saturday he had written a letter to Mr. Gillman, which is worth preserving here :—

"42, *Norfolk Street, Strand, Saturday Noon.*
"[*April* 13, 1816.]
"My dear Sir,
"The first half hour I was with you convinced me that I should owe my reception into your family exclusively to motives not less flattering to me than honourable to yourself. I trust we shall ever in matters of intellect be reciprocally serviceable to each other. Men of sense generally come to the same conclusions; but they are likely to contribute to each other's enlargement of view, in proportion to the distance or even opposition of the points from which they set out. Travel and the strange variety of situations and employments on which chance has thrown me, in the course of my life, might have made me a mere man of *observation*, if pain and sorrow and self-miscomplacence had not forced my mind in on itself, and so formed habits of *meditation*. It is now as much my nature to evolve the fact from the law, as that of a practical man to deduce the law from the fact.

"With respect to pecuniary remuneration, allow me to say, I must not at least be suffered to make any addition to your family expenses—though I cannot offer any thing that would be in any way adequate to my sense of the service; for that indeed there could not be a compensation, as it must be returned in kind, and by esteem and grateful affection.

"And now of myself. My ever wakeful reason, and the keenness of my moral feelings, will secure you from all unpleasant circumstances connected with me save only one, viz. the evasion of a specific madness. You will never *hear* any thing but truth from me :—

prior habits render it out of my power to tell an untruth, but unless carefully observed, I dare not promise that I should not, with regard to this detested poison, be capable of acting one. No sixty hours have yet passed without my having taken laudanum, though for the last week comparatively trifling doses. I have full belief that your anxiety need not be extended beyond the first week; I shall not, I must not, be permitted to leave your house, unless with you. Delicately or indelicately, this must be done, and both the servants and the assistant must receive absolute commands from you. The stimulus of conversation suspends the terror that haunts my mind; but when I am alone, the horrors I have suffered from laudanum, the degradation, the blighted utility, almost overwhelm me. If (as I feel for the *first time* a soothing confidence it will prove) I should leave you restored to my moral and bodily health, it is not myself only that will love and honour you; every friend I have, (and, thank God! in spite of this wretched vice, I have many and warm ones, who were friends of my youth, and have never deserted me,) will thank you with reverence. I have taken no notice of your kind apologies. If I could not be comfortable in your house, and with your family, I should deserve to be miserable. If you could make it convenient, I should wish to be with you by Monday evening, as it would prevent the necessity of taking fresh lodgings in town.

With respectful compliments to Mrs. Gillman and her sister, I remain, dear sir,

Your much obliged,
S. T. COLERIDGE."*

* Gillman, pp. 273-276.

Several publications of Coleridge, both in prose and verse, now followed each other in rapid succession; viz., the two Lay Sermons (*a*), the *Biographia Literaria* (*b*), *Sibylline Leaves* (*c*), *Zapolya* (*d*), and a new edition, or rather a *rifaccimento* of *The Friend* (*e*).

(*a*) *The Statesman's Manual ; or the Bible the best Guide to Political Skill and Foresight: a Lay Sermon, addressed to the higher classes of Society, with an Appendix, containing Comments and Essays connected with the Study of the Inspired Writings.* By S. T. Coleridge, Esq. London: Printed for Gale and Fenner, Paternoster Row, &c. 1816, pp. XLVII. 65.

"Blessed are ye that sow beside all Waters!" *A Lay Sermon, addressed to the higher and middle classes, on the existing distresses and discontents.* By S. T. Coleridge, Esq. London: Printed for Gale and Fenner, &c. 1817, XXXI, 134.

(*b*) *Biographia Literaria, or Biographical Sketches of my Literary Life and Opinions,* by S. T. Coleridge, Esq., 2 vols. London: Rest Fenner, Paternoster-row, 1817. Vol i. pp. 296, Vol. ii. pp. 309. The first volume and the second to page 144 were printed at Bristol by J. M. Gutch. The remainder of the second volume and the Title-pages were printed by Curtis of Camberwell.

(*c*) *Sibylline Leaves, A Collection of Poems,* by S. T. Coleridge, Esq. London: Rest Fenner, 23, Paternoster-row, 1817, pp. VIII. 303.

(*d*) *Zapolya : A Christmas Tale, in Two Parts : The Prelude entitled* The Usurper's Fortune ; *and the Sequel entitled* The Usurper's Fate. By S. T. Coleridge, Esq. London: Printed for Rest Fenner, Paternoster-row. 1817, pp. XII. 128.

(*e*) *The Friend : a Series of Essays, in Three Volumes, to aid in the formation of fixed principles in politics, morals, and religion, with literary amusements interspersed.* By S. T. Coleridge, Esq. London: Printed for Rest Fenner, Paternoster-row, 1818.

These six publications, unfortunately for Coleridge, were issued, not by Mr. Murray, of Albemarle-street, who had published his *Christabel*; but by the house of Gale and Fenner, afterwards Rest Fenner, or Fenner and Curtis, in Paternoster-row. A short time afterwards that house became bankrupt; and Coleridge lost all or nearly all the profits that would have accrued from the sale of these nine volumes of his writings.

The drama of *Zapolya* and the *Biographia Literaria* had been composed during Coleridge's retirement at Calne in 1814-15. *Zapolya* was dictated to his friend Mr. Morgan while walking up and down the room. It was submitted to Mr. Douglas Kinnaird, who was then the critic for Drury Lane. Mr. Kinnaird rejected the play, assigning some ludicrous objections to the metaphysics. On its publication, however, as a Christmas tale, it became so immediately popular that two thousand copies were sold in six weeks.

The *Biographia Literaria*, with the exception of the concluding sheets of the second volume, and the *Sibylline Leaves*, with the exception of the preliminary sheet (Title, Preface, Errata, &c.), had been printed at Bristol in 1815, nearly two years prior to their actual publication.

The *Sibylline Leaves* had been intended, as we have seen, to be preceded by another volume of verse, and accordingly on the printer's signatures of every sheet we find "Vol. II." appearing. This scheme, however, was abandoned, like so many of Coleridge's schemes, and the Second Volume was left without any first to accompany it. A sheet containing Title, Preface, three additional Poems,* and a leaf with a ter-

* *Time, Real and Imaginary*, *The Raven*, *A Christmas Tale*, and *Mutual Passion*.

ribly long list of Errata, but no Table of Contents, was printed in London, and the book was published, as we have already seen, by Fenner, in 1817. The date 1817, appended in our footnotes to any various reading, must be understood always to refer to this volume, though it will be well to remember that the date of printing was not 1817, but 1815.

"The following collection," says Coleridge in the Preface, "has been entitled SIBYLLINE LEAVES; in <small>Preface to Sibylline Leaves.</small> allusion to the fragmentary and widely scattered state in which they have been long suffered to remain. It contains the whole of the author's poetical compositions, from 1793 to the present date, with the exception of a few works not yet finished, and those published in the first edition of his Juvenile Poems, over which he has no control.* They may be divided into three classes: First, A selection from the Poems added to the second and third† editions, together with those originally published in the *Lyrical Ballads*, which after having remained many years out of print, have been omitted by Mr. Wordsworth in the recent collection of all his minor poems, and of course revert to the author. Second, Poems published at very different periods, in various obscure or perishable journals, &c., some with, some without the writer's

---

* One poem from this first edition was, however, (perhaps by inadvertence) reprinted in the *Sibylline Leaves*, as we shall presently see.—ED.

† No new poem was *added* to the third edition, though one or two pieces were restored from the first edition, which had been omitted in the second. Of the twelve poems added in the second edition (1797) nine reappeared in *Sibylline Leaves*.—ED.

consent; many imperfect, all incorrect. The third and last class is formed of Poems which have hitherto remained in manuscript. The whole is now presented to the reader collectively, with considerable additions and alterations, and as perfect as the author's judgment and powers could render them.

"In my Literary Life, it has been mentioned that, with the exception of this Preface, the SIBYLLINE LEAVES have been printed almost two years; and the necessity of troubling the reader with the list of Errata, which follows this preface, alone induces me to refer again to the circumstance, at the risk of ungenial feelings, from the recollection of its worthless causes. A few corrections of later date have been added.—Henceforward the author must be occupied by studies of a very different kind.

> Ite hinc, CAMŒNÆ! Vos quoque ite, suaves,
> Dulces CAMŒNÆ! Nam (fatebimur verum)
> Dulces fuistis!—Et tamen meas chartas
> Revisitote: sed pudenter et raro!
> VIRGIL. Catalect. vii."

We may here supply, what is wanting in the original edition, a list of the Contents of *Sibylline Leaves*. The pieces italicized were printed (as far as we have been able to discover) for the first time:—

The Rime of the Ancient Mariner.
The Foster-Mother's Tale.

Poems occasioned by Political Events or feelings connected with them.

Ode to the Departing Year.
France: An Ode.
Fears in Solitude.

Recantation. Illustrated in the Story of the Mad Ox.
Parliamentary Oscillators.*
Fire, Famine and Slaughter, a War Eclogue.
(*With an Apologetic Preface*).†

Love-Poems.

Love.‡
Lewti, or the Circassian Love-Chant.
The Picture, or the Lover's Resolution.
The Night-Scene: A Dramatic Fragment.
To an Unfortunate Woman, whom the Author had known in the days of her innocence.
To an Unfortunate Woman at the Theatre.
Lines composed in a Concert-room.
The Keepsake.
To a Lady with Falconer's Shipwreck.
To a Young Lady, on her recovery from a fever.
Something childish, but very natural.
Home-sick. Written in Germany.
Answer to a Child's Question.
The Visionary Hope.
The Happy Husband. A Fragment.
Recollections of Love.
On Revisiting the sea-shore, after long absence, under strong medical recommendation not to bathe.

* Dated 1794, and presumably printed in *The Morning Chronicle* in that year; but the volume of that date in the British Museum being imperfect, we have not been able to trace it.

† The Preface appears for the first time in *Sibylline Leaves.*

‡ Introduction to the Ballad of The Dark Ladie: see vol. ii. pp. 92-97 of the present edition.

Meditative Poems in Blank Verse.

Hymn before Sunrise, in the Vale of Chamouni.
Lines written in the Album at Elbingerode.
On observing a blossom on the 1st February, 1796.
The Eolian Harp, composed at Clevedon, Somersetshire.*
Reflections on leaving a place of Retirement.
To the Rev. George Coleridge, of Ottery St. Mary, with some Poems.
Inscription for a Fountain on a Heath.
A Tombless Epitaph.
This Lime-tree bower my prison.
To a friend who had declared his intention of writing no more poetry.
To a Gentleman. Composed on the night after his recitation of a Poem on the Growth of an Individual Mind.
The Nightingale; a Conversation Poem.
Frost at Midnight.
The Three Graves.

Odes and Miscellaneous Poems.

Dejection : An Ode.
Ode to Georgiana, Duchess of Devonshire.
Ode to Tranquillity.
To a Young Friend, on his proposing to domesticate with the Author.
Lines to W. L., Esq., while he sang a song to Purcell's Music.
To a Young Man of Fortune who abandoned himself to an indolent and causeless melancholy.

* This is the only piece from the *first* (1796) edition of Coleridge's Poems reprinted in *Sibylline Leaves.*

Sonnet to the River Otter.
Sonnet composed on a journey homeward, the Author having received intelligence of the birth of a son.
Sonnet to a friend who asked how I felt when the nurse first presented my infant to me.
The Virgin's Cradle-Hymn.
Epitaph on an Infant.
Melancholy : A Fragment.
Tell's Birth-place. Imitated from Stolberg.
A Christmas Carol.
Human Life. On the Denial of Immortality. A Fragment.
An Ode to the Rain.
The Visit of the Gods. Imitated from Schiller.
Elegy imitated from one of Akenside's Blank-verse Inscriptions.
The Destiny of Nations. A Vision.

To these should be added the three additional pieces printed in the preliminary sheet, viz. :

Time, Real and Imaginary.
The Raven, a Christmas Tale.
Mutual Passion, altered and modernized from an old Poet.

Of the thirteen presumably new pieces, or pieces which, not having traced them to any earlier source, I assume to have been first printed in the volume of *Sibylline Leaves*, the date of composition of at least four can be fixed with something like certainty at a considerably earlier period. *The Visionary Hope*, as we have already seen, is most probably the poem alluded to by Coleridge himself as having been written in 1803. *Recollections of Love* would seem, from the internal evidence of an allusion in the first two lines of the second stanza, to have been written at Keswick in the summer of 1806. The lines to Wordsworth on his Autobiographical Poem were also evidently written in the Lake district about the same period. *Time, Real and Imaginary* is confessedly a schoolboy poem.

This reduces to very narrow compass the quantity of verse produced by Coleridge during the last twenty years of his life. His poetical flights were henceforth, as he had intimated they would be, few and far between. Of the pieces printed for the first time in the Collected Editions of 1828-9 and 1834, very few can with certainty be pronounced to be the work of his later years, and many of them undoubtedly belong to a much earlier period. "It has been found impossible," says his daughter, "to ascertain the date of *Alice du Clos.*" The exquisite lines entitled *Work without Hope* were written early in 1827, and a portion at least of the poem called *Youth and Age* seems to have been composed about the same time. *The Garden of Boccaccio* is the happiest production of this later time, and in a very different style, the poem entitled *A Character* is worthy of Swift, in its scathing sarcasm and high-minded vindication of and apology for the aims of a life. Other pieces, such as the Lines to Kayser and the concluding Epitaph, are dated and belong to the last year or two of Coleridge's life.

De Quincey indeed considered that opium-eating proved fatal to the exercise of Coleridge's poetical powers. "We are of opinion that it killed Coleridge as a poet. 'The harp of Quantock' was silenced for ever by the torment of opium; but proportionably it roused and stung by misery his metaphysical ininstincts into more spasmodic life. Poetry can flourish only in the

Later Poems.

Fatal effect of opium on S. T. C. as a poet.

atmosphere of happiness. But subtle and perplexed investigations of difficult problems are amongst the commonest resources for beguiling the sense of misery."*

Coleridge, however, himself is reported to have said late in life:—"I could write as good verses now as ever I did, if I were perfectly free from vexations, and were in the *ad libitum* hearing of fine music, which has a sensible effect in harmonizing my thoughts, and in animating and, as it were, lubricating my inventive faculty."†

Shortly after his settlement at Highgate, Coleridge resumed his occupation of public lecturer. In the earlier months of 1818, he delivered a course of fourteen Lectures on Literature, which appear to have been more brilliant and more successful than any of his previous attempts. The lecture-room (in Flower de Luce Court) being near the Temple, many of the students were among his auditors. "He lectured," says Mr. Gillman, "from notes, which he had carefully made; yet it was obvious, that his audience was more delighted when, putting his notes aside, he spoke extempore. He was brilliant, fluent, and rapid; his words seemed to flow as from a person repeating with grace and energy some delightful poem. If, however, he sometimes paused, it was not for the want of words, but that he was seeking the most appropriate, or their most logical arrangement."

<small>Course of Lectures in 1818.</small>

It was after the delivery of the first of these Lectures that Coleridge became acquainted with his enthusi-

---

* *Coleridge and Opium-eating* (1844): De Quincey's Works, xi. 105, 106.

† *Table-Talk of S. T. C.*, vol. ii. p. 221 (under date July 6, 1833).

astic disciple, Thomas Allsop, with whom he was in constant correspondence for seven years afterwards, and who in 1836 published two volumes of *Letters, Conversations and Recollections of Coleridge*, frequently quoted in the course of the present volumes.

<small>Thomas Allsop.</small>

In 1821 Coleridge offered himself as an occasional contributor to Blackwood's Magazine;* but the papers he sent were of a fragmentary character and were never completed.

On May 18, 1825, Coleridge read a paper before the Royal Society of Literature, on "The Prometheus of Æschylus, an Essay preparatory to a series of Disquisitions respecting the Egyptian in connexion with the sacerdotal Theology and in contrast with the Mysteries of Ancient Greece." The promised "series of Disquisitions," however, that were to follow, were heard of no more.

In the same year, Coleridge published his *Aids to Reflection*—one of the most popular and best known of his prose works.†

In 1828 the monotony and even tenour of Coleridge's life under Mr. Gillman's roof at Highgate, were broken by the interesting episode of a tour up

---

* *Selections from Mr. Coleridge's Literary Correspondence,* —Blackwood's Edinburgh Magazine, October, 1821. More was promised, but more never appeared.

Ib.—January, 1822, a wild fragment in prose, entitled *The Historie and Gests of Maxilian.*

† *Aids to Reflection in the formation of a manly character on the several grounds of Prudence, Morality and Religion: illustrated by select passages from our elder Divines, especially from Archbishop Leighton.* By S. T. Coleridge. London: Printed for Taylor and Hessey, 1825. xvi. 404.

Tour up the Rhine with Wordsworth. the Rhine in company with Wordsworth and his daughter. Upon the banks of that beautiful river they passed a fortnight, chiefly under the hospitable roof of Mr. Aders of Gotesberg. Since Coleridge's final departure from the Lake District in 1810, the intercourse between himself and Wordsworth either personally or by letter had been very scant and intermittent, confined mainly to a passing call at Highgate on Wordsworth's occasional visits to London. Thus thrown together again, it may well be imagined with what solemn sadness and sweetness the thoughts of the two poets would revert to the earliest period of their friendship, and how at times, as to a great living poet,

"The two and thirty years were a mist that rolls away."

It was in 1828 also that the first collected edition appeared of Coleridge's Poetical and Dramatic Works, *Collected Poetical Works, 1828-9.* in three handsome octavo volumes, published by the late William Pickering. The same edition was re-issued in 1829, without alteration or addition, and it is under the latter date that it is referred to in one or two of the footnotes to these volumes.

The edition of 1828-9 was the last upon which Coleridge was able to bestow personal care and attention. *Edition of 1834.* The fuller and more complete edition issued by the same publisher in three smaller volumes in 1834 was arranged mainly, if not entirely, at the discretion of his nephew and son-in-law, Henry Nelson Coleridge,* who also edited Cole-

* Henry Nelson and Sara Coleridge (the daughter of the poet) were married September 3, 1829, at Crosthwaite Church,

ridge's *Table-Talk, Literary Remains, Confessions of an Inquiring Spirit*, &c., &c.

During the later years of Coleridge's life, Mr. Gillman's house at Highgate became a centre of attraction and curiosity to a number of ardent young minds, and among those who made pilgrimages to this shrine are not a few names that themselves afterwards became famous. In a lane near Highgate one day, "a loose, slack, not well-dressed youth" (by name John Keats) met Coleridge walking with a friend who knew them both, and who introduced them to each other. "After he had left us a little way," Coleridge related many years afterwards, he came back, and said: "Let me carry away the memory, Coleridge, of having pressed your hand!" With an instinctive and sad prescience Coleridge remarked when the boy-poet had departed (bearing that memory of *Tantum vidi* along with him) that there was death in that hand.* Keats meets Coleridge.

Hither to Highgate, in later years, would Hare and Maurice and Sterling repair, as loving disciples, to hang upon the great man's lips. Everybody remembers that wonderful chapter in the Life of John Sterling, in which Mr. Carlyle has described Coleridge's appearance and manner of talk in those latter times. Hither too an American pilgrim, Ralph Waldo Emer- Pilgrims to Highgate.

Keswick. Of their children, the twins Berkeley and Florence died in infancy; Herbert, who became distinguished as a philologist, died in 1861; Edith, edited her mother's Memoirs and Letters already quoted. Henry Nelson Coleridge died January 1843, and his accomplished wife on 3rd May, 1852.

* *Table-Talk of S. T. C.*, vol ii. pp. 89-90.

son, was drawn in 1833, and has left us a record of his visit hardly less graphic.

Of the marvellous eloquence and fluency of Coleridge's talk it is probable that no description or record, however, can convey anything like an adequate idea. Of the style and manner of it his own report of a speech he made before a brilliant assembly of guests at a dinner-party, forming a part of the Apologetic Preface to *Fire, Famine, and Slaughter*, would, I should think, give as good a notion as any.

Coleridge's last separate work, issued during his life-time, was an Essay on the Constitution of the Church and State.*

He contributed a number of pieces in prose and verse during the later years of his life to the then fashionable annuals, the *Literary Souvenir*, the *Bijou*, the *Keepsake*, the *Amulet*, *Friendship's Offering*, &c. These I have traced as far as possible; but I cannot be sure that I have traced them all. One song he seems to have given to John Sterling for the *Athenæum;* the *Water-Ballad*,† printed there in 1831 and now unearthed for the first time. *The Old Man's Sigh*‡ with a Prose Introduction, appeared in *Blackwood's Magazine* in the following year (1832).

The only remaining event that varied the even tenour of Coleridge's later days at Highgate was his visit to Cambridge, upon the occasion of the Scientific Meeting there, in June, 1833. "My emotions," he said, "at re-visiting the University, were at first over-

---

* *On the Constitution of the Church and State, according to the idea of each: with aids toward a right judgment on the late Catholic Bill.* By S. T. Coleridge, Esq., R.A. R.S.L. London : Hurst, Chance, and Co., 1830, pp. viii. 227.

† Vol. ii. pp. 30-56. ‡ See vol. ii. p. 302, *note*.

whelming. I could not speak for an hour; yet my feelings were upon the whole very pleasurable, and I have not passed, of late years at least, three days of such great enjoyment and healthful excitement of mind and body."*

Samuel Taylor Coleridge died at Highgate, July 25th, 1834, in the sixty-second year of his age, at the house where he had for eighteen years been so affectionately tended.

The life of Coleridge divides itself broadly into three distinct portions. 1. That earlier portion of it which belongs distinctly to the eighteenth century, in which all or nearly all the work by which he will be remembered as a poet was produced. 2. The prime of his manhood and middle age onwards to 1818, devoted mainly to political journalism, to æsthetic criticism, and to public lecturing; and, 3. The later years of his life at Highgate, entirely devoted to philosophy, metaphysics and theology. It is with the first period that we have been chiefly concerned here, and we have endeavoured to review it in some detail. The second and third periods we have passed over more lightly and rapidly.

It would not perhaps be too hazardous to affirm that if Coleridge had died in his thirtieth year, as Shelley did, and if his verse had been then collected, he would have stood quite as high as a poet as he now does. And in any estimate of modern poetry, the rank and importance of Coleridge's contributions to it can never be adequately or duly estimated without remembering that all the essential part of them had

---

* *Table-Talk*, ii. 200, *note*. See also " S. T. Coleridge at Trinity," in a volume entitled *Conversations at Cambridge*, published in 1836.

been produced long before Byron, Shelley, Keats, or even Scott had begun to write. Nor, again, will it be too bold to assert that these four great master-singers would never have produced the work they afterwards did, if Coleridge had not preceded them.

Much has been done, though much still remains to be done, towards the collection and arrangement of Coleridge's Prose Writings. The chief remaining desiderata in that department are—1. A collection of his scattered Letters to Poole, Southey, Cottle, Wordsworth, the two Wedgwoods, Allsop, and numerous others.* Unfortunately none of the letters of Coleridge to Lamb have been preserved. In some melancholy mood Lamb destroyed them all; and was so vexed with what he had done, that he never preserved any letters which he received afterwards.— 2. What De Quincey once suggested, a collection, as complete as could be made, of the still more widely scattered Marginalia written by Coleridge, sometimes in pencil, sometimes in ink, in his own books and in those of his friends. A very large number of these still remain unpublished; some are in the British Museum and many in private collections. By proper announcements in the right quarters and by assiduous application, access might doubtless be had to the majority of these. From the specimens already before the world, it might reasonably be argued that such a collection would form a *Corpus* of genial, penetrating, and discriminative criticism on the *belles lettres* that might be sought for vainly elsewhere in any modern publication.

* The *Canterbury Magazine* of September, 1834 (p. 121-131) and January, 1835 (p. 31-35) contains a series of interesting letters from S. T. C. from 1818 onwards.

In the meantime, the greatest desideratum of all—an edition of Coleridge's Poetical Works with some fair approximation to completeness and correctness—is, it is to be hoped, now partially though very tardily supplied in the present volumes. The Text of the present edition is founded on that published in three volumes by the late William Pickering in 1834. That edition, which was printed in the Poet's life-time, though not actually published until after his death, contained a number of Juvenile Poems then first collected, and here reproduced * with an additional piece, not before included.† In the present edition, the entire Contents of the Volume of Poems published by Coleridge in 1796, together with two Sonnets ‡ not previously included, and the twelve new pieces added in 1797, are for the first time given, without any omission whatsoever. A few Miscellaneous Pieces contributed to various publications in 1794-1797 close the first volume.

In the *Ancient Mariner*, and indeed in many other poems, a number of passages afterwards omitted are restored, within brackets, to their original place in the text. Some persons may consider this a rather hardy and hazardous procedure on the Editor's part; but it was not determined on without long and careful consideration. Wherever lines have been merely altered, the later reading is almost invariably given in the text, and the earlier reading, where of sufficient importance, in a footnote. In collecting these omitted lines and various readings, I have examined not only all the known early or original editions of Coleridge's separate publications, but, with one or two unim-

---

* Vol. i. pp. 1-36. † *Julia*, vol. i. pp. 3-4.
‡ Those to Robert Southey and William Godwin.

portant exceptions, all the newspapers, magazines, and annuals (as far as they are known to me) in which many of his finest poems first appeared. The second volume contains a considerable number of pieces not included in the ordinary editions and a few important poems, such as *A Stranger Minstrel* and the exquisite *Water Ballad*, not previously included in any edition.

I have omitted no piece of indubitable authenticity, or any part of one, either on the score of worthlessness or on any other score whatsoever; though I have relegated a few slight fragmentary or doubtful pieces to the Appendix. Sometimes the most apparently insignificant bagatelle will be found to shed unexpected light on the poet's mind and life. For these and for other reasons I trust I shall not be blamed for restoring in their integrity the whole of the Juvenile Pieces, the general immaturity of which I should at once be disposed to admit.

The text of the three original Dramas, and of the Translation of Schiller's *Wallenstein*, has been carefully collated with the original editions, in the same manner as the minor Poems. In the second scene of the fourth Act of *Zapolya*,* an important and hitherto inedited reading has been introduced into the text from a manuscript source; and in the Tragedy of *Remorse* the various readings of the original draught of the play (which came to light some four years ago) have been appended in foot-notes.

A few corruptions of the Text which have gradually crept into the later editions of Coleridge, have now to be noticed. These are not many in number; but some of them are very grievous.

* Vol. iv. pp. 270-271.

1. In *The Destiny of Nations* (vol. i. p. 208) "departing *for* their native shores" (the reading of the quarto *Joan of Arc*, and obviously the correct reading) is corrupted to "*from*," which entirely spoils the sense. This corruption originated in the *Sibylline Leaves* (which, as we have seen, abounds with *Errata*, corrected and uncorrected), and has been repeated in all subsequent editions of Coleridge, except the present.

Corruptions of Text.

2. In the Ode entitled *France* (vol. ii. p. 6):— "Her arm made mockery of the warrior's *ramp*"— is the reading of the two newspaper versions (1798-1802), of the original quarto edition (1798), and of *Sibylline Leaves*. The corruption of "tramp" for "ramp," which most miserably mars both the music and meaning of the passage, crept into the collected edition of 1828, and has been repeated ever since.* The date of "February 1798" is appended to this Ode in the original quarto and in *Sibylline Leaves*. In the later collected editions it has unaccountably changed to "February 1797."

3. *Fears in Solitude* (vol. ii. p. 16). "No speculation *on* contingency" is the correct reading of the original quarto and of *Sibylline Leaves*. For "on" *or* has been substituted in the later editions.

4. Introduction to the *Tale of the Dark Ladie* (vol. ii. p. 91)—"*unspiced* with politics or personality"

---

† As an instance how easily such corruptions may arise, it may not be impertinent to note that a reprint of the original newspaper version of this Ode in *The Spirit of the Public Journals for* 1798 reads "camp" in this line—
"Her arm made mockery of the warrior's *camp*,"
a reading, indeed, quite as eligible and intelligible as "tramp."

Corruptions of Text. —("unspired" in the *Morning Post*). The Editor of Coleridge's *Literary Remains* (vol. i. p. 51) prints "uninspired." That Coleridge wrote "unspiced" I entertain no doubt whatever.

5. *Lewti, or the Circassian Love-Chant* (vol. ii. p. 100). To this poem, in the ordinary editions, the date of "1795" is appended,—an error which clearly arose from a misprint in *Sibylline Leaves* (p. 127); where the piece is stated to be reprinted "from the *Morning Post*, 1795." *Lewti* appeared in the *Morning Post* of April 13, 1798, and it is difficult to believe that it was written so early as 1795.

6. *Apologetic Preface to Fire, Famine, and Slaughter* (vol. ii. p. 123). In a quotation from Jeremy Taylor occur the words "the *insolencies* of traitors and the violences of rebels"—so printed correctly in *Sibylline Leaves*. In the edition of 1834, and in the later editions, "insolencies" is corrupted to *indolence*—which of course makes utter nonsense of the passage.

7. For the date of 1818 affixed in the later editions to the Prose Introduction to the poem of *The Three Graves*, I am at a loss to account. It is not even the nominal date of the collection of *Sibylline Leaves*, where the poem was reprinted. But *The Three Graves* and the Introduction to it appeared in the sixth number of *The Friend*, in September, 1809. In the course of the Introduction, Coleridge speaks of having "composed the verses somewhat more than twelve years ago," which (1809-12) fixes the date of composition as = 1797. The false date of the ordinary editions is therefore as mischievous and misleading as it is unwarrantable and absurd.

8. *Ode to the Rain* (vol. ii. p. 264). Corruptions of Text.

"*We* three dear friends, in truth we Impatiently to be alone." [groan

This is the reading of *Sibylline Leaves*, in which the poem first appeared. It was not included in the collected editions of 1828-9 and 1834. The later editions read "*With* three dear friends "—completely to the destruction of the sense. I have traced the origin of this corruption to the *Literary Remains* of 1836, in which the poem was resuscitated.

9. *Alice du Clos* (vol. ii. p. 288) :—"And had not *Ellen* stay'd the race."—I confess myself unable to understand the introduction of this new name, and suspect it to be a slip of the pen or a misprint for "Alice." The poem first appeared in the collected edition of 1834. I have not, however, ventured to make an alteration for which there is no printed or manuscript authority; but have let it stand as it is.

10. *To Two Sisters : a Wanderer's Farewell* (vol. ii. p. 233). The date of 1817 appended to the fragment which is all that is printed of this poem in the ordinary editions, is obviously wrong. In a note printed in the edition of 1852, the names of the sisters are supplied on manuscript authority, and the erroneous date is repeated, as follows :—

On Taking Leave of——, 1817.

" 'To Mary Morgan and Charlotte Brent. Nov. 1817, St. James's square, Bristol.'—S. T. C."

The lines actually appeared in the *Courier* newspaper in December, 1807 ; and " Nov. 1817 " may therefore be a misprint for " Nov. 1807." We know, in fact, that Coleridge was at Bristol for some time at the former period (see *Cottle*, vol. ii., *sœpius*).

11. *A Character* (vol. ii. p. 337). " But for their rivals' baser blunder " is misprinted in the edition of 1834, " But for their rivals, baser blunder,"—a misprint perpetuated in some of the later editions. The true reading appears in an extract from the poem printed in Coleridge's *Table-Talk* (London, 1835), vol. ii. p. 50, and in the excellent one-volume edition of Coleridge's Poems published by the late William Pickering in 1844.

JUVENILE POEMS.

[With two or three exceptions duly indicated the Pieces in this division are entirely derived from the Edition of 1834, in which alone they have hitherto appeared.]

JUVENILE POEMS.

JULIA.

*——De medio fonte leporum
Surgit amari aliquid.*

JULIA was blest with beauty, wit, and grace:
   Small poets loved to sing her blooming face.
Before her altars, lo! a numerous train
Preferr'd their vows; yet all preferr'd in vain:
Till charming Florio, born to conquer, came
And touch'd the fair one with an equal flame.
The flame she felt, and ill could she conceal
What every look and action would reveal.
With boldness then, which seldom fails to move,
He pleads the cause of marriage and of love:
The course of Hymeneal joys he rounds,
The fair one's eyes dance pleasure at the sounds.
Nought now remain'd but 'Noes'—how little meant,
And the sweet coyness that endears consent.
The youth upon his knees enraptured fell:
The strange misfortune, oh! what words can tell?
Tell, ye neglected sylphs, who lap-dogs guard,
Why snatch'd ye not away your precious ward?

Why suffer'd ye the lover's weight to fall
On the ill-fated neck of much-loved Ball?
The favourite on his mistress casts his eyes,
Gives a short melancholy howl, and—dies!
Sacred his ashes lie, and long his rest!
Anger and grief divide poor Julia's breast.
Her eyes she fix'd on guilty Florio first,
On him the storm of angry grief must burst.
That storm he fled: he wooes a kinder fair,
Whose fond affections no dear puppies share.
'Twere vain to tell how Julia pined away;
Unhappy fair, that in one luckless day
(From future almanacks the day be crost!)
At once her lover and her lap-dog lost!*

1789.

---

* Printed in *A History of the Royal Foundation of Christ's Hospital*, by the Rev. William Trollope, M.A. (Lond. William Pickering, 1834), p. 192, preceded by the following remarks:—
"One of the first attempts of Coleridge, the most original of poets and the author of *Christabel*, will not be unacceptable to Blues either of past or present days; and should it meet the eye of his now matured and exalted genius, *non nunc hæc meminisse pigebit*. It was the practice of Mr. Boyer to excite the emulation of his scholars by allowing them to transcribe exercises of more than ordinary merit in a book kept for the purpose. From this book, which is still in existence, the verses are copied."

PHILEDON.

O curas hominum! O quantum est in rebus inane!

THE fervid Sun had more than halved the day,
When gloomy on his couch Philedon lay;
His feeble frame consumptive as his purse,
His aching head did wine and women curse;
His fortune ruin'd and his wealth decay'd,
Clamorous his duns, his gaming debts unpaid,
The youth indignant seized his tailor's bill,
And on its back thus wrote with moral quill.:
" Various as colours in the rainbow shown,
Or similar in emptiness alone,
How false, how vain are Man's pursuits below!
Wealth, Honour, Pleasure—what can ye bestow?
Yet see, how high and low, and young and old
Pursue the all delusive power of Gold.
Fond man! should all Peru thy empire own,
For thee tho' all Golconda's jewels shone,
What greater bliss could all this wealth supply?
What, but to eat and drink and sleep and die?
Go, tempt the stormy sea, the burning soil—
Go, waste the night in thought, the day in toil,
Dark frowns the rock, and fierce the tempests rave—
Thy ingots go the unconscious deep to pave!
Or thunder at thy door the midnight train,
Or Death shall knock that never knocks in vain.

Next Honour's sons come bustling on amain;
I laugh with pity at the idle train.
Infirm of soul! who think'st to lift thy name
Upon the waxen wings of human fame,—
Who for a sound, articulated breath—
Gazest undaunted in the face of death!
What art thou but a Meteor's glaring light—
Blazing a moment and then sunk in night?
Caprice which raised thee high shall hurl thee low,
Or envy blast the laurels on thy brow.
To such poor joys could ancient Honour lead
When empty fame was toiling Merit's meed;
To Modern Honour other lays belong;
Profuse of joy and Lord of right and wrong,
Honour can game, drink, riot in the stew,
Cut a friend's throat;—what cannot Honour do?
Ah me—the storm within can Honour still
For Julio's death, whom Honour made me kill?
Or will this lordly Honour tell the way
To pay those debts, which Honour makes me pay?
Or if with pistol and terrific threats
I make some traveller pay my Honour's debts,
A medicine for this wound can Honour give?
Ah, no! my Honour dies to make my Honour live.
But see! young Pleasure, and her train advance,
And joy and laughter wake the inebriate dance;
Around my neck she throws her fair white arms,
I meet her loves, and madden at her charms.
For the gay grape can joys celestial move,
And what so sweet below as Woman's love?

With such high transport every moment flies,
I curse Experience that he makes me wise ;
For at his frown the dear deliriums flew,
And the changed scene now wears a gloomy hue.
A hideous hag th' Enchantress Pleasure seems,
And all her joys appear but feverous dreams.
The vain resolve still broken and still made,
Disease and loathing and remorse invade ;
The charm is vanish'd and the bubble's broke,—
A slave to pleasure is a slave to smoke !"
Such lays repentant did the Muse supply ;
When as the Sun was hastening down the sky,
In glittering state twice fifty guineas come,—
His Mother's plate antique had raised the sum.
Forth leap'd Philedon of new life possest :—
'Twas Brookes's all till two,—'twas Hackett's all
    the rest !

ANTHEM

FOR THE CHILDREN OF CHRIST'S HOSPITAL.

SERAPHS ! around th' Eternal's seat who
    throng
  With tuneful ecstasies of praise :
O ! teach our feeble tongues like yours the song
  Of fervent gratitude to raise—
Like you, inspired with holy flame
To dwell on that Almighty name
Who bade the child of woe no longer sigh,
And Joy in tears o'erspread the widow's eye.

Th' all-gracious Parent hears the wretch's prayer;
   The meek tear strongly pleads on high;
Wan Resignation struggling with despair
   The Lord beholds with pitying eye;
Sees cheerless Want unpitied pine,
Disease on earth its head recline,
And bids Compassion seek the realms of woe
To heal the wounded, and to raise the low.

   She comes! she comes! the meek-eyed power
      I see
   With liberal hand that loves to bless;
The clouds of sorrow at her presence flee;
   Rejoice! rejoice! ye children of distress!
The beams that play around her head
Thro' Want's dark vale their radiance spread:
The young uncultured mind imbibes the ray,
And Vice reluctant quits th' expected prey.

   Cease, thou lorn mother! cease thy wailings
      drear;
   Ye babes! the unconscious sob forego;
Or let full gratitude now prompt the tear
   Which erst did sorrow force to flow.
Unkindly cold and tempest shrill
In life's morn oft the traveller chill,
But soon his path the sun of Love shall warm;
And each glad scene look brighter for the storm!
                      1789.

THE NOSE.

YE souls unused to lofty verse
  Who sweep the earth with lowly wing,
Like sand before the blast disperse—
  A Nose ! a mighty Nose I sing !
As erst Prometheus stole from heaven the fire
  To animate the wonder of his hand ;
Thus with unhallow'd hands, O muse, aspire,
  And from my subject snatch a burning brand !
So like the Nose I sing—my verse shall glow—
Like Phlegethon my verse in waves of fire shall
  flow !

  Light of this once all darksome spot
    Where now their glad course mortals run,
  First-born of Sirius begot
    Upon the focus of the sun—
I'll call thee ——! for such thy earthly name—
  What name so high, but what too low must be ?
Comets, when most they drink the solar flame
  Are but faint types and images of thee !
Burn madly, Fire ! o'er earth in ravage run,
Then blush for shame more red by fiercer ——
  outdone !

  I saw when from the turtle feast
    The thick dark smoke in volumes rose !
  I saw the darkness of the mist
    Encircle thee, O Nose !

Shorn of thy rays thou shott'st a fearful gleam
   (The turtle quiver'd with prophetic fright)
Gloomy and sullen thro' the night of steam :—
   So Satan's Nose when Dunstan urged to flight,
Glowing from gripe of red-hot pincers dread
Athwart the smokes of Hell disastrous twilight
   shed!*

   The Furies to madness my brain devote—
     In robes of ice my body wrap!
On billowy flames of fire I float,
   Hear ye my entrails how they snap?
Some power unseen forbids my lungs to breathe!
   What fire-clad meteors round me whizzing fly!
I vitrify thy torrid zone beneath,
   Proboscis fierce! I am calcined! I die!
Thus, like great Pliny, in Vesuvius' fire,
I perish in the blaze while I the blaze admire.
                           1789.

TO THE MUSE.

THO' no bold flights to thee belong;
   And tho' thy lays with conscious fear,
Shrink from Judgment's eye severe,
Yet much I thank thee, Spirit of my song!
For, lovely Muse! thy sweet employ
Exalts my soul, refines my breast,
Gives each pure pleasure keener zest,

---

* This stanza was printed in *The Morning Post*, January 2, 1798, headed " To the Lord Mayor's Nose."

And softens sorrow into pensive Joy.
From thee I learn'd the wish to bless,
From thee to commune with my heart;
From thee, dear Muse ! the gayer part,
To laugh with pity at the crowds that press
Where Fashion flaunts her robes by Folly spun,
Whose hues gay-varying wanton in the sun.
1789.

DESTRUCTION OF THE BASTILE.

I.

HEARD'ST thou yon universal cry,
    And dost thou linger still on Gallia's shore ?
Go, Tyranny ! beneath some barbarous sky
  Thy terrors lost and ruin'd power deplore !
    What tho' through many a groaning age
    Was felt thy keen suspicious rage,
    Yet Freedom roused by fierce Disdain
    Has wildly broke thy triple chain,
And like the storm which earth's deep entrails hide,
At length has burst its way and spread the ruins
  wide.

* * * * * * * *

IV.

In sighs their sickly breath was spent; each gleam
  Of Hope had ceased the long long day to cheèr ;
Or if delusive, in some flitting dream,
  It gave them to their friends and children dear—

  Awaked by lordly Insult's sound
  To all the doubled horrors round,
  Oft shrunk they from Oppression's band
  While anguish raised the desperate hand
For silent death ; or lost the mind's control,
Thro' every burning vein would tides of Frenzy
  roll.

V.

But cease, ye pitying bosoms, cease to bleed !
 Such scenes no more demand the tear humane ;
I see, I see ! glad Liberty succeed
  With every patriot virtue in her train !
   And mark yon peasant's raptured eyes ;
   Secure he views his harvests rise ;
   No fetter vile the mind shall know,
   And Eloquence shall fearless glow.
  Yes ! Liberty the soul of Life shall reign,
Shall throb in every pulse, shall flow thro' every
  vein !

VI.

Shall France alone a Despot spurn ?
 Shall she alone, O Freedom, boast thy care ?
Lo, round thy standard Belgia's heroes burn,
 Tho' Power's blood-stain'd streamers fire the air,
  And wider yet thy influence spread,
  Nor e'er recline thy weary head,
  Till every land from pole to pole
  Shall boast one independent soul !

And still, as erst, let favour'd Britain be
First ever of the first and freest of the free !

MUSIC.

HENCE, soul-dissolving Harmony
    That lead'st th' oblivious soul astray—
  Though thou sphere-descended be—
    Hence away !—
Thou mightier Goddess, thou demand'st my lay,
  Born when earth was seized with cholic ;
Or as more sapient sages say,
  What time the Legion diabolic
    Compell'd their beings to enshrine
    In bodies vile of herded swine,
    Precipitate adown the steep
    With hideous rout were plunging in the deep,
And hog and devil mingling grunt and yell
  Seized on the ear with horrible obtrusion ;—
Then if aright old legendaries tell,
  Wert thou begot by Discord on Confusion !

What tho' no name's sonorous power
Was given thee at thy natal hour !—
Yet oft I feel thy sacred might,
While concords wing their distant flight.
  Such power inspires thy holy son
    Sable clerk of Tiverton.
And oft where Otter sports his stream,
I hear thy banded offspring scream.

Thou Goddess! thou inspirest each throat;
'Tis thou who pour'st the scritch-owl note!
Transported hear'st thy children all
Scrape and blow and squeak and squall,
And while old Otter's steeple rings,
Clappest hoarse thy raven wings!

1790.

DEVONSHIRE ROADS.

THE indignant Bard composed this furious ode,
   As tired he dragg'd his way thro' Plimtree
      road!
  Crusted with filth and stuck in mire
  Dull sounds the Bard's bemudded lyre;
  Nathless Revenge and Ire the Poet goad
  To pour his imprecations on the road.

  Curst road! whose execrable way
  Was darkly shadow'd out in Milton's lay,
  When the sad fiends thro' Hell's sulphureous
      roads
  Took the first survey of their new abodes;
  Or when the fall'n Archangel fierce
  Dared through the realms of Night to pierce,
  What time the Bloodhound lured by Human
      scent
Thro' all Confusion's quagmires floundering went.

Nor cheering pipe, nor Bird's shrill note
Around thy dreary paths shall float;
Their boding songs shall scritch-owls pour
To fright the guilty shepherds sore,
Led by the wandering fires astray
Thro' the dank horrors of thy way!
While they their mud-lost sandals hunt
May all the curses, which they grunt
In raging moan like goaded hog,
Alight upon thee, damned Bog!

       1790.

INSIDE THE COACH.

'TIS hard on Bagshot Heath to try
 Unclosed to keep the weary eye;
But ah! Oblivion's nod to get
In rattling coach is harder yet.
Slumbrous God of half-shut eye!
Who lovest with limbs supine to lie;
Soother sweet of toil and care
Listen, listen to my prayer;
And to thy votary dispense
Thy soporific influence!
What tho' around thy drowsy head
The seven-fold cap of night be spread,
Yet lift that drowsy head awhile
And yawn propitiously a smile;
In drizzly rains poppean dews
O'er the tired inmates of the Coach diffuse;

And when thou'st charm'd our eyes to rest
Pillowing the chin upon the breast,
Bid many a dream from thy dominions
Wave its various-painted pinions,
Till ere the splendid visions close
We snore quartettes in ecstasy of nose.
While thus we urge our airy course,
O may no jolt's electric force
Our fancies from their steeds unhorse,
And call us from thy fairy reign
To dreary Bagshot Heath again!

1790.

MONODY ON A TEA-KETTLE.

O MUSE who sangest late another's pain,
    To griefs domestic turn thy coal-black steed!
With slowest steps thy funeral steed must go,
Nodding his head in all the pomp of woe:
Wide scatter round each dark and deadly weed,
And let the melancholy dirge complain,   [run)
(While bats shall shriek and dogs shall howling
The tea-kettle is spoilt and Coleridge is undone!

Your cheerful songs, ye unseen crickets, cease!
Let songs of grief your alter'd minds engage!
For he who sang responsive to your lay,
What time the joyous bubbles 'gan to play,

The sooty swain has felt the fire's fierce rage;—
Yes, he is gone, and all my woes increase;
I heard the water issuing from the wound—
No more the Tea shall pour its fragrant steams
    around!

O Goddess best beloved, delightful Tea! [vine?
With thee compared what yields the maddening
Sweet power! who know'st to spread the calm
    delight,
And the pure joy prolong to midmost night!
Ah! must I all thy varied sweets resign?
Enfolded close in grief thy form I see
No more wilt thou extend thy willing arms,
Receive the fervent Jove and yield him all thy
    charms!

How sink the mighty low by Fate opprest!—
Perhaps, O Kettle! thou by scornful toe
Rude urged t' ignoble place with plaintive din,
May'st rust obscure midst heaps of vulgar tin;—
As if no joy had ever seized my breast   [fly,—
When from thy spout the streams did arching
As if infused thou ne'er hadst known t' inspire
All the warm raptures of poetic fire!

But hark! or do I fancy the glad voice—
"What tho' the swain did wondrous charms dis-
    close—
(Not such did Memnon's sister sable drest)

Take these bright arms with royal face imprest,
A better Kettle shall thy soul rejoice,
And with Oblivion's wings o'erspread thy woes!"
Thus Fairy Hope can soothe distress and toil;
On empty Trivets she bids fancied Kettles boil!
1790.

ON RECEIVING AN ACCOUNT

THAT HIS ONLY SISTER'S DEATH WAS INEVITABLE.

THE tear which mourn'd a brother's fate scarce dry—
Pain after pain, and woe succeeding woe—
Is my heart destined for another blow?
O my sweet sister! and must thou too die?
Ah! how has Disappointment pour'd the tear
O'er infant Hope destroy'd by early frost!
How are ye gone, whom most my soul held dear!
Scarce had I loved you ere I mourn'd you lost;
Say, is this hollow eye, this heartless pain,
Fated to rove thro' Life's wide cheerless plain—
Nor father, brother, sister meet its ken—
My woes, my joys unshared! Ah! long ere then
On me thy icy dart, stern Death, be proved;—
Better to die, than live and not be loved!

ON SEEING A YOUTH

AFFECTIONATELY WELCOMED BY A SISTER.

I TOO a sister had! too cruel Death!
How sad remembrance bids my bosom heave!
Tranquil her soul, as sleeping Infant's breath;
Meek were her manners as a vernal Eve.
Knowledge, that frequent lifts the bloated mind,
Gave her the treasure of a lowly breast,
And Wit to venom'd Malice oft assign'd,
Dwelt in her bosom in a Turtle's nest.
Cease, busy Memory! cease to urge the dart;
Nor on my soul her love to me impress!
For oh I mourn in anguish—and my heart
Feels the keen pang, th' unutterable distress.
Yet wherefore grieve I that her sorrows cease,
For Life was misery, and the Grave is Peace!

PAIN.

ONCE could the Morn's first beams, the healthful
    breeze,
All Nature charm, and gay was every hour:—
But ah! not Music's self, nor fragrant bower
Can glad the trembling sense of wan disease.
Now that the frequent pangs my frame assail,

Now that my sleepless eyes are sunk and dim,
And seas of pain seem waving through each limb—
Ah what can all Life's gilded scenes avail?
I view the crowd, whom youth and health inspire,
Hear the loud laugh, and catch the sportive lay,
Then sigh and think—I too could laugh and play
And gaily sport it on the Muse's lyre,
Ere Tyrant Pain had chased away delight,
Ere the wild pulse throbb'd anguish thro' the night!

LIFE.

AS late I journey'd o'er the extensive plain
    Where native Otter sports his scanty stream,
Musing in torpid woe a sister's pain,
    The glorious prospect woke me from the dream.

At every step it widen'd to my sight,
    Wood, Meadow, verdant Hill, and dreary Steep.
Following in quick succession of delight,
    Till all—at once—did my eye ravish'd sweep!

May this (I cried) my course through Life portray!
New scenes of wisdom may each step display,
    And knowledge open as my days advance!
Till what time Death shall pour the undarken'd ray,
    My eye shall dart thro' infinite expanse,
And thought suspended lie in rapture's blissful
    trance.

SONNET.

ON QUITTING SCHOOL FOR COLLEGE.

FAREWELL parental scenes! a sad farewell!
   To you my grateful heart still fondly clings,
Tho' fluttering round on Fancy's burnish'd wings
Her tales of future Joy Hope loves to tell.
Adieu, adieu! ye much-loved cloisters pale!
Ah! would those happy days return again,
When 'neath your arches, free from every stain,
I heard of guilt and wonder'd at the tale!
Dear haunts! where oft my simple lays I sang,
Listening meanwhile the echoings of my feet,
Lingering I quit you, with as great a pang,
As when erewhile, my weeping childhood, torn
By early sorrow from my native seat,
Mingled its tears with hers—my widow'd Parent
   lorn.

A MATHEMATICAL POEM.

If Pegasus will let thee only ride him,
Spurning my clumsy efforts to o'erstride him,
Some fresh expedient the Muse will try,
And walk on stilts, although she cannot fly.

To the Rev. George Coleridge.

Dear Brother,

I have often been surprised that Mathematics, the quintessence of Truth, should have found admirers so few and so languid. Frequent consideration and minute scrutiny have at length unravelled the cause; viz. that though Reason is feasted, Imagination is starved; whilst Reason is luxuriating in its proper Paradise, Imagination is wearily travelling on a dreary desert. To assist Reason by the stimulus of Imagination is the design of the following production. In the execution of it much may be objectionable. The verse (particularly in the introduction of the ode) may be accused of unwarrantable liberties, but they are liberties equally homogeneal with the exactness of Mathematical disquisition, and the boldness of Pindaric daring. I have three strong champions to defend me against the attacks of Criticism: the Novelty, the Difficulty, and the Utility of the work. I may justly plume myself that I first have drawn the nymph Mathesis from the visionary caves of abstracted idea, and caused her to unite with Harmony. The first-born of this Union I now present to you; with interested motives indeed—as I expect to receive in return the more valuable offspring of your Muse.

Thine ever,
S. T. C.

March 31, 1791.

This is now—this was erst,
Proposition the first—and Problem the first.

I.

On a given finite line
Which must no way incline;
To describe an equi—
—lateral Tri—
—A, N, G, L, E.
Now let A. B.
Be the given line
Which must no way incline;
The great Mathematician.
Makes this Requisition,
That we describe an Equi—
—lateral Tri—
—angle on it:
Aid us, Reason—aid us, Wit!

II.

From the centre A. at the distance A. B.
   Describe the circle B. C. D.
   At the distance B. A. from B. the centre
The round A. C. E. to describe boldly venture.
     (Third postulate see.)
   And from the point C.
   In which the circles make a pother
   Cutting and slashing one another,
     Bid the straight lines a journeying go.
C. A. C. B. those lines will show.
   To the points, which by A. B. are reckon'd,
   And postulate the second
For Authority ye know.
     A. B. C.
     Triumphant shall be
   An Equilateral Triangle,
Not Peter Pindar carp, nor Zoilus can wrangle.

III.

Because the point A. is the centre
   Of the circular B. C. D.
And because the point B. is the centre
   Of the circular A. C. E.
A. C. to A. B. and B. C. to B. A.
Harmoniously equal for ever must stay;
   Then C. A. and B. C.
   Both extend the kind hand
     To the basis, A. B.

Unambitiously join'd in Equality's Band.
But to the same powers, when two powers are equal,
    My mind forebodes the sequel;
My mind does some celestial impulse teach,
    And equalizes each to each.
Thus C. A. with B. C. strikes the same sure alliance,
. That C. A. and B. C. had with A. B. before;
    And in mutual affiance
      None attempting to soar
      Above another,
    The unanimous three
  C. A. and B. C. and A. B.
All are equal, each to his brother,
    Preserving the balance of power so true :
Ah ! the like would the proud Autocratix* do !
  At taxes impending not Britain would tremble,
  Nor Prussia struggle her fear to dissemble;
    Nor the Mahomet-sprung wight
      The great Mussulman
      Would stain his Divan
With Urine the soft-flowing daughter of Fright.

IV.

But rein your stallion in, too daring Nine !
Should Empires bloat the scientific line ?
Or with dishevell'd hair all madly do ye run
For transport that your task is done?

---

    * Empress of Russia.

For done it is—the cause is tried !
And Proposition, gentle maid,
Who soothly ask'd stern Demonstration's aid,
   Has proved her right, and A. B. C.
   Of Angles three
   Is shown to be of equal side ;
And now our weary steed to rest in fine,
'Tis raised upon A. B. the straight, the given line.

INTRODUCTION TO

A GREEK PRIZE ODE

ON THE SLAVE TRADE

(1791).*

Ὦ σκότου πύλας Θάνατε, προλείπων
Ἐς γένος σπεύδοις ὑποζευχθὲν Ἄτᾳ·
Οὐ ξενισθήσῃ γενύων σπαραγμοῖς,
        Οὐδ' ὀλολύγμῳ,

---

* Coleridge gained Sir William Browne's gold medal for this Ode in the summer of 1791, a few months after entering at Jesus College. When printing it five years afterwards he says that "the ideas are better than the language or metre in which they are conveyed."

" Porson," says De Quincey, (*Tait's Magazine*, Sept. 1834), " was accustomed, meanly enough, to ridicule the Greek *lexis* of this Ode, which was to break a fly upon the wheel. The Ode was clever enough for a boy; but to such skill in Greek as could have enabled him to compose with critical accuracy, Coleridge never made pretensions.—ED.

JUVENILE POEMS.

Ἀλλὰ καὶ κύκλοισι χορροιτύποισι,
Κ'ἀσμάτων χαρᾷ· φοβερὸς μὲν ἐσσὶ
Ἀλλ' ὁμῶς Ἐλευθερίᾳ συνοικεῖς,
    Στυγνὲ Τύραννε!

Δασκίοις ἐπὶ πτερύγεσσι σῇσι
Ἄ! θαλάσσιον καθορῶντες οἶδμα
Αἰθεροπλάγτοις ὑπὸ ποσσ' ἀνεῖσι
    Πατρίδ' ἐπ' αἶαν.

Ἔνθα μὰν Ἔρασαι Ἐρωμένῇσιν
Ἀμφὶ πηγῇσιν κιτρίνων ὑπ' ἄλσων,
Ὅσσ' ὑπὸ βροτοῖς ἔπαθον βροτοὶ, τὰ
    Δεινὰ λέγοντι.

LITERAL TRANSLATION.

 Leaving the gates of darkness, O Death! hasten thou to a race yoked with misery! Thou wilt not be received with lacerations of cheeks, nor with funereal ululation—but with circling dances and the joy of songs. Thou art terrible indeed, yet thou dwellest with Liberty, stern Genius! Borne on thy dark pinions over the swelling of Ocean, they return to their native country. There by the side of fountains beneath citron-groves, the lovers tell to their beloved what horrors, being men, they had endured from men.

         S. T. C.

TIME, REAL AND IMAGINARY.*

AN ALLEGORY.

ON the wide level of a mountain's head,
    (I knew not where, but 'twas some faery place)
Their pinions, ostrich-like, for sails outspread,
Two lovely children run an endless race,
    A sister and a brother!
    This far outstripp'd the other;
  Yet ever runs she with reverted face,
  And looks and listens for the boy behind:
    For he, alas! is blind!
O'er rough and smooth with even step he pass'd,
And knows not whether he be first or last.

---

* By imaginary Time I meant the state of a schoolboy's mind when on his return to school he projects his being in his day-dreams, and lives in his next holidays, six months hence; and this I contrasted with real Time. [Preface to *Sibylline Leaves*, in which this piece was first published.]

THE RAVEN.*

A CHRISTMAS TALE, TOLD BY A SCHOOL-BOY TO HIS LITTLE BROTHERS AND SISTERS.

UNDERNEATH an old oak tree
 There was of swine a huge company,
That grunted as they crunch'd the mast:
For that was ripe, and fell full fast.
Then they trotted away, for the wind grew high:
One acorn they left, and no more might you spy.
Next came a Raven, that liked not such folly:
He belong'd, they did say, to the witch Melancholy!
Blacker was he than blackest jet,
Flew low in the rain, and his feathers not wet.
He pick'd up the acorn and buried it straight
By the side of a river both deep and great.
 Where then did the Raven go?
 He went high and low,
Over hill, over dale, did the black Raven go.
 Many Autumns, many Springs
 Travell'd he with wandering wings:

---

* Printed in *The Morning Post*, March 10, 1798, and reprinted in its present form in *Sibylline Leaves*, with the following apologetic remarks:—"At the request of the friends of my youth, who still remain my friends, and who were pleased with the wildness of the composition's, I have added two schoolboy poems. Surely malice itself will scarcely attribute their insertion to any other motive than the wish to keep alive the recollections from early life."

Many Summers, many Winters—
I can't tell half his adventures.*
At length he came back, and with him a She,
And the acorn was grown to a tall oak tree.
They built them a nest in the topmost bough,
And young ones they had, and were happy enow.
But soon came a woodman in leathern guise,
His brow, like a pent-house, hung over his eyes.
He'd an axe in his hand, not a word he spoke,
But with many a hem ! and a sturdy stroke,
At length he brought down the poor Raven's own oak.
His young ones were kill'd ; for they could not depart,
And their mother did die of a broken heart.

The boughs from the trunk the woodman did sever ;
And they floated it down on the course of the river,
They saw'd it in planks, and its bark they did strip,
And with this tree and others they made a good ship.
The ship, it was launch'd ; but in sight of the land
Such a storm there did rise as no ship could withstand.

* Seventeen or eighteen years ago, an artist of some celebrity was so pleased with this doggerel that he amused himself with the thought of making a Child's Picture Book of it; but he could not hit on a picture for these four lines. I suggested a *roundabout* with four seats, and the four seasons, as children, with Time for the showman. [Note by S.T.C. in *Sibylline Leaves*, 1817. Did this Child's Picture Book ever appear?]

It bulged on a rock, and the waves rush'd in fast:
Round and round flew the Raven, and caw'd to
 the blast.

He heard the last shriek of the perishing souls—
See! see! o'er the topmast the mad water rolls!
 Right glad was the Raven, and off he went fleet,
And Death riding home on a cloud he did meet,
And he thank'd him again and again for this treat:
 They had taken his all, and Revenge was sweet!
[We must not think so; but forget and forgive,
And what Heaven gives life to, we'll still let it live?]

WITH FIELDING'S AMELIA.

VIRTUES and Woes alike too great for man
 In the soft tale oft claim the useless sigh;
For vain the attempt to realize the plan,
 On Folly's wings must Imitation fly.
With other aim has Fielding here display'd
 Each social duty and each social care;
With just yet vivid colouring portray'd
 What every wife should be, what many are.
And sure the Parent of a race so sweet
 With double pleasure on the page shall dwell,
Each scene with sympathising breast shall meet,
 While Reason still with smiles delights to tell
Maternal hope, that her loved progeny
In all but sorrows shall Amelias be!

HAPPINESS.

ON wide or narrow scale shall Man
    Most happily describe life's plan?
Say shall he bloom and wither there,
Where first his infant buds appear;
Or upwards dart with soaring force,
And tempt some more ambitious course?
  Obedient now to Hope's command,
I bid each humble wish expand,
And fair and bright Life's prospects seem,
While Hope displays her cheering beam,
And Fancy's vivid colourings stream,
While Emulation stands me nigh
The Goddess of the eager eye.
  With foot advanced and anxious heart
Now for the fancied goal I start :—
Ah! why will Reason intervene
Me and my promised joys between!
She stops my course, she chains my speed,
While thus her forceful words proceed :—
" Ah! listen, youth, ere yet too late,
What evils on thy course may wait!
To bow the head, to bend the knee,
A minion of Servility,
At low Pride's frequent frowns to sigh,
And watch the glance in Folly's eye;
To toil intense, yet toil in vain,
And feel with what a hollow pain

Pale Disappointment hangs her head
O'er darling Expectation dead!
" The scene is changed and Fortune's gale
Shall belly out each prosperous sail.
Yet sudden wealth full well I know
Did never happiness bestow.
That wealth to which we were not born
Dooms us to sorrow or to scorn.
Behold yon flock which long had trod
O'er the short grass of Devon's sod,
To Lincoln's rank rich meads transferr'd,
And in their fate thy own be fear'd;
Through every limb contagions fly,
Deform'd and choked they burst and die.
" When Luxury opens wide her arms,
And smiling wooes thee to those charms,
Whose fascination thousands own,
Shall thy brows wear the stoic frown?
And when her goblet she extends
Which maddening myriads press around,
What power divine thy soul befriends
That thou should'st dash it to the ground?—
No, thou shalt drink, and thou shalt know
Her transient bliss, her lasting woe,
Her maniac joys, that know no measure,
And riot rude and painted pleasure;—
Till (sad reverse!) the Enchantress vile
To frowns converts her magic smile;
Her train impatient to destroy,
Observe her frown with gloomy joy;

On thee with harpy fangs they seize
The hideous offspring of Disease,
Swoln Dropsy ignorant of Rest,
And Fever garb'd in scarlet vest,
Consumption driving the quick hearse,
And Gout that howls the frequent curse,
With Apoplex of heavy head
That surely aims his dart of lead.
  "But say Life's joys unmix'd were given
To thee some favourite of Heaven :
Within, without, tho' all were health—
Yet what e'en thus are Fame, Power, Wealth,
But sounds that variously express,
What's thine already—Happiness !
'Tis thine the converse deep to hold
With all the famous sons of old ;
And thine the happy waking dream
While Hope pursues some favourite theme,
As oft when Night o'er Heaven is spread,
Round this maternal seat you tread,
Where far from splendour, far from riot,
In silence wrapt sleeps careless quiet.
'Tis thine with fancy oft to talk,
And thine the peaceful evening walk ;
And what to thee the sweetest are—
The setting sun, the evening star—
The tints, which live along the sky,
And Moon that meets thy raptured eye,
Where oft the tear shall grateful start,
Dear silent pleasures of the Heart !

Ah! Being blest, for Heaven shall lend
To share thy simple joys a friend!
Ah! doubly blest, if Love supply
His influence to complete thy joy,
If chance some lovely maid thou find
To read thy visage in thy mind.
   " One blessing more demands thy care :—
Once more to Heaven address the prayer :
For humble independence pray
The guardian genius of thy way;
Whom (sages say) in days of yore
Meek Competence to Wisdom bore,
So shall thy little vessel glide
With a fair breeze adown the tide,
And Hope, if e'er thou 'ginst to sorrow
Remind thee of some fair to-morrow,
Till Death shall close thy tranquil eye
While Faith proclaims " thou shalt not die !"

ON IMITATION.

ALL are not born to soar—and ah! how few
   In tracks where Wisdom leads their paths pursue!
Contagious when to wit or wealth allied,
Folly and Vice diffuse their venom wide.
On Folly every fool his talent tries;
It asks some toil to imitate the wise;
Tho' few like Fox can speak—like Pitt can think—
Yet all like Fox can game—like Pitt can drink.

PROGRESS OF VICE.

DEEP in the gulf of Vice and Woe
    Leaps man at once with headlong throw?
Him inborn Truth and Virtue guide,
  Whose guards are shame and conscious pride;
In some gay hour Vice steals into the breast;
Perchance she wears some softer Virtue's vest.
  By unperceived degrees she tempts to stray,
Till far from Virtue's path she leads the feet away.

  Then swift the soul to disenthral
  Will Memory the past recal,
  And fear before the Victim's eyes
  Bid future ills and dangers rise.   [bine—
But hark! the voice, the lyre, their charms com-
Gay sparkles in the cup the generous wine;
Th' inebriate dance—the fair frail nymph
    inspires,   [retires.
And Virtue vanquish'd—scorn'd—with hasty flight

  But soon to tempt the pleasures cease;
  Yet shame forbids return to peace,
  And stern necessity will force
  Still to urge on the desperate course.
The drear black paths of Vice the wretch must
  try,
Where Conscience flashes horror on each eye,
Where Hate—where Murder scowl—where starts
  Affright!
Ah! close the scene—ah! close—for dreadful is
  the sight.

POEMS COLLECTED
IN 1796-1797.

PREFACE

TO POEMS PUBLISHED IN 1796.

POEMS on various subjects written at different times and prompted by very different feelings; but which will be read at one time and under the influence of one set of feelings—this is a heavy disadvantage: for we love or admire a poet in proportion as he develops our own sentiments and emotions, or reminds us of our own knowledge.

Compositions resembling those of the present volume are not unfrequently condemned for their querulous egotism. But egotism is to be condemned then only when it offends against time and place, as in a history or an epic poem. To censure it in a monody or sonnet is almost as absurd as to dislike a circle for being round. Why then write Sonnets or Monodies? Because they give me pleasure when perhaps nothing else could. After the more violent emotions of sorrow the mind demands amusement and can find it in employment alone; but full of its late sufferings, it can endure no employment not in some measure connected with them. Forcibly to turn away our attention to general subjects is a painful and most often an unavailing effort.

> " But O! how grateful to a wounded heart,
> The tale of misery to impart—
> From others' eyes bid artless sorrows flow,
> And raise esteem upon the base of woe!"
> SHAW.

The communicativeness of our nature leads us to describe our own sorrows; in the endeavour to describe them, intellectual activity is exerted; and from intellectual activity there results a pleasure, which is gradually associated, and mingles as a corrective, with the painful subject of the description. " True !" (it may be answered) " but how is the Public interested in your sorrows or your description?" We are for ever attributing personal unities to imaginary aggregates. What is the Public but a term for a number of scattered individuals? of whom as many will be interested in these sorrows, as have experienced the same or similar.

> " Holy be the lay
> Which mourning soothes the mourner on his way."

If I could judge of others by myself, I should not hesitate to affirm, that the most interesting passages in all writings are those in which the author develops his own feelings. The sweet voice of Cona* never sounds so sweetly as when it speaks of itself; and I should almost suspect that man of an unkindly heart, who could read the opening of the third book of the Paradise Lost without peculiar emotion. By a law of our nature, he who labours under a strong feeling is impelled to seek for sympathy; but a poet's feelings are all strong. *Quicquid amet valde amat.* Akenside therefore speaks with philosophical accuracy when he classes Love and Poetry, as producing the same effects:

> " Love and the wish of Poets when their tongue
> Would teach to others' bosoms what so charms
> Their own."   PLEASURES OF IMAGINATION.

* Ossian.

There is one species of egotism which is truly disgusting; not that which leads us to communicate our feelings to others, but that which would reduce the feelings of others to an identity with our own. The atheist, who exclaims, "pshaw!" when he glances his eye on the praises of Deity, is an egotist : an old man, when he speaks contemptuously of Love-verses, is an egotist : and the sleek favourites of fortune are egotists, when they condemn all " melancholy, discontented " verses. Surely it would be candid not merely to ask whether the poem pleases ourselves, but to consider whether or no there may not be others to whom it is well calculated to give an innocent pleasure. With what anxiety every fashionable author avoids the word *I!*—now he transforms himself into a third person; "the present writer" now multiplies himself and swells into "we"; and all this is the watchfulness of guilt. Conscious that this said *I* is perpetually intruding on his mind and that it monopolizes his heart, he is prudishly solicitous that it may not escape from his lips.

This disinterestedness of phrase is in general commensurate with selfishness of feeling : men old and hackneyed in the ways of the world are scrupulous avoiders of egotism.

Of the following Poems a considerable number are styled "Effusions,"* in defiance of Churchill's line

" Effusion on effusion *pour* away."

I could recollect no title more descriptive of the manner and matter of the Poems—I might indeed

* In the later editions, however, the word "Sonnet" was substituted.—ED.

have called the majority of them Sonnets—but they do not possess that *oneness* of thought which I deem indispensable in a Sonnet—and (not a very honourable motive perhaps) I was fearful that the title "Sonnet" might have reminded my reader of the Poems of the Rev. W. L. Bowles—a comparison with whom would have sunk me below that mediocrity on the surface of which I am at present enabled to float.

Some of the verses allude to an intended emigration to America on the scheme of an abandonment of individual property.

I shall only add that each of my readers will, I hope, remember that these poems on various subjects, which he reads at one time and under the influence of one set of feelings, were written at different times and prompted by very different feelings; and therefore that the supposed inferiority of one poem to another may sometimes be owing to the temper of mind in which he happens to peruse it.

PREFACE TO THE SECOND EDITION

PUBLISHED IN 1797.

I return my acknowledgments to the different Reviewers for the assistance which they have afforded me in detecting my poetic deficiencies. I have endeavoured to avail myself of their remarks: one third of the former Volume I have omitted, and the imperfections of the re-published part must be considered as errors of taste, not faults of carelessness.

My poems have been rightly charged with a profusion of double-epithets, and a general turgidness. I have pruned the double-epithets with no sparing hand; and used my best efforts to tame the swell and glitter both of thought and diction. This latter fault however had insinuated itself into my "Religious Musings" with such intricacy of union, that sometimes I have omitted to disentangle the weed from the fear of snapping the flower. A third and heavier accusation has been brought against me, that of obscurity; but not, I think, with equal justice. An author is obscure when his conceptions are dim and imperfect, and his language incorrect, or inappropriate, or involved. A poem that abounds in allusions, like the Bard of Gray, or one that impersonates high and abstract truths, like Collins's Ode on the Poetical Character, claims not to be popular—but should be acquitted of obscurity. The deficiency is in the reader. But this is a charge which every poet whose imagination is warm and rapid must expect from his contemporaries. Milton did not escape it; and it was adduced with virulence against Gray and Collins. We now hear no more of it: not that their poems are better understood at present than they were at their first publication; but their fame is established; and a critic would accuse himself of frigidity or inattention who should profess not to understand them. But a living writer is yet *sub judice*; and if we cannot follow his conceptions or enter into his feelings, it is more consoling to our pride to consider him as lost beneath than as soaring above us. If any man expect from my poems the same easiness of style which he admires in a drinking-song, for him I have not written. *Intelligibilia, non intellectum adfero.*

I expect neither profit nor general fame by my writings; and I consider myself as having been amply repaid without either. Poetry has been to me its own "exceeding great reward:" it has soothed my afflictions; it has multiplied and refined my enjoyments; it has endeared solitude; and it has given me the habit of wishing to discover the Good and the Beautiful in all that meets and surrounds me.

Stowey, May 1797.

POSTSCRIPT

TO THE EDITION OF 1797.

I have excepted the following Poems* from those which I had determined to omit. Some intelligent friends particularly requested it, observing that what most delighted me when I was "young in *writing* poetry would probably best please those who are young in *reading* poetry: and a man must learn to be *pleased* with a subject before he can yield that attention to it which is requisite in order to acquire a just taste." I, however, was fully convinced that he who gives to the press what he does not thoroughly approve in his own closet commits an act of disrespect both against himself and his fellow-citizens. The request and the reasoning would not, therefore, have influenced me had they not been assisted by other motives. The first in order of these verses which I have thus endeavoured to *reprieve* from immediate oblivion was originally addressed "To the Author of Poems published anonymously at Bristol." A second edition of these poems has lately appeared with the Author's name prefixed; and I could not refuse myself the gratification of seeing the name of that man among my poems, without whose kindness they would probably have remained unpublished; and to whom I know myself greatly and variously obliged as

* *Lines to Joseph Cottle, On an Autumnal Evening, In the Manner of Spenser, The Composition of a Kiss, To an Infant, On the Christening of a Friend's Child.*

a Poet, a Man and a Christian. The second is entitled "An Effusion on an Autumnal Evening, Written in Early Youth." In a note to this poem I had asserted that the tale of Florio in Mr. Rogers's "Pleasures of Memory" was to be found in the *Lochleven* of Bruce.* I did (and still do) perceive a certain likeness between the two stories; but certainly not a sufficient one to justify my assertion. I feel it my duty, therefore, to apologize to the Author and the Public for this rashness; and my sense of honesty would not have been satisfied by the bare omission of the note. No one can see more clearly the *littleness* and futility of imagining plagiarisms in the works of men of genius; but *nemo omnibus horis sapit;* and my mind at the time of writing that note was sick and sore with anxiety, and weakened through much suffering. I have not the most distant knowledge of Mr. Rogers, except as a correct and elegant Poet. If any of my readers should know him personally, they would oblige me by informing him that I have expiated a sentence of unfounded detraction by an unsolicited and self-originating apology.

Having from these motives re-admitted two, and those the longest of the poems I had omitted, I yielded a passport to the three others which were recommended by the greatest number of votes.

* "The tale of Florio in "The Pleasures of Memory" is to be found in *Lochleven*, a poem of great merit by Michael Bruce. In Mr. Rogers's poem the names are Florio and Julia; in the *Lochleven* Lomond and Levina, and this is all the difference."

GENEVIEVE.*

MAID of my Love, sweet Genevieve!
   In Beauty's light you glide along;
Your eye is like the star of eve,
   And sweet your voice as seraph's song.
Yet not your heavenly beauty gives
   This heart with passion soft to glow:
Within your soul a voice there lives!
   It bids you hear the tale of woe.
When sinking low the sufferer wan
   Beholds no hand outstretch'd to save,
Fair as the bosom of the swan
   That rises graceful o'er the wave,
I've seen your breast with pity heave,
And therefore love I you, sweet Genevieve!

SONNET.

TO THE AUTUMNAL MOON.

MILD Splendour of the various-vested Night!
   Mother of wildly-working visions! hail!
I watch thy gliding, while with watery light
Thy weak eye glimmers through a fleecy veil;
And when thou lovest thy pale orb to shroud

---

* Printed in the volume of 1796 with the following note:—
"This little poem was written when the Author was a boy."

Behind the gather'd blackness lost on high;
And when thou dartest from the wind-rent cloud
Thy placid lightning o'er the awaken'd sky.
Ah such is Hope! as changeful and as fair!
Now dimly peering on the wistful sight;
Now hid behind the dragon-wing'd Despair:
But soon emerging in her radiant might
She o'er the sorrow-clouded breast of Care
Sails, like a meteor kindling in its flight.

ABSENCE.

A FAREWELL ODE ON QUITTING SCHOOL FOR JESUS
COLLEGE, CAMBRIDGE.

WHERE graced with many a classic spoil
    Cam rolls his reverend stream along,
I haste to urge the learned toil
That sternly chides my love-lorn song:
Ah me! too mindful of the days
Illumed by Passion's orient rays,
When Peace, and Cheerfulness, and Health
Enrich'd me with the best of wealth.

Ah fair Delights! that o'er my soul
    On Memory's wing, like shadows fly!
Ah flowers! which Joy from Eden stole
    While Innocence stood smiling by!—
But cease, fond Heart! this bootless moan:

Those Hours on rapid Pinions flown
Shall yet return, by Absence crown'd,
And scatter livelier roses round.

The Sun who ne'er remits his fires
　On heedless eyes may pour the day:
The Moon, that oft from Heaven retires,
　Endears her renovated ray.
What though she leave the sky unblest
To mourn awhile in murky vest?
When she relumes her lovely light,
We bless the Wanderer of the Night.

SONGS OF THE PIXIES.

THE PIXIES, in the superstition of Devonshire, are a race of beings invisibly small, and harmless or friendly to man. At a small distance from a village in that county, half way up a wood-covered hill, is an excavation called the Pixies' Parlour. The roots of old trees form its ceiling; and on its sides are innumerable cyphers, among which the author discovered his own and those of his brothers, cut by the hand of their childhood. At the foot of the hill flows the river Otter.

To this place the Author, during the summer months of the year 1793, conducted a party of young ladies; one of whom, of stature elegantly small and of complexion colourless yet clear, was proclaimed the Faery Queen. On which occasion the following Irregular Ode was written.

I.

WHOM the untaught Shepherds call
    Pixies in their madrigal,
Fancy's children, here we dwell:
Welcome, Ladies! to our cell.
Here the wren of softest note
    Builds its nest and warbles well;
Here the blackbird strains his throat;
    Welcome, Ladies! to our cell.

II.

When fades the moon to shadowy-pale,*
And scuds the cloud before the gale,
Ere the morn, all gem-bedight,†
Hath streak'd the East with rosy light,
We sip the furze-flower's fragrant dews
Clad in robes of rainbow hues :
[Richer than the deepen'd bloom
That glows on Summer's scented plume ;]
Or sport amid the shooting gleams
To the tune of distant-tinkling teams,‡
While lusty Labour scouting sorrow
Bids the Dame a glad good-morrow,
Who jogs the accustom'd road along,
And paces cheery to her cheering song.

III.

But not our filmy pinion
We scorch amid the blaze of day,
When Noontide's fiery-tressed minion,
    Flashes the fervid ray.
    Aye from the sultry heat
    We to the cave retreat
O'ercanopied by huge roots intertwined
With wildest texture, blacken'd o'er with age :

---

* " All shadowy-pale," in the early editions.
† Ere morn with living gems bedight
  Purples the East with streaky light.—1796.
‡ Or sport amid the rosy gleam
  Soothed by the distant-tinkling team.—1796.

Round them their mantle green the ivies bind,
    Beneath whose foliage pale
    Fann'd by the unfrequent gale
We shield us from the Tyrant's mid-day rage.

IV.

Thither, while the murmuring throng
Of wild-bees hum their drowsy song,
By Indolence and Fancy brought,
A youthful Bard, " unknown to Fame,"
Wooes the Queen of Solemn Thought,
And heaves the gentle misery of a sigh
    Gazing with tearful eye,
    As round our sandy grot appear
    Many a rudely-sculptured name
    To pensive Memory dear!
Weaving gay dreams of sunny-tinctured hue,
    We glance before his view:
O'er his hush'd soul our soothing witcheries shed,
And twine the future garland* round his head.

V.

    When Evening's dusky car
    Crown'd with her dewy star
Steals o'er the fading sky in shadowy flight;
    On leaves of aspen trees
    We tremble to the breeze
Veil'd from the grosser ken of mortal sight.
    Or, haply, at the visionary hour,

---

* Our faery garlands.—1796.

Along our wildly-bower'd sequester'd walk,
We listen to the enamour'd rustic's talk ;
Heave with the heavings of the maiden's breast,
Where young-eyed Loves have hid* their turtle
    nest ;
   Or guide of soul-subduing power
The glance, that from the half-confessing eye†
Darts the fond question or the soft reply.

VI.

Or through the mystic ringlets of the vale
We flash our faery feet in gamesome prank ;
Or, silent-sandal'd, pay our defter court,
Circling the Spirit of the Western Gale,
Where wearied with his flower-caressing sport,
   Supine he slumbers on a violet bank ;
Then with quaint music hymn the parting gleam
By lonely Otter's sleep-persuading stream ;
Or where his wave with loud unquiet song
Dash'd o'er the rocky channel froths along ;
Or where, his silver waters smoothed to rest,
The tall tree's shadow sleeps upon his breast.

VII.

   Hence thou lingerer, Light !
   Eve saddens into Night.
Mother of wildly-working dreams ! we view
   The sombre hours, that round thee stand
   With down-cast eyes (a duteous band !)

---

* Have built.—1796.
† Th' electric flash that from the melting eye.—*ib.*

Their dark robes dripping with the heavy dew.
  Sorceress of the ebon throne !
  Thy power the Pixies own,
  When round thy raven brow
  Heaven's lucent roses glow,
And clouds in watery colours drest
Float in light drapery o'er thy sable vest :
What time the pale moon sheds a softer day
Mellowing the woods beneath its pensive beam :
For mid the quivering light 'tis ours to play,
Aye dancing to the cadence of the stream.

VIII.

  Welcome, Ladies ! to the cell
  Where the blameless Pixies dwell :
But thou, sweet Nymph ! proclaim'd our Faery
    Queen,
  With what obeisance meet
  Thy presence shall we greet ?
For lo ! attendant on thy steps are seen
  Graceful Ease in artless stole,
  And white-robed Purity of soul,
   With Honour's softer mien ;
Mirth of the loosely-flowing hair,
And meek-eyed Pity eloquently fair,
  Whose tearful cheeks are lovely to the view
  As snow-drop wet with dew.

IX.

Unboastful Maid ! though now the Lily pale
 Transparent grace thy beauties meek ;
Yet ere again along the impurpling vale,

The purpling vale and elfin-haunted grove,
Young Zephyr his fresh flowers profusely throws,
  We'll tinge with livelier hues thy cheek ;
And haply from the nectar-breathing Rose
    Extract a Blush for Love !

MONODY ON THE DEATH OF CHATTERTON.

O WHAT a wonder seems the fear of death,
  Seeing how gladly we all sink to sleep,
Babes, Children, Youths, and Men,
Night following night for threescore years and ten !
But doubly strange, where life is but a breath
To sigh and pant with, up Want's rugged steep.

Away, Grim Phantom ! Scorpion King, away !
Reserve thy terrors and thy stings display
For coward Wealth and Guilt in robes of State !
Lo ! by the grave I stand of one, for whom
A prodigal nature and a niggard doom
(That all bestowing, this withholding all,)
Made each chance knell from distant spire or dome
Sound like a seeking Mother's anxious call,
Return, poor Child ! Home, weary truant, home !*
Thee, Chatterton ! these unblest stones protect
From want, and the bleak freezings of neglect.

  * The original opening of this Monody (as printed in the Volumes of 1796, 1797, and 1803) was as follows :—

*Too long before the vexing Storm-blast driven
Here hast thou found repose ! beneath this sod !
Thou ! O vain word ! thou dwell'st not with the clod !
Amid the shining Host of the Forgiven
Thou at the throne of mercy and thy God
The triumph of redeeming Love dost hymn
(Believe it, O my Soul !) to harps of Seraphim.

Yet oft, perforce, ('tis suffering Nature's call)
I weep that heaven-born Genius so should fall ;
And oft, in Fancy's saddest hour, my soul
Averted shudders at the poison'd bowl.
Now groans my sickening heart, as still I view
    Thy corse of livid hue ;
Now indignation checks the feeble sigh,   [eye !
Or flashes through the tear† that glistens in mine

> " When faint and sad o'er Sorrow's desart wild
> Slow journeys onward poor Misfortune's child,
> When fades each lovely form by Fancy drest,
> And inly pines the self-consuming breast ;
> No scourge of scorpions in thy right arm dread,
> No helmed terrors nodding o'er thy head.
> Assume, O Death, the cherub wings of Peace,
> And bid the heart-sick Wanderer's anguish cease !"

* The original version (1796) continues thus :—
  " Escaped the sore wounds of Affliction's rod
    Meek at the throne of Mercy, and of God,
    Perchance thou raisest high th' enraptured hymn
      Amid the blaze of Seraphim !
    Yet oft ('tis Nature's bosom-startling call)," &c.

† And now a flash of indignation high
  Darts thro' the tear, &c.   1796.

MONODY ON CHATTERTON.

Is this the land of song-ennobled line?
Is this the land, where Genius ne'er in vain
    Pour'd forth his lofty strain?
Ah me! yet Spenser, gentlest bard divine,
Beneath chill Disappointment's shade,
His weary limbs in lonely anguish laid;
    And o'er her darling dead
    Pity hopeless hung her head,
While "mid the pelting of that merciless storm,"
Sunk to the cold earth Otway's famish'd form!

Sublime of thought, and confident of fame,
From vales where Avon winds the Minstrel* came.
    Light-hearted youth! aye, as he hastes along,
    He meditates the future song,
How dauntless Ælla fray'd the Dacyan foe;
    And while the numbers flowing strong
    In eddies whirl, in surges throng,
Exulting in the spirits' genial throe
In tides of power his life-blood seems to flow.†

---

    * Avon, a river near Bristol; the birth-place of Chatterton.
    † How dauntless Ælla fray'd the Dacyan foes;
        And, as floating high in air
        Glitter the sunny visions fair
    His eyes dance rapture, and his bosom glows!
                             1796.
  In the editions of 1797 and 1803 the poem continues here—
      "Ah! where are fled the charms," &c.,
the whole of the intermediate passage being omitted.

And now his cheeks with deeper ardours flame,
His eyes have glorious meanings, that declare
More than the light of outward day shines there,
A holier triumph and a sterner aim!
Wings grow within him; and he soars above
Or Bard's or Minstrel's lay of war or love.*
Friend to the friendless, to the sufferer health,
He hears the widow's prayer, the good man's praise;
To scenes of bliss transmutes his fancied wealth,
And young and old shall now see happy days.
On many a waste he bids trim gardens rise,
Gives the blue sky to many a prisoner's eyes;
And now in wrath he grasps the patriot steel,†
And her own iron rod he makes Oppression feel.
Sweet Flower of Hope! free Nature's genial child!
That didst so fair disclose thy early bloom,
Filling the wide air with a rich perfume!
For thee in vain all heavenly aspects smiled;
From the hard world brief respite could they win—
The frost nipp'd sharp without, the canker prey'd
    within!‡

* The above six lines were a later addition.

† Friend to the friendless, to the sick man health,
  With generous joy he views th' *ideal* wealth;
  He hears the widow's heaven-breathed prayer of praise;
  He marks the shelter'd orphan's tearful gaze;
  Or, where the sorrow-shrivell'd captive lay
  Pours the bright blaze of Freedom's noon-tide ray:
  And now, indignant, "grasps the patriot steel."—1796.
        (See *Lines on the Man of Ross*.)

‡ The above six lines are a later substitution for the following passage in the original version:—

Ah! where are fled the charms of vernal Grace,
And Joy's wild gleams that lighten'd o'er thy face?*
Youth of tumultuous soul, and haggard eye!
Thy wasted form, thy hurried steps I view,
On thy wan forehead starts the lethal dew,
And oh! the anguish of that shuddering sigh!†

   Such were the struggles of the gloomy hour,
      When Care, of wither'd brow,
   Prepared the poison's death-cold power:
Already to thy lips was raised the bowl,
   When near thee stood Affection meek
   (Her bosom bare, and wildly pale her cheek)
Thy sullen gaze she bade thee roll
On scenes that well might melt thy soul;

   " Clad in Nature's rich array
     And bright in all her tender hues
  Sweet tree of Hope! thou loveliest child of Spring,
  How fair didst thou disclose thine early bloom
  Loading the west-winds with its soft perfume!
  And Fancy, elfin form of gorgeous wing,
    On every blossom hung her fostering dews,
    That, changeful, wanton'd to the orient day!
  But soon upon thy poor unshelter'd head
  Did Penury her sickly mildew shed:
  And soon the scathing Lightning bade thee stand
  In frowning horror o'er the blighted land!"

* And Joy's wild gleams, light-flashing o'er thy face.
                                 1803.
† On thy cold forehead starts the anguish'd dew:
   And dreadful was that bosom-rending sigh!—1796.

Thy native cot she flash'd upon thy view,
Thy native cot, where still, at close of day,
Peace smiling sate, and listen'd to thy lay;
Thy Sister's shrieks she bade thee hear,
And mark thy mother's thrilling tear;
  See, see her breast's convulsive throe,
  Her silent agony of woe!
Ah! dash the poison'd chalice from thy hand!

And thou hadst dash'd it, at her soft command,
But that Despair and Indignation rose,
And told again the story of thy woes;
Told the keen insult of the unfeeling heart,
The dread dependence on the low-born mind;
Told every pang, with which thy soul must smart,
Neglect, and grinning Scorn, and Want combined!
Recoiling quick, thou badest the friend of pain
Roll the black tide of Death through every freez-
  ing vein!

    O Spirit blest!
Whether the Eternal's throne around,
Amidst the blaze of Seraphim,
Thou pourest forth the grateful hymn;
Or soaring thro' the blest domain
Enrapturest Angels with thy strain,—
Grant me, like thee, the lyre to sound,
Like thee with fire divine to glow;—
But ah! when rage the waves of woe,

Grant me with firmer breast to meet their hate,
And soar beyond the storm with upright eye elate!*
Ye woods! that wave o'er Avon's rocky steep,
To Fancy's ear sweet is your murmuring deep!
For here she loves the cypress wreath to weave;
Watching, with wistful eye, the saddening tints of eve.
Here, far from men, amid this pathless grove,
In solemn thought the Minstrel wont to rove,
Like star-beam on the slow sequester'd tide
Lone-glittering, through the high tree branching wide.
And here, in Inspiration's eager hour,
When most the big soul feels the mastering power,†
 These wilds, these caverns roaming o'er,
 Round which the screaming sea-gulls soar,
With wild unequal steps he pass'd along,
Oft pouring on the winds a broken song:
Anon, upon some rough rock's fearful brow
Would pause abrupt—and gaze upon the waves
 below.

Poor Chatterton! he sorrows for thy fate [late.
Who would have praised and loved thee, ere too
Poor Chatterton! farewell! of darkest hues
This chaplet cast I on thy unshaped tomb;
But dare no longer on the sad theme muse,
Lest kindred woes persuade a kindred doom:

 * The whole of the above paragraph is a later addition.
 † The maddening power.—1796.

For oh! big gall-drops, shook from Folly's wing,
Have blacken'd the fair promise of my spring;
And the stern Fate transpierced with viewless dart
The last pale Hope that shiver'd at my heart!

Hence, gloomy thoughts! no more my soul shall dwell
On joys that were! no more endure to weigh
The shame and anguish of the evil day,
Wisely forgetful! O'er the ocean swell
Sublime of Hope I seek the cottaged dell
Where Virtue calm with careless step may stray;
And, dancing to the moon-light roundelay,
The wizard passions weave a holy spell!

O Chatterton! that thou wert yet alive!
Sure thou would'st spread the canvass to the gale,
And love with us the tinkling team to drive
O'er peaceful Freedom's undivided dale;
And we, at sober eve, would round thee throng,
Would hang, enraptured, on thy stately song,
And greet with smiles the young-eyed Poesy
All deftly mask'd as hoar Antiquity.

Alas, vain Phantasies! the fleeting brood
Of Woe self-solaced in her dreamy mood!
Yet will I love to follow the sweet dream
Where Susquehana pours his untamed stream;
And on some hill, whose forest-frowning side
Waves o'er the murmurs of his calmer tide,

Will raise a solemn Cenotaph to thee,
Sweet Harper of time-shrouded Minstrelsy!
And there, soothed sadly by the dirgeful wind,
Muse on the sore ills I had left behind.

October, 1794.

LINES ON AN AUTUMNAL EVENING.*

O THOU wild Fancy, check thy wing! No more
Those thin white flakes, those purple clouds explore!
Nor there with happy spirits speed thy flight
Bathed in rich amber-glowing floods of light;
Nor in yon gleam, where slow descends the day,
With western peasants hail the morning ray!
Ah! rather bid the perish'd pleasures move,
A shadowy train, across the soul of Love!
O'er Disappointment's wintry desert fling
Each flower that wreathed the dewy locks of Spring,
When blushing, like a bride, from Hope's trim bower
She leapt, awaken'd by the pattering shower.

Now sheds the sinking Sun a deeper gleam,
Aid, lovely Sorceress! aid thy Poet's dream!
With faery wand O bid the Maid arise,
Chaste Joyance dancing in her bright-blue eyes;

* Original title, "Written in early youth, the time, an Autumnal Evening."

As erst when from the Muses' calm abode
I came, with Learning's meed not unbestow'd;
When as she twined a laurel round my brow,
And met my kiss, and half return'd my vow,
O'er all my frame shot rapid my thrill'd heart,
And every nerve confess'd the electric dart.

O dear Deceit! I see the Maiden rise,
Chaste Joyance dancing in her bright-blue eyes!
When first the lark high-soaring swells his throat,
Mocks the tired eye, and scatters the loud note,
I trace her footsteps on the accustom'd lawn,
I mark her glancing mid the gleams of dawn.
When the bent flower beneath the night-dew weeps
And on the lake the silver lustre sleeps,
Amid the paly radiance soft and sad
She meets my lonely path in moon-beams clad.
With her along the streamlet's brink I rove;
With her I list the warblings of the grove;
And seems in each low wind her voice to float,
Lone-whispering Pity in each soothing note!

Spirits of Love! ye heard her name! Obey
The powerful spell, and to my haunt repair.
Whether on clustering pinions ye are there,
Where rich snows blossom on the Myrtle-trees,
Or with fond languishment around my fair
Sigh in the loose luxuriance of her hair;
O heed the spell, and hither wing your way,
Like far-off music, voyaging the breeze!

Spirits! to you the infant Maid was given
Form'd by the wondrous Alchemy of Heaven!
No fairer Maid does Love's wide empire know,
No fairer Maid e'er heaved the bosom's snow.
A thousand Loves around her forehead fly;
A thousand Loves sit melting in her eye;
Love lights her smile—in Joy's red nectar dips
His myrtle flower,* and plants it on her lips.
[Tender, serene, and all devoid of guile,
Soft is her soul as sleeping infants' smile:]
She speaks! and hark that passion-warbled song—
Still, Fancy! still that voice, those notes prolong.
As sweet as when that voice with rapturous falls
Shall wake† the soften'd echoes of Heaven's Halls!

O (have I sigh'd) were mine the wizard's rod,
Or mine the power of Proteus, changeful God!
A flower-entangled Arbour I would seem
To shield my Love from Noontide's sultry beam:
Or bloom a Myrtle, from whose odorous boughs
My Love might weave gay garlands for her brows.
When Twilight stole across the fading vale,
To fan my Love I'd be the Evening Gale;

---

* In Joy's bright nectar dips
  The flamy rose, &c. 1796.

† Still, Fancy! still those mazy notes prolong,
  Sweet as th' angelic harps whose rapturous falls
  Awake the soften'd echoes, &c. 1796.

Mourn in the soft folds of her swelling vest,
And flutter my faint pinions on her breast!
On Seraph wing I'd float a Dream by night,
To soothe my Love with shadows of delight :—
Or soar aloft to be the Spangled Skies,
And gaze upon her with a thousand eyes!

As when the savage, who his drowsy frame
Had bask'd beneath the Sun's unclouded flame,
Awakes amid the troubles of the air,
The skiey deluge, and white lightning's glare—
Aghast he scours before the tempest's sweep,
And sad recalls the sunny hour of sleep :—
So toss'd by storms along Life's wildering way,
Mine eye reverted views that cloudless day,
When by my native brook I wont to rove,
While Hope with kisses nursed the Infant Love.

Dear native brook! like Peace, so placidly
Smoothing through fertile fields thy current meek!
Dear native brook! where first young Poesy
Stared wildly-eager in her noontide dream!
Where blameless pleasures dimple Quiet's cheek,
As water-lilies ripple thy slow stream !*

---

* In *The Watchman*, of April 2, 1796, the above sixteen lines, beginning
   " As the tired savage who his drowsy frame"
appear under the title of " Recollection," and continue with ten

Dear native haunts! where Virtue still is gay,
Where Friendship's fix'd star sheds a mellow'd ray,
Where Love a crown of thornless Roses wears,
Where soften'd Sorrow smiles within her tears ;
And Memory, with a Vestal's chaste employ,
Unceasing feeds the lambent flame of joy !
No more your sky-larks melting from the sight
Shall thrill the attuned heart-string with delight—
No more shall deck your pensive Pleasures sweet
With wreaths of sober hue my evening seat.
Yet dear to Fancy's eye your varied scene
Of wood, hill, dale, and sparkling brook between !
Yet sweet to Fancy's ear the warbled song,
That soars on Morning's wing your vales among.

Scenes of my Hope ! the aching eye ye leave
Like yon bright hues that paint the clouds of eve !
Tearful and saddening with the sadden'd blaze
Mine eye the gleam pursues with wistful gaze :—
Sees shades on shades with deeper tint impend,
Till chill and damp the moonless night descend.

lines afterwards inserted in the Sonnet to the River Otter, closing thus :—
" Ah! fair though faint those forms of memory seem,
  Like Heaven's bright bow on thy smooth evening stream."

THE ROSE.

AS late each flower that sweetest blows
   I pluck'd, the Garden's pride!
Within the petals of a Rose
   A sleeping Love I spied.

Around his brows a beamy wreath
   Of many a lucent hue;
All purple glow'd his cheek, beneath,
   Inebriate with dew.

I softly seized the unguarded Power,
   Nor scared his balmy rest:
And placed him, caged within the flower,
   On spotless Sara's breast.

But when unweeting of the guile
   Awoke the prisoner sweet,
He struggled to escape awhile
   And stamp'd his faery feet.

Ah! soon the soul-entrancing sight
   Subdued the impatient boy!
He gazed! he thrill'd with deep delight!
   Then clapp'd his wings for joy.

" And O!" he cried—" of magic kind
   What charms this Throne endear!
Some other Love let Venus find—
   I'll fix my empire here."

THE KISS.

ONE kiss, dear maid! I said and sigh'd—
  Your scorn the little boon denied.
Ah why refuse the blameless bliss?
Can danger lurk within a kiss?
Yon viewless wanderer of the vale,
The Spirit of the Western Gale,
At Morning's break, at Evening's close
Inhales the sweetness of the Rose,
And hovers o'er the uninjured bloom
Sighing back the soft perfume.
Vigour to the Zephyr's wing
Her nectar-breathing kisses fling;
And He the glitter of the Dew
Scatters on the Rose's hue.
Bashful lo! she bends her head,
And darts a blush of deeper Red!

Too well those lovely lips disclose
The triumphs of the opening Rose;
O fair! O graceful! bid them prove
As passive to the breath of Love.
In tender accents, faint and low,
Well-pleased I hear the whisper'd "No!"
The whisper'd "No"—how little meant!
Sweet Falsehood that endears Consent!

For on those lovely lips the while
Dawns the soft relenting smile,
And tempts with feign'd dissuasion coy
The gentle violence of Joy.

TO A YOUNG ASS.

ITS MOTHER BEING TETHERED NEAR IT.

POOR little foal of an oppressed race !
    I love the languid patience of thy face :
And oft with gentle hand I give thee bread,
And clap thy ragged coat, and pat thy head.
But what thy dulled spirits hath dismay'd,
That never thou dost sport along the glade?
And (most unlike the nature of things young)
That earthward still thy moveless head is hung?
Do thy prophetic fears anticipate,
Meek Child of Misery ! thy future fate?
The starving meal, and all the thousand aches
" Which patient Merit of the Unworthy takes?"
Or is thy sad heart thrill'd with filial pain
To see thy wretched mother's shorten'd chain?
And, truly very piteous is her Lot—
Chain'd to a log within a narrow spot,
Where the close-eaten grass is scarcely seen,
While sweet around her waves the tempting green !

Poor Ass ! thy master should have learnt to show
Pity—best taught by fellowship of Woe
For much I fear me that He lives like thee,
Half famish'd in a land of Luxury !
How askingly its footsteps hither bend,*
It seems to say, " And have I then one friend ?"
Innocent foal ! thou poor despised forlorn !
I hail thee brother—spite of the fool's scorn !
And fain would take thee with me, in the Dell
Of Peace and mild Equality to dwell,
Where Toil shall call the charmer Health his bride,
And Laughter tickle Plenty's ribless side !
How thou wouldst toss thy heels in gamesome play,
And frisk about, as lamb or kitten gay !
Yea ! and more musically sweet to me
Thy dissonant harsh bray of joy would be,
Than warbled melodies that soothe to rest
The aching of pale Fashion's vacant breast ! †

December, 1794.

* Toward me bend—1796.

† The tumult of some SCOUNDREL Monarch's breast !—*Ib.*

[The line that now stands in the text was substituted in the edition of 1797.]

THE SIGH.

WHEN Youth his faery reign began
    Ere sorrow had proclaim'd me man;
While Peace the present hour beguiled,
And all the lovely Prospect smiled;
Then Mary! 'mid my lightsome glee
I heaved the painless Sigh for thee.

And when, along the waves of woe,
My harass'd Heart was doom'd to know
The frantic burst of Outrage keen,
And the slow Pang that gnaws unseen;
Then shipwreck'd on Life's stormy sea
I heaved an anguish'd Sigh for thee!

But soon Reflection's power imprest
A stiller sadness on my breast;
And sickly Hope with waning eye
Was well content to droop and die:
I yielded to the stern decree,
Yet heaved a languid Sigh for thee!

And though in distant climes to roam,
A wanderer from my native home,
I fain would soothe the sense of Care,
And lull to sleep the Joys that were,
Thy Image may not banish'd be—
Still, Mary! still I sigh for thee.

June, 1794.

EPITAPH ON AN INFANT.

ERE Sin could blight or Sorrow fade,
    Death came with friendly care;
The opening bud to Heaven convey'd,
And bade it blossom there.

LINES

WRITTEN AT THE KING'S ARMS, ROSS, FORMERLY THE HOUSE OF THE "MAN OF ROSS."

RICHER than Miser o'er his countless hoards,
    Nobler than Kings, or king-polluted Lords,
Here dwelt the Man of Ross! O Traveller, hear!
Departed Merit claims a reverent tear.
Friend to the friendless, to the sick man health,
With generous joy he view'd his modest wealth;
He heard the widow's heaven-breathed prayer of
    praise,
He mark'd the shelter'd orphan's tearful gaze,
Or where the sorrow-shrivell'd captive lay,
Pour'd the bright blaze of Freedom's noon-tide ray.*

---

* The above six lines occur in the edition of 1796 in the Monody on the Death of Chatterton. In the edition of 1797 they were omitted from that poem and transferred to the present one. In the edition of 1803 they disappeared altogether.—ED.

Beneath this roof if thy cheer'd moments pass,*
Fill to the good man's name one grateful glass :
To higher zest shall Memory wake thy soul,
And Virtue mingle in the ennobled bowl.
But if, like me, through life's distressful scene
Lonely and sad thy pilgrimage hath been ;
And if thy breast with heart-sick anguish fraught,
Thou journeyest onward tempest-toss'd in thought ;
Here cheat thy cares ! in generous visions melt,
And dream of goodness, thou hast never felt !

LINES

TO A BEAUTIFUL SPRING IN A VILLAGE.

ONCE more, sweet Stream ! with slow foot
    wandering near,
I bless thy milky waters cold and clear.
Escaped the flashing of the noontide hours,
With one fresh garland of Pierian flowers
(Ere from thy zephyr-haunted brink I turn)
My languid hand shall wreath thy mossy urn.
For not through pathless grove with murmur rude
Thou soothest the sad wood-nymph, Solitude ;
Nor thine unseen in cavern depths to well,
The hermit-fountain of some dripping cell !

---

* If 'neath this roof thy wine-cheer'd moments pass.—1803.
 [An alteration extorted from the author by Charles Lamb, who saw the edition of 1803 through the press. Coleridge afterwards restored the original reading.—ED.]

Pride of the Vale ! thy useful streams supply
The scatter'd cots and peaceful hamlet nigh.
The elfin tribe around thy friendly banks
With infant uproar and soul-soothing pranks,
Released from school, their little hearts at rest,
Launch paper navies on thy waveless breast.
The rustic here at eve with pensive look
Whistling lorn ditties leans upon his crook,
Or starting pauses with hope-mingled dread
To list the much-loved maid's accustom'd tread :
She, vainly mindful of her dame's command,
Loiters, the long-fill'd pitcher in her hand.

Unboastful Stream ! thy fount with pebbled falls
The faded form of past delight recalls,
What time the morning sun of Hope arose,
And all was joy ; save when another's woes
A transient gloom upon my soul imprest,
Like passing clouds impictured on thy breast.
Life's current then ran sparkling to the noon,
Or silvery stole beneath the pensive Moon :
Ah ! now it works rude brakes and thorns among,
Or o'er the rough rock bursts and foams along !

LINES ON A FRIEND

WHO DIED OF A FRENZY FEVER INDUCED BY CALUMNIOUS REPORTS.

EDMUND ! thy grave with aching eye I scan,
   And inly groan for Heaven's poor outcast—
                                      [Man !

'Tis tempest all or gloom : in early youth
If gifted with the Ithuriel lance of Truth
We force to start amid her feign'd caress
Vice, siren-hag ! in native ugliness ;
A Brother's fate will haply rouse the tear,
And on we go in heaviness and fear !
But if our fond hearts call to Pleasure's bower
Some pigmy Folly in a careless hour,
The faithless guest shall stamp the enchanted
    ground,
And mingled forms of Misery rise around :
Heart-fretting Fear, with pallid look aghast,
That courts the future woe to hide the past ;
Remorse, the poison'd arrow in his side,
And loud lewd Mirth, to Anguish close allied :
Till Frenzy, fierce-eyed child of moping Pain,
Darts her hot lightning-flash athwart the brain.

Rest, injured shade ! Shall Slander squatting near
Spit her cold venom in a dead Man's ear ?
'Twas thine to feel the sympathetic glow
In Merit's joy, and Poverty's meek woe ;
Thine all that cheer the moment as it flies,
The zoneless Cares, and smiling Courtesies.
Nursed in thy heart the firmer Virtues grew,
And in thy heart they wither'd ! Such chill dew
Wan Indolence on each young blossom shed ;
And Vanity her filmy net-work spread,
With eye that roll'd around in asking gaze,
And tongue that traffick'd in the trade of praise.
Thy follies such ! the hard world mark'd them well !

Were they more wise, the proud who never fell?
Rest, injured shade! the poor man's grateful prayer
On heaven-ward wing thy wounded soul shall bear.*

As oft at twilight gloom thy grave I pass,
And sit me down upon its recent grass,
With introverted eye I contemplate
Similitude of soul, perhaps of—fate!
To me hath Heaven with bounteous hand assign'd
Energic Reason and a shaping mind,
The daring ken of Truth, the Patriot's part,
And Pity's sigh, that breathes the gentle heart—
Sloth-jaundiced all! and from my graspless hand
Drop Friendship's precious pearls, like hour-glass
    sand.
I weep, yet stoop not! the faint anguish flows,
A dreamy pang in Morning's feverous doze.

Is this piled earth our Being's passless mound?
Tell me, cold grave! is death with poppies
    crown'd?
Tired Sentinel! mid fitful starts I nod,
And fain would sleep, though pillow'd on a clod!

November, 1794.

* The poor man's prayer of praise
On heavenward wing thy wounded Soul shall raise.—1796.

TO A YOUNG LADY,

WITH A POEM ON THE FRENCH REVOLUTION.

MUCH on my early youth I love to dwell,
    Ere yet I bade that friendly dome farewell,
Where first, beneath the echoing cloisters pale,
I heard of guilt and wonder'd at the tale!
Yet though the hours flew by on careless wing,
Full heavily of Sorrow would I sing.
Aye as the star of evening flung its beam
In broken radiance on the wavy stream,
My soul amid the pensive twilight gloom   [tomb.
Mourn'd with the breeze, O Lee Boo!* o'er thy
Where'er I wander'd, Pity still was near,
Breathed from the heart and glisten'd in the tear:
No knell that toll'd but fill'd my anxious eye,
And suffering Nature wept that *one* should die!†

Thus to sad sympathies I soothed my breast,
Calm, as the rainbow in the weeping West:
When slumbering Freedom roused by high Disdain
With giant fury burst her triple chain!
Fierce on her front the blasting Dog-star glow'd;
Her banners, like a midnight meteor, flow'd;

---

* Lee Boo, the son of Abba Thule, Prince of the Pelew Islands, came over to England with Captain Wilson, died of the small-pox, and is buried in Greenwich Churchyard. See Keate's Account.   † Southey's Retrospect.

Amid the yelling of the storm-rent skies
She came, and scatter'd battles from her eyes!
Then Exultation waked the patriot fire
And swept with wild hand the Tyrtæan lyre :*
Red from the Tyrant's wound I shook the lance,
And strode in joy the reeking plains of France!

Fall'n is the oppressor, friendless, ghastly, low,†
And my heart aches, though Mercy struck the blow.
With wearied thought once more I seek the shade,
Where peaceful Virtue weaves the myrtle braid.
And O! if Eyes whose holy glances roll,
Swift messengers, and eloquent of soul ;‡
If Smiles more winning, and a gentler Mien
Than the love-wilder'd Maniac's brain hath seen
Shaping celestial forms in vacant air,
If these demand the impassion'd Poet's care—
If Mirth and soften'd Sense and Wit refined,
The blameless features of a lovely mind ;
Then haply shall my trembling hand assign
No fading wreath to Beauty's saintly shrine.
Nor, Sara! thou these early flowers refuse—
Ne'er lurk'd thè snake beneath their simple hues ;
No purple bloom the Child of Nature brings
From Flattery's night-shade: as he feels he sings.

September, 1792.

* And swept with wilder hand th' Alcæan lyre :—1796.
† In ghastly horror lie th' oppressors low.—*Ib.*
‡ The eloquent messengers of the pure soul.—*Ib.*

IMITATED FROM THE WELSH.

IF while my passion I impart
   You deem my words untrue,
O place your hand upon my heart—
   Feel how it throbs for you!

Ah no! reject the thoughtless claim
   In pity to your Lover!
That thrilling touch would aid the flame
   It wishes to discover.

TO AN INFANT.

AH! cease thy tears and sobs, my little Life!
   I did but snatch away the unclasp'd knife:
Some safer toy will soon arrest thine eye,
And to quick laughter change this peevish cry!
Poor stumbler on the rocky coast of woe,
Tutor'd by pain each source of pain to know!
Alike the foodful fruit and scorching fire
Awake thy eager grasp and young desire;
Alike the Good, the Ill offend thy sight,
And rouse the stormy sense of shrill affright!
Untaught, yet wise! mid all thy brief alarms
Thou closely clingest to thy Mother's arms,
Nestling thy little face in that fond breast
Whose anxious heavings lull thee to thy rest!

Man's breathing miniature ! thou makest me sigh—
A babe art thou—and such a thing am I !
To anger rapid and as soon appeased,
For trifles mourning and by trifles pleased,
Break Friendship's mirror with a tetchy blow,
Yet snatch what coals of fire on Pleasure's altar
    glow !

O thou that rearest with celestial aim
The future seraph in my mortal frame,
Thrice holy Faith ! whatever thorns I meet
As on I totter with unpractised feet,
Still let me stretch my arms and cling to thee,
Meek nurse of souls through their long infancy !

LINES

WRITTEN AT SHURTON BARS, NEAR BRIDGEWATER,
SEPTEMBER, 1795, IN ANSWER TO A
LETTER FROM BRISTOL.

> Good verse most good, and bad verse then seems better
> Received from absent friend by way of letter.
> For what so sweet can labour'd lays impart
> As one rude rhyme warm from a friendly heart ?—ANON.

NOR travels my meandering eye
    The starry wilderness on high ;
  Nor now with curious sight
I mark the glowworm, as I pass,

Move with "green radiance"* through the grass,
   An emerald of light.

O ever present to my view !
My wafted spirit is with you,
   And soothes your boding fears :
I see you all oppress'd with gloom
Sit lonely in that cheerless room—
   Ah me ! you are in tears !

Beloved woman ! did you fly
Chill'd Friendship's dark disliking eye,
   Or Mirth's untimely din ?
With cruel weight these trifles press
A temper sore with tenderness,
   When aches the void within.

---

* The expression "green radiance" is borrowed from Mr. Wordsworth, a poet whose versification is occasionally harsh and his diction too frequently obscure; but whom I deem unrivalled among the writers of the present day in manly sentiment, novel imagery, and vivid colouring. (Note by S. T. C. in the editions of 1796—97.) [This criticism refers to the two juvenile poems of "The Evening Walk" and "Descriptive Sketches" (1793), which were all that Wordsworth had then published. The expression quoted by Coleridge occurs in the former of these pieces :—

"Delighted with the glowworm's harmless ray,
   Toss'd light from hand to hand; while on the ground
   Small circles of green radiance gleam around."]

In a copy of the second edition of his Poems, now in the possession of Mr. Frederick Locker, Coleridge has written as follows, under this allusion of his to Wordsworth :—

"This note was written before I had ever seen Mr. Wordsworth, *atque utinam opera ejus tantum noveram.*"

But why with sable wand unblest
Should Fancy rouse within my breast
   Dim-visaged shapes of Dread?
Untenanting its beauteous clay
My Sara's soul has wing'd its way,
   And hovers round my head!

I felt it prompt the tender dream,
When slowly sank the day's last gleam;
   You roused each gentler sense,
As sighing o'er the blossom's bloom
Meek Evening wakes its soft perfume
   With viewless influence.

And hark, my love! The sea-breeze moans
Through yon reft house! O'er rolling stones
   In bold ambitious sweep,
The onward-surging tides supply
The silence of the cloudless sky
   With mimic thunders deep.

Dark reddening from the channell'd Isle*
(Where stands one solitary pile
   Unslated by the blast)
The watchfire, like a sullen star
Twinkles to many a dozing tar
   Rude cradled on the mast.

---

* The Holmes, in the Bristol Channel.

Even there—beneath that light-house tower—
In the tumultuous evil hour
   Ere Peace with Sara came,
Time was, I should have thought it sweet
To count the echoings of my feet,
   And watch the storm-vex'd flame.

And there in black soul-jaundiced fit
A sad gloom-pamper'd Man to sit,
   And listen to the roar:
When mountain surges bellowing deep
With an uncouth monster leap
   Plunged foaming on the shore.

Then by the lightning's blaze to mark
Some toiling tempest-shatter'd bark;
   Her vain distress-guns hear;
And when a second sheet of light
Flash'd o'er the blackness of the night—
   To see no vessel there!

But Fancy now more gaily sings;
Or if awhile she droop her wings,
   As skylarks 'mid the corn,
On summer fields she grounds her breast:
The oblivious poppy o'er her nest
   Nods, till returning morn.

O mark those smiling tears, that swell
The open'd rose! From heaven they fell,

And with the sun-beam blend.
Blest visitations from above,
Such are the tender woes of Love
　Fostering the heart they bend!

When stormy Midnight howling round
Beats on our roof with clattering sound,
　To me your arms you'll stretch:
Great God! you'll say—To us so kind,
O shelter from this loud bleak wind
　The houseless, friendless wretch!

The tears that tremble down your cheek,
Shall bathe my kisses chaste and meek
　In pity's dew divine;
And from your heart the sighs that steal
Shall make your rising bosom feel
　The answering swell of mine!

How oft, my Love! with shapings sweet
I paint the moment, we shall meet!
　With eager speed I dart—
I seize you in the vacant air,
And fancy with a husband's care
　I press you to my heart!

'Tis said, in Summer's evening hour
Flashes the golden-colour'd flower*

---

* In Sweden a very curious phenomenon has been observed on certain flowers by M. Haggern, lecturer in natural history.

A fair electric flame:
And so shall flash my love-charged eye
When all the heart's big ecstasy
Shoots rapid through the frame!

LINES *

TO A FRIEND IN ANSWER TO A MELANCHOLY LETTER.

AWAY those cloudy looks, that labouring sigh,
 The peevish offspring of a sickly hour!

> One evening he perceived a faint flash of light repeatedly dart from a marigold. Surprised at such an uncommon appearance, he resolved to examine it with attention; and, to be assured it was no deception of the eye, he placed a man near him, with orders to make a signal at the moment when he observed the light. They both saw it constantly at the same moment. The light was most brilliant on marigolds of an orange or flame colour, but scarcely visible on pale ones. The flash was frequently seen on the same flower two or three times in quick succession, but more commonly at intervals of several minutes; and when several flowers in the same place emitted their light together, it could be observed at a considerable distance. This phenomenon was remarked in the months of July and August at sunset, and for half an hour, when the atmosphere was clear; but after a rainy day, or when the air was loaded with vapours, nothing of it was seen. The following flowers emitted flashes, more or less vivid, in this order:—1, the marigold, *galendula officinalis*; 2, monk's-hood, *tropœlum majus*; 3, the orange lily, *lilium bulbiferum*; 4, the Indian pink, *tagetes patula, & erecta*. From the rapidity of the flash and other circumstances, it may be conjectured that there is something of electricity in this phenomenon. (*Note of* 1796.)

Nor meanly thus complain of Fortune's power,
When the blind gamester throws a luckless die.

Yon setting sun flashes a mournful gleam
   Behind those broken clouds, his stormy train :
   To-morrow shall the many-colour'd main
In brightness roll beneath his orient beam !

Wild, as the autumnal gust, the hand of Time
   Flies o'er his mystic lyre : in shadowy dance
   The alternate groups of Joy and Grief advance
Responsive to his varying strains sublime !

Bears on its wing each hour a load of Fate ; [led
   The swain, who, lull'd by Seine's mild murmurs,
   His weary oxen to their nightly shed,
To-day may rule a tempest-troubled State.

Nor shall not Fortune with a vengeful smile
   Survey the sanguinary despot's might,
   And haply hurl the pageant from his height
Unwept to wander in some savage isle.

There shivering sad beneath the tempest's frown
   Round his tired limbs to wrap the purple vest ;
   And mix'd with nails and beads, an equal jest !
Barter for food the jewels of his crown.

RELIGIOUS MUSINGS:

A DESULTORY POEM, WRITTEN ON THE CHRISTMAS EVE OF 1794.

THIS is the time, when most divine to hear,
  The voice of adoration rouses me,
As with a Cherub's trump: and high upborne,
Yea, mingling with the choir, I seem to view
The vision of the heavenly multitude,
Who hymn'd the song of peace o'er Bethlehem's
    fields!
Yet thou more bright than all the angel blaze,
That harbinger'd thy birth, Thou Man of Woes!
Despised Galilean! For the great
Invisible (by symbols only seen)
With a peculiar and surpassing light
Shines from the visage of the oppress'd good man,
When heedless of himself the scourged Saint
Mourns for the oppressor. Fair the vernal mead,
Fair the high grove, the sea, the sun, the stars;
True impress each of their creating Sire!
Yet nor high grove, nor many-colour'd mead,
Nor the green Ocean with his thousand isles,
Nor the starr'd azure, nor the sovran sun,
E'er with such majesty of portraiture
Imaged the supreme beauty uncreate,
As thou, meek Saviour! at the fearful hour

When thy insulted anguish wing'd the prayer
Harp'd by Archangels, when they sing of mercy !
Which when the Almighty heard from forth his
   throne
Diviner light fill'd Heaven with ecstasy !*
Heaven's hymnings paused : and Hell her yawning
   mouth
Closed a brief moment.

* This poem originally opened thus in the edition of 1796 :—
This is the time, when most divine to hear,
As with a cherub's " loud uplifted " trump
The voice of adoration my thrill'd heart
Rouses ! And with the rushing noise of wings
Transports my spirit to the favour'd fields
Of Bethlehem, there in shepherd's guise to sit
Sublime of ecstasy, and mark entranced
The glory-streaming Vision throng the night.
Ah ! not more radiant nor loud harmonies
Hymning more unimaginably sweet
With choral songs around th' Eternal Mind,
The constellated company of worlds
Danced jubilant : what time the startling East
Saw from her dark womb leap her flamy Child !
Glory to God in the highest ! peace on earth !

Yet thou more biight than all that angel blaze,
Despised Galilæan ! Man of woes !
For chiefly in the oppressed good man's face
The Great Invisible (by symbols seen)
Shines with peculiar and concentred light,
When all of self regardless the scourged saint
Mourns for th' oppressor. O thou meekest Man !
Meek Man and lowliest of the Sons of Men !

Lovely was the death
Of Him whose life was love ! Holy with power
He on the thought-benighted Sceptic beam'd
Manifest Godhead, melting into day
What floating mists of dark idolatry
Broke and misshaped the omnipresent Sire :
And first by Fear uncharm'd the drowsed Soul.*
Till of its nobler nature it 'gan feel
Dim recollections ; and thence soar'd to Hope,
Strong to believe whate'er of mystic good
The Eternal dooms for His immortal sons.
From Hope and firmer Faith to perfect Love
Attracted and absorb'd : and centred there
God only to behold, and know, and feel,
Till by exclusive consciousness of God
All self-annihilated it shall make †

    Who thee beheld thy imaged Father saw.
    His power and wisdom from thy awful eye
    Blended their beams, and loftier Love sate there
    Musing on human weal, and that dread hour
    When thy insulted anguish wing'd the prayer
    Harp'd by archangels, when they sing of mercy !
    Which when th' Almighty heard, from forth his throne
    Diviner light flash'd ecstasy o'er heaven ! &c.

*   What mists dim-floating of idolatry
   Split and misshaped the omnipresent Sire :
   And first by terror, mercy's startling prelude,
   Uncharm'd the spirit spell-bound with earthy lusts, &c.

                                  1796.

† See this demonstrated by Hartley, vol. i. p. 114 and vol. ii. p. 329. See it likewise proved and freed from the

God its identity : God all in all !
We and our Father one !

              And blest are they,
Who in this fleshly World, the elect of Heaven,
Their strong eye darting through the deeds of men,
Adore with steadfast unpresuming gaze
Him Nature's essence, mind, and energy !
And gazing, trembling, patiently ascend
Treading beneath their feet all visible things
As steps, that upward to their Father's throne
Lead gradual—else nor glorified nor loved.
They nor contempt embosom nor revenge :
For they dare know of what may seem deform
The Supreme Fair sole operant : in whose sight
All things are pure, his strong controlling love
Alike from all educing perfect good.
Theirs too celestial courage, inly arm'd—
Dwarfing Earth's giant brood, what time they muse
On their great Father, great beyond compare !
And marching onwards view high o'er their heads
His waving banners of Omnipotence.

Who the Creator love, created might
Dread not : within their tents no terrors walk.
For they are holy things before the Lord

charge of mysticism by Pistorius in his Notes and Additions to part ii. of Hartley on Man, Addition the 18th, vol. iii. p. 653 of Hartley, 8vo. edition.

Aye unprofaned, though Earth should league with
    Hell!
God's altar grasping with an eager hand
Fear, the wild-visaged, pale, eye-starting wretch,
Sure-refuged hears his hot pursuing fiends
Yell at vain distance. Soon refresh'd from Heaven
He calms the throb and tempest of his heart.
His countenance settles; a soft solemn bliss
Swims in his eye—his swimming eye upraised:
And Faith's whole armour glitters on his limbs!
And thus transfigured with a dreadless awe,
A solemn hush of soul, meek he beholds
All things of terrible seeming: yea, unmoved
Views e'en the immitigable ministers
That shower down vengeance on these latter days.
For kindling with intenser Deity
From the celestial Mercy-seat they come,
And at the renovating wells of Love
Have fill'd their vials with salutary wrath,*
To sickly Nature more medicinal

* Yea, and there,
Unshudder'd, unaghasted, he shall view,
E'en the Seven Spirits, who in the latter day
Will shower hot pestilence on the sons of men.
For he shall know, his heart shall understand,
That kindling with intenser Deity
They from the Mercy-seat, like rosy flames,
From God's celestial Mercy-seat will flash,
And at the wells of renovating love
Fill their seven vials with salutary wrath, &c.—1796.

Than what soft balm the weeping good man pours
Into the lone despoiled traveller's wounds!

Thus from the Elect, regenerate through faith,
Pass the dark passions and what thirsty Cares *
Drink up the Spirit, and the dim regards
Self-centre.   Lo they vanish! or acquire
New names, new features—by supernal grace
Enrobed with Light, and naturalized in Heaven.
As when a shepherd on a vernal morn
Through some thick fog creeps timorous with slow
    foot,
Darkling he fixes on the immediate road
His downward eye: all else of fairest kind
Hid or deform'd.   But lo! the bursting Sun!
Touch'd by the enchantment of that sudden beam
Straight the black vapour melteth, and in globes
Of dewy glitter gems each plant and tree;
On every leaf, on every blade it hangs!
Dance glad the new-born intermingling rays,
And wide around the landscape streams with glory!

There is one Mind, one omnipresent Mind,
Omnific.   His most holy name is Love.

* Our evil passions under the influence of religion, become innocent, and may be made to animate our virtue—in the same manner as the thick mist, melted by the sun, increases the light which it had before excluded. In the preceding paragraph, agreeably to this truth, we had allegorically narrated the transfiguration of fear into holy awe.

Truth of subliming import ! with the which
Who feeds and saturates his constant soul,
He from his small particular orbit flies
With blest outstarting ! From himself he flies,
Stands in the sun, and with no partial gaze
Views all creation; and he loves it all,
And blesses it, and calls it very good !
This is indeed to dwell with the Most High !
Cherubs and rapture-trembling Seraphim
Can press no nearer to the Almighty's throne.
But that we roam unconscious, or with hearts
Unfeeling of our universal Sire,
And that in His vast family no Cain
Injures uninjured (in her best-aim'd blow
Victorious murder a blind suicide)
Haply for this some younger Angel now
Looks down on human nature : and, behold !
A sea of blood bestrew'd with wrecks, where mad
Embattling interests on each other rush
With unhelm'd rage !

     'Tis the sublime of man,
Our noontide majesty, to know ourselves
Parts and proportions of one wondrous whole !
This fraternizes man, this constitutes
Our charities and bearings. But 'tis God
Diffused through all, that doth make all one whole;
This the worst superstition, him except*

 * If to make aught but the Supreme Reality the object of final pursuit be superstition: if the attributing of sublime pro-

Aught to desire, Supreme Reality!
The plenitude and permanence of bliss!
O Fiends of Superstition! not that oft
The erring priest hath stain'd with brother's blood
Your grisly idols, not for this may wrath
Thunder against you from the Holy One!
But o'er some plain that steameth to the sun,
Peopled with death; or where more hideous Trade
Loud-laughing packs his bales of human anguish;*
I will raise up a mourning, O ye Fiends!
And curse your spells that film the eye of Faith,
Hiding the present God; whose presence lost,
The moral world's cohesion, we become

perties to things or persons, which those things or persons neither do nor can possess, be superstition; then avarice and ambition are superstitions, and he who wishes to estimate the evils of superstition should transport himself not to the temple of the Mexican Deities, but to the plains of Flanders, or the coast of Africa.—Such is the sentiment conveyed in this and the subsequent lines.

<blockquote>
* Your pitiless rites have floated with man's blood
The skull-piled temple, not for this shall wrath
Thunder against you from the Holy One!
But (whether ye th' unclimbing bigot mock
With secondary Gods, or if more pleased
Ye petrify th' imbrothell'd Atheist's heart,
The Atheist your worst slave) I o'er some plain
Peopled with death, and to the silent sun
Steaming with tyrant-murder'd multitudes;
Or where mid groans and shrieks loud-laughing Trade
More hideous packs his bales of living anguish, &c.
1796.
</blockquote>

An anarchy of Spirits ! Toy-bewitch'd,
Made blind by lusts, disherited of soul,
No common centre Man, no common sire
Knoweth ! A sordid solitary thing,
Mid countless brethren with a lonely heart
Through courts and cities the smooth savage roams
Feeling himself, his own low self the whole ;
When he by sacred sympathy might make
The whole one self ! self, that no alien knows !
Self, far diffused as Fancy's wing can travel !
Self, spreading still ! Oblivious of its own,
Yet all of all possessing ! This is Faith !
This the Messiah's destined victory !
But first offences needs must come ! Even now*
(Black hell laughs horrible—to hear the scoff !)
Thee to defend, meek Galilean ! Thee
And thy mild laws of Love unutterable,

* January 21st, 1794, in the debate on the address to his Majesty, on the speech from the throne, the Earl of Guildford moved an amendment to the following effect :—" That the House hoped his Majesty would seize the earliest opportunity to conclude a peace with France," &c. This motion was opposed by the Duke of Portland, who " considered the war to be merely grounded on one principle—the preservation of the Christian religion." May 30th, 1794, the Duke of Bedford moved a number of resolutions, with a view to the establishment of a peace with France. He was opposed (among others) by Lord Abingdon in these remarkable words : " The best road to peace, my Lords, is war ! and war carried on in the same manner in which we are taught to worship our Creator, namely, with all our souls, and with all our minds, and with all our hearts, and with all our strength."

Mistrust and enmity have burst the bands
Of social peace : and listening treachery lurks
With pious fraud to snare a brother's life ;
And childless widows o'er the groaning land
Wail numberless; and orphans weep for bread
Thee to defend, dear Saviour of mankind !
Thee, Lamb of God ! Thee, blameless Prince of
    Peace !
From all sides rush the thirsty brood of War—
Austria, and that foul Woman of the North,
The lustful murderess of her wedded lord !
And he, connatural mind !* whom (in their songs
So bards of elder time had haply feign'd)
Some Fury fondled in her hate to man,
Bidding her serpent hair in mazy surge †
Lick his young face, and at his mouth imbreathe
Horrible sympathy ! And leagued with these
Each petty German princeling, nursed in gore !
Soul-harden'd barterers of human blood ! ‡
Death's prime slave-merchants ! Scorpion-whips of
    Fate !
Nor least in savagery of holy zeal,

---

  * The despot who received the wages of an hireling that he might act the part of a swindler, and who skulked from his impotent attacks on the liberties of France to perpetrate more successful iniquity in the plains of Poland.
  † In tortuous fold.—1796.
  ‡ The father of the present Prince of Hesse Cassel supported himself and his strumpets at Paris by the vast sums which he received from the British Government during the American war for the flesh of his subjects. (*Note of* 1796.)

Apt for the yoke, the race degenerate,
Whom Britain erst had blush'd to call her sons !
Thee to defend the Moloch priest prefers
The prayer of hate, and bellows to the herd
That Deity, accomplice Deity
In the fierce jealousy of waken'd wrath
Will go forth with our armies and our fleets
To scatter the red ruin on their foes !
O blasphemy ! to mingle fiendish deeds
With blessedness !

    Lord of unsleeping Love,*
From everlasting Thou ! We shall not die.
These, even these, in mercy didst thou form,
Teachers of Good through Evil, by brief wrong
Making Truth lovely, and her future might
Magnetic o'er the fix'd untrembling heart.

In the primeval age a dateless while
The vacant Shepherd wander'd with his flock,
Pitching his tent where'er the green grass waved.

 * Art thou not from everlasting, O Lord, my God, mine Holy One ? We shall not die. O Lord, thou hast ordained them for judgment, &c.—*Habakkuk*, i. 12. In this paragraph the author recals himself from his indignation against the instruments of evil, to contemplate the *uses* of these evils in the great process of Divine benevolence. In the first age men were innocent from ignorance of vice ; they fell that by the knowledge of consequences they might attain intellectual security, *i.e.*, Virtue, which is a wise and strong-nerved innocence.

But soon Imagination conjured up
A host of new desires : with busy aim,
Each for himself, Earth's eager children toil'd.
So Property began, twy-streaming fount,
Whence Vice and Virtue flow, honey and gall.
Hence the soft couch, and many-colour'd robe,
The timbrel, and arch'd dome and costly feast,
With all the inventive arts, that nursed the soul
To forms of beauty, and by sensual wants
Unsensualized the mind, which in the means·
Learnt to forget the grossness of the end,
Best pleasured with its own activity.
And hence Disease that withers manhood's arm,
The dagger'd Envy, spirit-quenching Want,
Warriors, and Lords, and Priests*—all the sore ills
That vex and desolate our mortal life.

* I deem that the teaching of the gospel for hire is wrong ; because it gives the teacher an improper bias in favour of particular opinions on a subject where it is of the last importance that the mind should be perfectly unbiassed. Such is my private opinion ; but I mean not to censure all hired teachers, many among whom I know, and venerate as the best and wisest of men—God forbid that I should think of these, when I use the word Priest, a name after which any other term of abhorrence would appear an anti-climax. By a Priest I mean a man who holding the scourge of power in his right hand and a Bible (translated by authority) in his left, doth necessarily cause the Bible and the scourge to be associated ideas, and so produces that temper of mind that leads to infidelity—infidelity which, judging of Revelation by the doctrines and practices of established Churches, honours God by rejecting Christ.

Wide-wasting ills! yet each the immediate source
Of mightier good. Their keen necessities
To ceaseless action goading human thought
Have made Earth's reasoning animal her Lord;
And the pale-featured Sage's trembling hand
Strong as a host of armed Deities,
Such as the blind Ionian fabled erst.

From avarice thus, from luxury and war
Sprang heavenly science; and from science freedom.
O'er waken'd realms Philosophers and Bards
Spread in concentric circles : they whose souls,
Conscious of their high dignities from God,
Brook not wealth's rivalry! and they who long
Enamour'd with the charms of order hate
The unseemly disproportion : and whoe'er
Turn with mild sorrow from the victor's car
And the low puppetry of thrones, to muse
On that blest triumph, when the patriot Sage*
Call'd the red lightnings from the o'er-rushing cloud
And dash'd the beauteous terrors on the earth
Smiling majestic. Such a phalanx ne'er
Measured firm paces to the calming sound
Of Spartan flute! These on the fated day,
When, stung to rage by pity, eloquent men
Have roused with pealing voice the unnumber'd
    tribes
That toil and groan and bleed, hungry and blind—
These hush'd awhile with patient eye serene

* Dr. Franklin.

RELIGIOUS MUSINGS. 101

Shall watch the mad careering of the storm ;
Then o'er the wild and wavy chaos rush
And tame the outrageous mass, with plastic might
Moulding confusion to such perfect forms,
As erst were wont,—bright visions of the day !—
To float before them, when, the summer noon,
Beneath some arch'd romantic rock reclined
They felt the sea-breeze lift their youthful locks ;
Or in the month of blossoms, at mild eve,
Wandering with desultory feet inhaled
The wafted perfumes, and the flocks and woods
And many-tinted streams and setting sun
With all his gorgeous company of clouds
Ecstatic gazed ! then homeward as they stray'd
Cast the sad eye to earth, and inly mused
Why there was misery in a world so fair.

Ah ! far removed from all that glads the sense,
From all that softens or ennobles Man,
The wretched Many ! Bent beneath their loads
They gape at pageant Power, nor recognise
Their cots' transmuted plunder ! From the tree
Of Knowledge, ere the vernal sap had risen
Rudely disbranched ! Blest Society !*
Fitliest depictured by some sun-scorch'd waste,
Where oft majestic through the tainted noon
The Simoom sails, before whose purple pomp
Who falls not prostrate dies !† And where by
    night,

* O *blest* Society.—1796. Evil Society.—1803.
† Bruce's Travels, vol. iv. p. 557.

Fast by each precious fountain on green herbs
The lion couches; or hyæna dips,
Deep in the lucid stream his bloody jaws;
Or serpent plants* his vast moon-glittering bulk,
Caught in whose monstrous twine Behemoth† yells,
His bones loud-crashing!

    O ye numberless,
Whom foul Oppression's ruffian gluttony
Drives from life's plenteous feast! O thou poor
  wretch
Who nursed in darkness ånd made wild by want,
Roamest for prey, yea thy unnatural hand
Dost lift to deeds of blood! O pale-eyed form,
The victim of seduction, doom'd to know
Polluted nights and days of blasphemy;
Who in loathed orgies with lewd wassailers
Must gaily laugh, while thy remember'd home
Gnaws like a viper at thy secret heart!
O aged women! ye who weekly catch
The morsel toss'd by law-forced charity,
And die so slowly, that none call it murder!
O loathly suppliants! ye, that unreceived
Totter heart-broken from the closing gates
Of the full Lazar-house; or, gazing, stand
Sick with despair! O ye to glory's field

---

 * Rolls.—1796.
 † Behemoth, in Hebrew, signifies wild beasts in general. Some believe it is the elephant, some the hippopotamus; some affirm it is the wild bull. Poetically, it designates any large quadruped.

Forced or ensnared, who, as ye gasp in death,
Bleed with new wounds beneath the vulture's
    beak !*
O thou poor widow, who in dreams dost view
Thy husband's mangled corse, and from short doze
Start'st with a shriek ; or in thy half-thatch'd cot
Waked by the wintry night-storm, wet and cold
Cower'st o'er thy screaming baby ! Rest awhile
Children of wretchedness ! More groans must rise,
More blood must stream, or ere your wrongs be full.
Yet is the day of retribution nigh :
The Lamb of God hath open'd the fifth seal
And upward rush on swiftest wing of fire
The innumerable multitude of Wrongs
By man on man inflicted ! Rest awhile,
Children of wretchedness ! The hour is nigh
And lo ! the great, the rich, the mighty Men,
The Kings and the chief Captains of the World,
With all that fix'd on high like stars of Heaven
Shot baleful influence, shall be cast to earth,
Vile and down-trodden, as the untimely fruit
Shook from the fig-tree by a sudden storm.
Even now the storm begins :† each gentle name,

---

* O loathly-visaged suppliants! ye that oft
   Rack'd with disease, from the unopen'd gate
   Of the full Lazar-house, heart-broken crawl!
   O ye to scepter'd Glory's gore-drench'd field
   Forced or ensnared, who swept by Slaughter's scythe,
   (Stern nurse of Vultures !) steam in putrid heaps !
                                                1796.
† This passage alludes to the French Revolution, and the

Faith and meek Piety, with fearful joy
Tremble far-off—for lo ! the giant Frenzy
Uprooting empires with his whirlwind arm
Mocketh high Heaven ; burst hideous from the cell
Where the old hag, unconquerable, huge,
Creation's eyeless drudge, black Ruin, sits
Nursing the impatient earthquake.

                                          O return !
Pure Faith ! meek Piety ! The abhorred Form
Whose scarlet robe was stiff with earthly pomp,
Who drank iniquity in cups of gold,
Whose names were many and all blasphemous,
Hath met the horrible judgment ! Whence that
    cry ?
The mighty army of foul Spirits shriek'd
Disherited of earth ! For she hath fall'n
On whose black front was written Mystery;
She that reel'd heavily, whose wine was blood ;
She that work'd whoredom with the Demon Power,
And from the dark embrace all evil things
Brought forth and nurtured : mitred Atheism !
And patient Folly who on bended knee
Gives back the steel that stabb'd him ; and pale
    Fear
Haunted by ghastlier shapings than surround

subsequent paragraph to the downfall of Religious Establishments. I am convinced that the Babylon of the Apocalypse does not apply to Rome exclusively; but to the union of Religion with Power and Wealth, wherever it is found.

Moon-blasted Madness when he yells at midnight!
Return pure Faith! return meek Piety!
The kingdoms of the world are yours: each heart
Self-govern'd, the vast family of Love
Raised from the common earth by common toil
Enjoy the equal produce. Such delights
As float to earth, permitted visitants!
When in some hour of solemn jubilee
The massy gates of Paradise are thrown
Wide open, and forth come in fragments wild .
Sweet echoes of unearthly melodies,*
And odours snatch'd from beds of amaranth,
And they, that from the crystal river of life
Spring up on freshen'd wing, ambrosial gales!
The favour'd good man in his lonely walk
Perceives them, and his silent spirit drinks
Strange bliss which he shall recognise in heaven.
And such delights, such strange beatitudes
Seize on my young anticipating heart
When that blest future rushes on my view!
For in his own and in his Father's might
The Saviour comes! While as the Thousand
    Years †

  * When on some solemn jubilee of Saints
    The sapphire-blazing gates of Paradise
    Are thrown wide open, and thence voyage forth
    Detachments wild of seraph-warbled airs, &c.
                                     1796.

† The Millenium—in which I suppose that man will continue to enjoy the highest glory, of which his human nature is capable; that all who in past ages have endeavoured to

Lead up their mystic dance, the Desert shouts !
Old Ocean claps his hands ! The mighty Dead *
Rise to new life, whoe'er from earliest time
With conscious zeal had urged Love's wondrous
    plan,
Coadjutors of God. To Milton's trump
The high groves of the renovated Earth †
Unbosom their glad echoes : inly hush'd,
Adoring Newton his serener eye
Raises to heaven : and he of mortal kind
Wisest, he‡ first who mark'd the ideal tribes
Up the fine fibres through the sentient brain. §
Lo ! Priestley there, patriot, and saint, and sage,
Him, full of years, from his loved native land ||

ameliorate the state of man, will rise and enjoy the fruits and flowers, the imperceptible seeds of which they had sown in their former life; and that the wicked will during the same period be suffering the remedies adapted to their several bad habits. I suppose that this period will be followed by the passing away of this Earth, and by our entering the state of pure intellect; when all Creation shall rest from its labours.

   * The Saviour comes ! While as to solemn strains
     The thousand years lead up their mystic dance,
     Old Ocean claps his hands ! the Desert shouts !
     And soft gales wafted from the haunts of Spring
     Melt the primeval North ! The mighty Dead, &c.
                        1796.
   † The odorous groves of Earth reparadised.—*Ib.*
   ‡ David Hartley.
   § Down the fine fibres from the sentient brain
     Roll subtly-surging. Pressing on his steps, &c.
                        1796.
   || Lo ! Priestley there patriot and saint and sage
     Whom that my fleshly eye hath never seen.

Statesmen blood-stain'd and priests idolatrous
By dark lies maddening the blind multitude
Drove with vain hate. Calm, pitying he retired,
And mused expectant on these promised years.

O Years ! the blest pre-eminence of Saints !
Ye sweep athwart my gaze, so heavenly bright,
The wings that veil the adoring Seraphs' eyes,
What time they bend before the Jasper Throne *
Reflect no lovelier hues ! Yet ye depart,†
And all beyond is darkness ! Heights most
    strange,
Whence Fancy falls, fluttering her idle wing.
For who of woman born may paint the hour,
When seized in his mid course, the Sun shall wane
Making noon ghastly ! Who of woman born
May image in the workings of his thought,‡
How the black-visaged, red-eyed Fiend outstretch'd§

> A childish pang of impotent regret
> Hath thrill'd my heart. Him from his native land, &c.
>   1796.

* Rev. chap. iv. v. 2 and 3.—And immediately I was in the Spirit: and behold, a Throne was set in Heaven and one sat on the Throne. And he that sat was to look upon like a jasper and a sardine stone, &c.

> † Sweeping before the rapt prophetic gaze
> Bright as what glories of the jasper throne,
> Stream from the gorgeous and face-veiling plumes
> Of Spirits adoring. Ye, blest years ! must end, &c.
>   1796.

‡ May image in his wildly-working thought.—*Ib.*

§ The final destruction impersonated.

Beneath the unsteady feet of Nature groans,
In feverous slumbers—destined then to wake,
When fiery whirlwinds thunder his dread name
And Angels shout, Destruction! How his arm
The last great Spirit* lifting high in air
Shall swear by Him, the ever-living One,
Time is no more!

     Believe thou, O my soul,
Life is a vision shadowy of Truth;
And vice, and anguish, and the wormy grave,
Shapes of a dream! The veiling clouds retire,
And lo! the Throne of the redeeming God
Forth flashing unimaginable day
Wraps in one blaze earth, heaven, and deepest hell.†
Contemplant Spirits! ye that hover o'er
With untired gaze the immeasurable fount
Ebullient with creative Deity!
And ye of plastic power, that interfused
Roll through the grosser and material mass
In organizing surge! Holies of God!
(And what if Monads of the infinite mind?)
I haply journeying my immortal course
Shall sometime join your mystic choir! Till then
I discipline my young and novice thought ‡
In ministeries of heart-stirring song,

 * The mighty Spirit.—1796.

 † This paragraph is intelligible to those, who, like the Author, believe and feel the sublime system of Berkeley; and the doctrine of the final happiness of all men.

 ‡ My young noviciate thought.—1796.

And aye on Meditation's heavenward wing
Soaring aloft I breathe the empyreal air
Of Love, omnific, omnipresent Love,
Whose day-spring rises glorious in my soul
As the great Sun, when he his influence
Sheds on the frost-bound waters—The glad stream
Flows to the ray and warbles as it flows.

TO THE

REV. W. J. H.*

WHILE TEACHING A YOUNG LADY SOME SONG-
TUNES ON HIS FLUTE.

I.

HUSH! ye clamorous Cares! be mute!
   Again, dear Harmonist! again
Thro' the hollow of thy flute
   Breathe that passion-warbled strain:
Till Memory each form shall bring
   The loveliest of her shadowy throng;
And Hope, that soars on sky-lark wing,
   Carol wild her gladdest song!

II.

O skill'd with magic spell to roll
The thrilling tones, that concentrate the soul!

---

* The Rev. W. J. Hort, a Unitarian clergyman, and in 1794 second master in Mr. (afterwards Dr.) Estlin's school, St. Michael's Hill. Bristol.—ED.

Breathe thro' thy flute those tender notes again,
While near thee sits the chaste-eyed Maiden mild;
And bid her raise the Poet's kindred strain
In soft impassion'd voice, correctly wild.

III.

In Freedom's undivided dell,
Where Toil and Health with mellow'd Love shall
    dwell,
  Far from folly, far from men,
  In the rude romantic glen,
  Up the cliff, and thro' the glade,
  Wandering with the dear-loved maid,
  I shall listen to the lay,
  And ponder on thee far away
Still, as she bids those thrilling notes aspire
(" Making my fond attuned heart her lyre "),
Thy honour'd form, my Friend! shall re-appear,
And I will thank thee with a raptured tear.

TO A FRIEND,

TOGETHER WITH AN UNFINISHED POEM.

THUS far my scanty brain hath built the rhyme
    Elaborate and swelling: yet the heart
Not owns it. From thy spirit-breathing powers
I ask not now, my friend! the aiding verse,
Tedious to thee, and from thy anxious thought
Of dissonant mood. In fancy (well I know)

From business wandering far and local cares,
Thou creepest round a dear-loved Sister's bed
With noiseless step, and watchest the faint look,
Soothing each pang with fond solicitude,
And tenderest tones medicinal of love.
I too a Sister had, an only Sister—
She loved me dearly, and I doted on her!
To her I pour'd forth all my puny sorrows,
(As sick Patient in his Nurse's arms)
And of the heart those hidden maladies
That even from Friendship's eye will shrink
   ashamed.
O! I have woke at midnight, and have wept,
Because she was not!—Cheerily, dear Charles!
Thou thy best friend shalt cherish many a year:
Such warm presagings feel I of high Hope.
For not uninterested the dear Maid
I've view'd—her soul affectionate yet wise,
Her polish'd wit as mild as lambent glories
That play around a sainted infant's head.
He knows (the Spirit that in secret sees,
Of whose omniscient and all-spreading Love
Aught to* implore were impotence of mind)
That my mute thoughts are sad before his throne,

---

  * I utterly recant the sentiment contained in the lines
    "Of whose omniscient and all-spreading Love
     Aught to implore were impotence of mind,"
it being written in Scripture, "Ask, and it shall be given you," and my human reason being moreover convinced of the propriety of offering petitions as well as thanksgivings to Deity.—(*Note of* 1797.)

Prepared, when he his healing ray vouchsafes,
To pour forth thanksgiving with lifted heart,
And praise Him Gracious with a Brother's Joy!

December, 1794.

TO THE NIGHTINGALE.

SISTER of love-lorn Poets, Philomel!
   How many Bards in city garret pent,
While at their window they with downward eye
Mark the faint lamp-beam on the kennell'd mud,
And listen to the drowsy cry of Watchmen,
(Those hoarse unfeather'd Nightingales of Time!)
How many wretched Bards address *thy* name,
And hers, the full-orb'd Queen that shines above.
But I *do* hear thee, and the high bough mark,
Within whose mild moon-mellow'd foliage hid
Thou warblest sad thy pity-pleading strains.
O! I have listen'd, till my working soul,
Waked by those strains to thousand phantasies,
Absorb'd hath ceased to listen! Therefore oft,
I hymn thy name: and with a proud delight
Oft will I tell thee, Minstrel of the Moon!
"Most musical, most melancholy" Bird!
That all thy soft diversities of tone,
Tho' sweeter far than the delicious airs
That vibrate from a white-arm'd Lady's harp,
What time the languishment of lonely love
Melts in her eye, and heaves her breast of snow,

Are not so sweet as is the voice of her,
My Sara—best beloved of human kind !
When breathing the pure soul of tenderness
She thrills me with the Husband's promised name !

THE COMPOSITION OF A KISS.

CUPID, if storying Legends tell aright,
   Once framed a rich Elixir of Delight.
A Chalice o'er love-kindled flames he fix'd,
And in it Nectar and Ambrosia mix'd :
With these the magic dews which Evening brings,
Brush'd from the Idalian star by faery wings :
Each tender pledge of sacred Faith he join'd,
Each gentler Pleasure of th' unspotted mind—
Day-dreams, whose tints with sportive brightness
    glow,
And Hope, the blameless parasite of Woe.
The eyeless Chemist heard the process rise,
The steamy Chalice bubbled up in sighs ;
Sweet sounds transpired, as when the enamour'd
    Dove
Pours the soft murmuring of responsive Love.
The finish'd work might Envy vainly blame,
And " Kisses " was the precious Compound's
    name.
With half the God his Cyprian Mother blest,
And breathed on Sara's lovelier lips the rest.

LINES

COMPOSED WHILE CLIMBING THE LEFT ASCENT OF BROCKLEY COOMB, SOMERSETSHIRE, MAY, 1795.

WITH many a pause and oft reverted eye
    I climb the Coomb's ascent: sweet songsters near
Warble in shade their wild-wood melody:
Far off the unvarying Cuckoo soothes my ear.
Up scour the startling stragglers of the flock
That on green plots o'er precipices browse:
From the deep fissures * of the naked rock
The Yew-tree bursts! Beneath its dark green
    boughs
(Mid which the May-thorn blends its blossoms
    white)
Where broad smooth stones jut out in mossy seats,
I rest:—and now have gain'd the topmost site.
Ah! what a luxury of landscape meets
My gaze! Proud towers, and cots more dear to me,
Elm-shadow'd fields, and prospect-bounding sea!
Deep sighs my lonely heart: I drop the tear:
Enchanting spot! O were my Sara here!

    * Forced fissures.—1796.

LINES

IN THE MANNER OF SPENSER.

O PEACE, that on a lilied bank dost love
 To rest thine head beneath an olive-tree,
I would that from the pinions of thy dove
One quill withouten pain ypluck'd might be!
For O! I wish my Sara's frowns to flee,
And fain to her some soothing song would write,
Lest she resent my rude discourtesy,
Who vow'd to meet her ere the morning light,
But broke my plighted word—ah! false and
 recreant wight!

Last night as I my weary head did pillow
With thoughts of my dissever'd Fair engrost,
Chill Fancy droop'd wreathing herself with willow,
As though my breast entomb'd a pining ghost.
" From some blest couch, young Rapture's bridal
 boast,
Rejected Slumber! hither wing thy way;
But leave me with the matin hour, at most!
As night-closed floweret to the orient ray, *
My sad heart will expand, when I the Maid
 survey."

* Like snowdrop opening to the solar ray.—1796.
(This, however, is altered in the Errata to the reading in the text.)

But Love, who heard the silence of my thought,
Contrived a too successful wile, I ween :
And whisper'd to himself, with malice fraught—
" Too long our Slave the Damsel's smiles hath
    seen :
To-morrow shall he ken her alter'd mien !"
He spake, and ambush'd lay, till on my bed
The morning shot her dewy glances keen,
When as I 'gan to lift my drowsy head—
" Now, Bard ! I'll work thee woe !" the laughing
    Elfin said.

Sleep, softly-breathing God ! his downy wing
Was fluttering now, as quickly to depart ;
When twang'd an arrow from Love's mystic string,
With pathless wound it pierced him to the heart.
Was there some magic in the Elfin's dart ?
Or did he strike my couch with wizard lance ?
For straight so fair a Form did upwards start
(No fairer deck'd the bowers of old Romance)
That Sleep enamour'd grew, nor moved from his
    sweet trance !

My Sara came, with gentlest look divine ;
Bright shone her eye, yet tender was its beam :
I felt the pressure of her lip to mine !
Whispering we went, and Love was all our theme—
Love pure and spotless, as at first, I deem,
He sprang from Heaven ! Such joys with Sleep
    did 'bide,
That I the living image of my dream

Fondly forgot. Too late I woke, and sigh'd—
" O ! how shall I behold my Love at even-tide !"

IMITATED FROM OSSIAN.

THE stream with languid murmur creeps,
   In Lumin's flowery vale :
Beneath the dew the Lily weeps
   Slow-waving to the gale.

" Cease, restless gale ! " it seems to say,
   " Nor wake me with thy sighing !
The honours of my vernal day
   On rapid wing are flying.

" To-morrow shall the Traveller come
   Who late beheld me blooming :
His searching eye shall vainly roam
   The dreary vale of Lumin."

With eager gaze and wetted cheek
   My wonted haunts along,
Thus, faithful Maiden ! thou shalt seek
   The Youth of simplest song.

But I along the breeze shall roll
   The voice of feeble power ;
And dwell, the Moon-beam of thy soul,
   In Slumber's nightly hour.

THE COMPLAINT OF NINATHOMA.

FROM THE SAME.

HOW long will ye round me be swelling,
    O ye blue-tumbling waves of the sea?
Not always in caves was my dwelling,
    Nor beneath the cold blast of the tree.
Through the high-sounding halls of Cathloma
    In the steps of my beauty I stray'd;
The warriors beheld Ninathoma,
    And they blessed the white-bosom'd Maid!

A Ghost! by my cavern it darted!
    In moon-beams the Spirit was drest—
For lovely appear the departed
    When they visit the dreams of my rest!
But disturb'd by the tempest's commotion
    Fleet the shadowy forms of delight—
Ah cease, thou shrill blast of the Ocean!
    To howl through my cavern by night.

THE HOUR

WHEN WE SHALL MEET AGAIN.

(Composed during Illness, and in Absence.) *

DIM Hour! that sleep'st on pillowing clouds afar,
O rise and yoke the Turtles to thy car!
Bend o'er the traces, blame each lingering Dove,
And give me to the bosom of my Love!
My gentle Love, caressing and carest,
With heaving heart shall cradle me to rest!
Shed the warm tear-drop from her smiling eyes,
Lull with fond woe, and medicine me with sighs!
While finely-flushing float her kisses meek,
Like melted rubies, o'er my pallid cheek.
Chill'd by the night, the drooping Rose of May
Mourns the long absence of the lovely Day;
Young Day returning at her promised hour
Weeps o'er the sorrows of her favourite Flower;
Weeps the soft dew, the balmy gale she sighs,
And darts a trembling lustre from her eyes.
New life and joy th' expanding floweret feels:
His pitying Mistress mourns, and mourning heals!

---

* Printed in *The Watchman*, March 17, 1796, and in the second and third editions of the Early Poems (1797, 1803).

WRITTEN AFTER

A WALK BEFORE SUPPER.

THO' much averse, dear Jack, to flicker,
    To find a likeness for friend V—ker,
I've made thro' Earth, and Air, and Sea,
A Voyage of Discovery!
And let me add (to ward off strife)
For V—ker and for V—ker's Wife—
She large and round beyond belief,
A superfluity of beef!
Her mind and body of a piece,
And both composed of kitchen-grease.
In short, Dame Truth might safely dub her
Vulgarity enshrined in blubber!
He, meagre bit of littleness,
All snuff, and musk, and politesse;
So thin, that strip him of his clothing,
He'd totter on the edge of Nothing!
In case of foe, he well might hide
Snug in the collops of her side.

Ah then what simile will suit?
Spindle-leg in great jack-boot?
Pismire crawling in a rut?
Or a spigot in a butt?
Thus I humm'd and ha'd awhile,
When Madam Memory with a smile
Thus twitch'd my ear—" Why sure, I ween,

TO JOSEPH COTTLE.

In London streets thou oft hast seen
The very image of this pair :
A little Ape with huge She-Bear
Link'd by hapless chain together :
An unlick'd mass the one—the other
An antic huge with nimble crupper ——— "
But stop, my Muse ! for here comes supper.

TO THE
AUTHOR OF POEMS
PUBLISHED ANONYMOUSLY AT BRISTOL,

In September, 1795.*

UNBOASTFUL BARD ! whose verse † concise
    yet clear
Tunes to smooth melody unconquer'd sense,
May your fame fadeless live, as "never-sere"
The Ivy wreathes yon Oak, whose broad defence
Embowers me from Noon's sultry influence !
For, like that nameless Rivulet stealing by,
Your modest verse to musing Quiet dear
Is rich with tints heaven-borrow'd : the charm'd eye
Shall gaze undazzled there, and love the soften'd sky.

Circling the base of the Poetic mount
A stream there is, which rolls in lazy flow

   * Joseph Cottle.
   † My honour'd Friend! whose verse, &c.—1797.

Its coal-black waters from Oblivion's fount:
The vapour-poison'd Birds, that fly too low,
Fall with dead swoop, and to the bottom go.
Escaped that heavy stream on pinion fleet
Beneath the Mountain's lofty-frowning brow,
Ere aught of perilous ascent you meet,
A mead of mildest charm delays th' unlabouring
    feet.

Not there the cloud-climb'd rock, sublime and vast,
That like some giant king, o'er-glooms the hill;
Nor there the Pine-grove to the midnight blast
Makes solemn music! But th' unceasing rill
To the soft Wren or Lark's descending trill
Murmurs sweet undersong 'mid jasmine bowers.
In this same pleasant meadow, at your will
I ween, you wander'd—there collecting flowers
Of sober tint, and herbs of medicinable powers!

There for the monarch-murder'd Soldier's tomb
You wove th' unfinish'd* wreath of saddest hues;
And to that holier† chaplet added bloom
Besprinkling it with Jordan's cleansing dews.
But lo your ‡ Henderson awakes the Muse——
His Spirit beckon'd from the mountain's height!
You left the plain and soar'd mid richer views!
So Nature mourn'd when sunk the First Day's light,
With stars, unseen before, spangling her robe of
    night!

* War, a Fragment.   † John the Baptist, a poem.
    ‡ Monody on John Henderson.

Still soar, my Friend, those richer views among,
Strong, rapid, fervent, flashing Fancy's beam !
Virtue and Truth shall love your gentler song ;
But Poesy demands th' impassion'd theme :
Waked by Heaven's silent dews at Eve's mild gleam
What balmy sweets Pomona breathes around !
But if the vext air rush a stormy stream
Or Autumn's shrill gust moan in plaintive sound,
With fruits and flowers she loads the tempest-
    honour'd ground.

THE SILVER THIMBLE.

THE PRODUCTION OF A YOUNG LADY, ADDRESSED
TO THE AUTHOR OF THE POEMS ALLUDED
TO IN THE PRECEDING EPISTLE.

She had lost her Silver Thimble, and her complaint being accidentally overheard by him, her Friend, he immediately sent her four others to take her choice of.

AS oft mine eye with careless glance
    Has gallop'd thro' some old romance,
Of speaking Birds and Steeds with wings,
Giants and Dwarfs, and Fiends and Kings ;
Beyond the rest with more attentive care
I've loved to read of elfin-favour'd Fair——
How if she long'd for aught beneath the sky
And suffer'd to escape one votive sigh,

Wafted along on viewless pinions aery
It laid itself obsequious at her feet:
Such things, I thought, one might not hope to meet
Save in the dear delicious land of Faery!
But now (by proof I know it well)
There's still some peril in free wishing——
Politeness is a licensed *spell*,
And *you*, dear Sir! the Arch-magician.

You much perplex'd me by the various set:
They were indeed an elegant quartette!
My mind went to and fro, and waver'd long;
At length I've chosen (Samuel thinks me wrong)
That, around whose azure rim
Silver figures seem to swim,
Like fleece-white clouds, that on the skiey Blue,
Waked by no breeze, the self-same shapes retain;
Or ocean-Nymphs with limbs of snowy hue
Slow-floating o'er the calm cerulean plain.

Just such a one, *mon cher ami*,
(The finger shield of industry)
Th' inventive Gods, I deem, to Pallas gave
What time the vain Arachne, madly brave,
Challenged the blue-eyed Virgin of the sky
A duel in embroider'd work to try.
And hence the thimbled Finger of grave Pallas
To th' erring Needle's point was more than callous.
But ah the poor Arachne! She unarm'd
Blundering thro' hasty eagerness, alarm'd
With all a *Rival's* hopes, a *Mortal's* fears,

Still miss'd the stitch, and stain'd the web with tears.
Unnumber'd punctures small yet sore
Full fretfully the maiden bore,
Till she her lily finger found
Crimson'd with many a tiny wound;
And to her eyes, suffused with watery woe,
Her flower-embroider'd web danced dim, I wist,
Like blossom'd shrubs in a quick-moving mist:
Till vanquish'd the despairing Maid sunk low.

O Bard! whom sure no common Muse inspires,
I heard your Verse that glows with vestal fires!
And I from unwatch'd needle's erring point
Had surely suffer'd on each finger joint
Those wounds, which erst did poor Arachne meet;
While he, the much-loved object of my choice,
(My bosom thrilling with enthusiast heat)
Pour'd on mine ear with deep impressive voice,
How the great Prophet of the Desert stood
And preach'd of penitence by Jordan's Flood;
On War; or else the legendary lays
In simplest measures hymn'd to Alla's praise;
Or what the Bard from his heart's inmost stores
O'er his *Friend's* grave in loftier numbers pours:
Yes, Bard polite! you but obey'd the laws
Of Justice, when the thimble you had sent;
What wounds your thought-bewildering Muse might cause
'Tis well your finger-shielding gifts prevent.
                                                    SARA.

SONNETS.

INTRODUCTION TO THE SONNETS.*

THE composition of the Sonnet has been regulated by Boileau in his Art of Poetry, and since Boileau, by William Preston, in the elegant preface to his Amatory Poems : the rules, which they would establish, are founded on the practice of Petrarch. I have never yet been able to discover sense, nature, or poetic fancy in Petrarch's poems; they appear to me all one cold glitter of heavy conceits and metaphysical abstractions.† However, Petrarch, although not the inventor of the Sonnet, was the first who made it popular ; and his countrymen have taken *his* poems as the model. Charlotte Smith and Bowles are they who first made the Sonnet popular among the present English : I am justified therefore by analogy in deducing its laws from *their* compositions.

The Sonnet then is a small poem, in which some lonely feeling is developed. It is limited to a *particular* number of lines, in order that the reader's mind

---

* Prefixed to a small Selection of Sonnets by himself and others, privately printed by Coleridge in 1796, afterwards transferred to the Second Edition of his Poems, 1797, and retained in the Third, 1803.

† A piece of petulant presumption, of which I should be more ashamed if I did not flatter myself that it stands alone in my writings. The best of the joke is that at the time I wrote it, I did not understand a word of Italian, and could therefore judge of this divine Poet only by bald translations of some half-dozen of his Sonnets. (M.S. Note by S. T. C. in a copy of the edition of 1797, now in the possession of Mr. Frederick Locker.)

having expected the close at the place in which he finds it, may rest satisfied; and that so the poem may acquire, as it were, a *Totality*,—in plainer phrase, may become a *Whole*. It is confined to fourteen lines, because as some particular number is necessary, and that particular number must be a small one, it may as well be fourteen as any other number. When no reason can be adduced against a thing, Custom is a sufficient reason for it. Perhaps, if the Sonnet were comprised in less than fourteen lines, it would become a serious Epigram; if it extended to more, it would encroach on the province of the Elegy. Poems, in which no lonely feeling is developed, are not Sonnets because the Author has chosen to write them in fourteen lines: they should rather be entitled Odes, or Songs, or Inscriptions. The greater part of Warton's Sonnets are severe and masterly likenesses of the style of the Greek ἐπίγραμματα.

In a Sonnet then we require a development of some lonely feeling, by whatever cause it may have been excited; but those Sonnets appear to me the most exquisite, in which moral sentiments, affections, or feelings, are deduced from, and associated with, the scenery of Nature. Such compositions generate a kind of thought highly favourable to delicacy of character. They create a sweet and indissoluble union between the intellectual and the material world. Easily remembered from their briefness, and interesting alike to the eye and the affections, these are the poems which we can "lay up in our heart and our soul," and repeat them "when we walk by the way, and when we lie down, and when we rise up." Hence the Sonnets of Bowles derive their marked superiority over all other Sonnets; hence they domesticate with the heart, and become, as it were, a part of our identity.

Respecting the metre of a Sonnet, the Writer should consult his own convenience.—Rhymes, many or few, or no rhymes at all—whatever the chastity of his ear may prefer, whatever the rapid expression of his feelings will permit;—all these things are left at his own disposal. A sameness in the final sound of its words is the great and grievous defect of the Italian language. That rule, therefore, which the Italians have established, of exactly *four* different sounds in the Sonnet, seems to have arisen from their wish to have *as many*, not from any dread of finding *more*. But surely it is ridiculous to make the *defect* of a foreign language a reason for our not availing ourselves of one of the marked excellencies of our own. "The Sonnet," says Preston, " will ever be cultivated by those who write on tender, pathetic subjects. It is peculiarly adapted to the state of a man violently agitated by a real passion, and wanting composure and vigour of mind to methodize his thought. It is fitted to express a momentary burst of passion," &c. Now, if there be one species of composition more difficult and artificial than another, it is an English Sonnet on the Italian Model. Adapted to the agitations of a real passion! Express momentary bursts of feeling in it! I should sooner expect to write pathetic *Axes* or *pour forth Extempore Eggs and Altars!* But the best confutation of such idle rules is to be found in the Sonnets of those who have observed them, in their inverted sentences, their quaint phrases, and incongruous mixture of obsolete and Spenserian words: and when, at last, the thing is toiled and hammered into fit shape, it is in general racked and tortured Prose rather than any thing resembling Poetry.

INTRODUCTION TO SONNETS.

The Sonnet has been ever a favourite species of composition with me; but I am conscious that I have not succeeded in it. From a large number I have retained such only as seemed not beneath mediocrity. Whatever more is said of them, *ponamus lucro*.

SONNETS

ON EMINENT CHARACTERS.*

I.—STANHOPE.

NOT, STANHOPE! with the Patriot's doubtful name
I mock thy worth—Friend of the Human Race!
Since scorning Faction's low and partial aim
Aloof thou wendest in·thy stately pace,
Thyself redeeming from that leprous stain,
Nobility: and aye unterrified
Pourest thine Abdiel warnings on the train
That sit complotting with rebellious pride
'Gainst † *Her* who from the Almighty's bosom leapt
With whirlwind arm, fierce Minister of Love!
Wherefore, ere Virtue o'er thy tomb hath wept,
Angels shall lead thee to the Throne above:
And thou from forth its clouds shalt hear the voice,
Champion of Freedom and her God! rejoice!

* The following series of Sonnets were originally printed in *The Morning Chronicle* in December 1794 and January 1795. With the exception of those to Godwin and Southey, they were included in the collected Poems of 1796.

† Gallic Liberty.

II.—BURKE.

AS late I lay in Slumber's shadowy vale,
  With wetted cheek and in a mourner's guise,
I saw the sainted form of Freedom rise:
She spake! not sadder moans the autumnal gale.
" Great Son of Genius! sweet to me thy name,
Ere in an evil hour with alter'd voice
Thou badest Oppression's hireling crew rejoice,
Blasting with wizard spell my laurell'd fame.
Yet never, BURKE! thou drank'st Corruption's bowl!
Thee stormy Pity and the cherish'd lure
Of Pomp, and proud precipitance of soul
Wilder'd with meteor fires.* Ah Spirit pure!
That Error's mist had left thy purged eye:
So might I clasp thee with a Mother's joy!"

III.—PRIESTLEY.

THO' roused by that dark Vizir Riot rude
  Have driven† our PRIESTLEY o'er the ocean swell;
Tho' Superstition and her wolfish brood
Bay his mild radiance, impotent and fell;
Calm in his halls of brightness he shall dwell!
For lo! Religion at his strong behest

---

* Urged on with wildering fires.—1794.
† Tho' King-bred rage, with lawless uproar rude,
   Hath driven, &c.—*Ib.*

Starts with mild anger* from the Papal spell,
And flings to Earth her tinsel-glittering vest,
Her mitred state and cumbrous pomp unholy;
And Justice wakes to bid th' Oppressor wail
Insulting aye the wrongs of patient Folly; †
And from her dark retreat by Wisdom won
Meek Nature slowly lifts her matron veil
To smile with fondness on her gazing son!

IV.—LA FAYETTE.

AS when far off the warbled strains are heard
That soar on Morning's wing the vales among;
Within his cage th' imprison'd matin bird
Swells the full chorus with a generous song:
He bathes no pinion in the dewy light,
No Father's joy, no Lover's bliss he shares,
Yet still the rising radiance cheers his sight—
His fellows' freedom soothes the Captive's cares!
Thou, FAYETTE! who didst wake with startling voice
Life's better sun from that long wintry night,
Thus in thy Country's triumphs shalt rejoice
And mock with raptures high the dungeon's might:
For lo! the morning struggles into day,
And Slavery's spectres shriek and vanish from the
    ray!

* Disdainful rouses from the Papal spell.—1794.
† That ground th' ensnared soul of patient Folly.—*Ib.*

V.—KOSCIUSKO.

O WHAT a loud and fearful shriek was there,
   As though a thousand souls one death-groan
     pour'd !
Ah me ! they saw beneath a hireling's sword
Their Kosciusko fall ! Through the swart air *
(As pauses the tired Cossack's barbarous yell
Of triumph) on the chill and midnight gale
Rises with frantic burst or sådder swell
The dirge of murder'd Hope ! while Freedom pale
Bends in such anguish o'er her destined bier,
As if from eldest time some Spirit meek
Had gather'd in a mystic urn each tear
That ever on a Patriot's furrow'd cheek
Fit channel found, and she had drain'd the bowl
In the mere wilfulness and sick despair of soul!†

   * Great Kosciusko 'neath an hireling's sword
     His country view'd.—Hark thro' the listening air.
                                                        1794.
     Fall'n Kosciusko ! Thro' the burthen'd air.—1796.
† That ever furrow'd a sad Patriot's cheek ;
     And she had drench'd the sorrows of the bowl
     Ev'n till she reel'd, intoxicate of soul !—1794.

VI.—PITT.

NOT always should the tear's ambrosial dew
　　Roll its soft anguish down thy furrow'd cheek!
Not always heaven-breathed tones of suppliance meek
.Beseem thee, Mercy! Yon dark Scowler view,
Who with proud words of dear-loved Freedom came—
More blasting than the mildew from the South!
And kiss'd his country with Iscariot mouth
(Ah! foul apostate from his Father's fame!) *
Then fix'd her on the cross of deep distress,
And at safe distance marks the thirsty lance
Pierce her big side! But O! if some strange trance
The eye-lids of thy stern-brow'd Sister † press,
Seize, Mercy! thou more terrible the brand, ‡
And hurl her thunderbolts with fiercer hand!

* (Staining most foul a godlike Father's name.)—1794.
† Justice.
‡ Seize thou, more terrible, th' avenging brand.—1794.

VII.—TO THE REV. W. L. BOWLES.*

[FIRST VERSION.] †

MY heart has thank'd thee, Bowles, for those soft strains
That on the still air floating, tremblingly
Waked in me Fancy, Love and Sympathy!
For hence, not callous to a brother's pains
Thro' youth's gay prime and thornless paths I went;
And, when the *darker* day of life began
And I did roam, a thought-bewilder'd man!
Thy kindred lays an healing solace lent
Each lonely pang with dreamy joys combined
And stole from vain Regret her scorpion stings;

---

* Author of "Sonnets and other Poems," published by Dilly. To Mr. Bowles's poetry I have always thought the following remark from Maximus Tyrius peculiarly applicable :—" I am not now treating of that poetry which is estimated by the pleasure it affords to the ear—the ear having been corrupted, and the judgment-seat of the perceptions; but of that which proceeds from the intellectual Helicon, that which is *dignified*, and appertaining to *human* feelings, and entering into the soul."—The 13th Sonnet for exquisite delicacy of painting; the 19th for tender simplicity; and the 25th for manly pathos, are compositions of perhaps unrivalled merit. Yet while I am selecting these I almost accuse myself of causeless partiality; for surely never was a writer so equal in excellence!

[Note by S. T. C., 1794.]

† As originally printed in *The Morning Chronicle*, Dec. 26th, 1794.

While shadowy Pleasure, with mysterious wings
Brooded the wavy and tumultuous mind,
Like that great Spirit, who with plastic sweep
Moved on the darkness of the formless Deep!

[SECOND VERSION.]

MY heart has thank'd thee, BOWLES, for those
soft strains
Whose sadness soothes me, like the murmuring
Of wild bees in the sunny showers of spring!*
For hence not callous to the mourner's pains
Thro' youth's gay prime and thornless paths I went:
And when the *darker* day of life began,
And I did roam, a thought-bewilder'd man!
Their mild and manliest melancholy lent
A mingled charm, which oft the pang consign'd
To slumber, tho' the big tear it renew'd:
Bidding such strange mysterious pleasure brood
Over the wavy and tumultuous mind,
As made the soul enamour'd of her woe:
No common praise, dear Bard! to thee I owe!

* This simile is transferred from the Sonnet to Southey, which was not reprinted in the Collected Poems. ED.

VIII.—MRS. SIDDONS.*

AS when a child on some long winter's night
Affrighted clinging to its Grandam's knees
With eager wondering and perturb'd delight

---

* A curious question, not easily soluble, arises as to the authorship of this Sonnet. It was unquestionably printed as the eighth of the Series of *Sonnets on Eminent Characters*, with the customary signature of S.T.C., in the *Morning Chronicle* of Monday, Dec. 29, 1794. But it also undoubtedly appeared in the first edition of Coleridge's collected Poems (1796, p. 51), with the initials C.L., and was among the pieces in Lamb's portion of the joint volume of 1797 (p. 224). From the third edition of Coleridge's Poems (1803) the contributions of Lamb and Lloyd were omitted; but, although Lamb himself saw this edition through the press, the Sonnet to Mrs. Siddons was retained; and Lamb certainly did not include it among his own Sonnets when collecting his Works in 1818.

Is it possible that Coleridge in the first instance playfully fathered the Sonnet which Lamb had written and communicated to him at one of their meetings at the " Salutation ?" If by Lamb, this Sonnet is by some time his earliest known appearance in print. That it should by error or oversight be attributed to Lamb in the edition of 1796 is intelligible enough; but that that error should be deliberately repeated in 1797 for no apparent reason is hardly credible. If it were accounted unworthy of either writer, it might have been quietly dropped. But then we have the troublesome fact of its retention in the edition of 1803—an edition purporting to contain the productions of Coleridge alone. Lamb indulged in several playful tricks as editor of that volume: his own waifs and strays being now sent adrift, as it were, did he decide that this Sonnet at least should resume the paternity with which it had been honoured at its first appearance in the world? At any

Listens strange tales of fearful dark decrees*
Mutter'd to wretch by necromantic spell ;
Or of those hags, who † at the witching time

rate, even if it were written by Lamb, its inclusion in the volume of 1803 among his own compositions, cannot fairly be adduced as "one of a thousand instances of Coleridge's partial and uncertain memory" (see Note in Poems of S. T. Coleridge, edited by Derwent and Sara Coleridge: Moxon, 1852, p. 383.) He was simply in that case the victim of a hoax.

Even Lamb's correspondence with Coleridge, though it contains two allusions to the above Sonnet does not, on account of their ambiguity of expression, fully or finally settle this *vexata quæstio*. "I love my Sonnets because they are the reflected images of my own feelings at different times. I charge you, Coleridge, spare my ewe-lambs. When my blank verse is finished, or any long fancy poem, *propino tibi alterandum, cut-up-andum, abridgandum*, just what you will with it; but spare my ewe-lambs! That to Mrs. Siddons now you were welcome to improve, if it had been worth it; but I say unto you again, Coleridge, spare my ewe-lambs!" "Do you not write in the *Critical?* for I observed in an article of this month's a line quoted out of that Sonnet to Mrs. Siddons—
'With eager wondering, and perturb'd delight;'
and a line from *that* Sonnet would not readily have occurred to a stranger. That Sonnet, Coleridge, brings afresh to my mind the time when you wrote those on Bowles, Priestley, Burke: 'twas two Christmases ago," &c. (C. L. to S. T. C., June 10, 1796.)

After all, the most probable solution of the matter is that the original draught of the Sonnet was Lamb's; but that Coleridge (as we know that he did in the case of other Sonnets of his friend) so touched and retouched it as to make it almost entirely his own; until Lamb may have felt and inwardly exclaimed "*Vix ea nostra voco!*"—ED.

* Dark tales of fearful strange decrees.—1794.
† Of Warlock Hags that, &c.—*Ib.*

Of murky midnight ride the air sublime,
And mingle foul embrace with fiends of Hell :
Cold Horror drinks its blood ! Anon the tear
More gentle starts, to hear the Beldame tell
Of pretty babes, that loved each other dear,
Murder'd by cruel Uncle's mandate fell :
Even such the shivering joys thy tones impart,
Even so thou, SIDDONS ! meltest my sad heart !

IX.—TO WILLIAM GODWIN,

AUTHOR OF "POLITICAL JUSTICE."

O FORM'D t' illume a sunless world forlorn
    As o'er the chill and dusky brow of Night
In Finland's wintry skies the mimic morn *
Electric pours a stream of rosy light,—
Pleased have I mark'd Oppression, terror-pale,
Since thro' the windings of her dark machine
Thy steady eye has shot its glances keen—
" And bade th' all-lovely scenes at distance hail."
Nor will I not thy holy guidance bless,
And hymn thee, GODWIN ! with an ardent lay ;
For that thy voice, in Passion's stormy day,
When wild I roam'd the bleak heath of distress,
Bade the bright form of Justice meet my way,
And told me that her name was Happiness.†

* Aurora Borealis.

† *Morning Chronicle*, January 10, 1795. In little more than a year, and before the publication of his first collection of Poems, Coleridge's opinion of Godwin had under-

X.—TO ROBERT SOUTHEY,

OF BALIOL COLLEGE, OXFORD, AUTHOR OF THE "RETROSPECT," AND OTHER POEMS.

SOUTHEY ! thy melodies steal o'er mine ear
  Like far-off joyance, or the murmuring
Of wild bees in the sunny showers of Spring—
Sounds of such mingled import as may cheer
The lonely breast, yet rouse a mindful tear :
Waked by the Song doth Hope-born Fancy fling
Rich showers of dewy fragrance from her wing,
Till sickly Passion's drooping Myrtles sere
Blossom anew ! But O ! more thrill'd, I prize
Thy sadder strains that bid in Memory's dream
The faded forms of past Delight arise ;
Then soft, on Love's pale cheek, the tearful gleam
Of Pleasure smiles—as faint yet beauteous lies
The imaged Rainbow on a willowy stream.*

gone an entire change. In the fifth number of *The Watchman* (April 2, 1796) he writes : " I consider Mr. Godwin's principles as vicious, and his book as a pandar to sensuality. Once I thought otherwise—nay, even addressed a complimentary sonnet to the Author in the *Morning Chronicle*, of which I confess with much moral and poetical contrition that the lines and the subject were equally bad."

* *Morning Chronicle*, January 14, 1795. This Sonnet is now first reprinted since its original appearance. It was rather a stretch of imagination or of friendship to designate Robert Southey as an " eminent character " in the early days of 1795, eminent as he afterwards became,—ED.

XI.

TO RICHARD BRINSLEY SHERIDAN, Esq.

IT was some spirit SHERIDAN! that breathed
  O'er thy young mind such wildly-various power!
My soul hath mark'd thee in her shaping hour,
Thy temples with Hymettian* flowerets wreathed :
And sweet thy voice, as when o'er Laura's bier
Sad music trembled thro' Vauclusa's glade ;

---

* *Hymettian Flowerets.*—Hymettus a mountain near Athens. celebrated for its honey. This alludes to Mr. Sheridan's classical attainments, and the following four lines to the exquisite sweetness and almost *Italian* delicacy of his Poetry. In Shakespeare's "Lover's Complaint" there is a fine Stanza almost prophetically characteristic of Mr. Sheridan :—

> "So on the tip of his subduing tongue
>   All kind of argument and question deep,
>   All replication prompt and reason strong
>   For his advantage still did wake and sleep
>   To make the weeper laugh, the laugher weep:
>   He had the dialect and different skill,
>   Catching all passions in his craft of will:
>   That he did in the general bosom reign
>   Of young and old."

[Alas! for the quarrels of authors! Coleridge was not always destined to speak of Sheridan in such *honeyed* words.—Vide Preface to *Remorse*.]

>   Was it some spirit, Sheridan, that breathed
>   His *various* influence on thy natal hour ?
>   My fancy bodies forth the Guardian power
>   His temples with Hymettian flowerets, &c.—1795.

Sweet, as at dawn the love-lorn serenade
That wafts soft dreams to Slumber's listening ear.
Now Patriot Rage and Indignation high
Swell the full tones! And now thine eye-beams dance
Meanings of Scorn and Wit's quaint Revelry!
Writhes inly from the bosom-probing glance
Th' Apostate by the brainless rout adored,
As erst that elder Fiend beneath great Michael's
    sword.

XII.—ERSKINE.

WHEN British Freedom for a happier land
    Spread her broad wings, that flutter'd with
    affright,
ERSKINE! thy voice she heard, and paused her flight
Sublime of hope! For dreadless thou didst stand
(Thy censer glowing with the hallow'd flame)
An hireless Priest before th' insulted shrine,
And at her altar pour'd'st the stream divine
Of unmatch'd eloquence. Therefore thy name
Her Sons shall venerate, and cheer thy breast
With blessings heaven-ward breathed. And when
    the doom
Of Nature bids thee rise beyond the tomb
Thy light shall shine: as sunk beneath the West
Tho' the great Summer Sun eludes our gaze,
Still burns wide Heaven with his distended blaze.

MISCELLANEOUS SONNETS.

I.

THOU gentle Look, that didst my soul beguile,
   Why hast thou left me? Still in some fond
     dream
Revisit my sad heart, auspicious smile!
As falls on closing flowers the lunar beam:
What time, in sickly mood, at parting day
I lay me down and think of happier years;
Of Joys, that glimmer'd in Hope's twilight ray,
Then left me darkling in a vale of tears.
O pleasant days of Hope—for ever flown!
Could I recal you!—But that thought is vain.
Availeth not Persuasion's sweetest tone
To lure the fleet-wing'd travellers back again:
Yet fair, tho' faint, their images shall gleam
Like the bright Rainbow on an evening stream.

II.—TO THE RIVER OTTER.

DEAR native Brook! wild Streamlet of the West!
   How many various-fated Years have past,
 What blissful and what anguish'd hours, since last
I skimm'd the smooth thin stone along thy breast,
   Numbering its light leaps! Yet so deep imprest
Sink the sweet scenes of Childhood, that mine eyes
I never shut amid the sunny blaze,
   But straight with all their tints thy waters rise,

Thy crossing plank, thy margin's willowy maze,
  And bedded sand that vein'd with various dyes
 Gleam'd thro' thy bright transparence to the gaze !*
  Visions of Childhood ! oft have ye beguiled
Lone Manhood's cares, yet waking fondest sighs,
  Ah ! that once more I were a careless Child !

III.

SWEET Mercy ! how my very heart has bled
  To see thee, poor Old Man ! and thy grey hairs
Hoar with the snowy blast ; while no one cares
To clothe thy shrivell'd limbs and palsied head.
My Father ! throw away this tatter'd vest
  That mocks thy shivering ! take my garment—use
  A young man's arm ! I'll melt these frozen dews
That hang from thy white beard and numb thy breast.
My Sara too shall tend thee, like a child :
  And thou shalt talk, in our fireside's recess,
  Of purple Pride, that scowls on Wretchedness.—
He did not scowl, the Galilæan mild,
  Who met the Lazar turn'd from rich man's doors
  And call'd him friend, and wept upon his sores ! †

---

* The above ten lines are almost literatim from a poem printed in *The Watchman* entitled *Recollection*, itself a *rifaccimento* of a portion of the *Lines on an Autumnal Evening*.—ED.

† For the rough sketch of this Sonnet the Author professed himself indebted to Mr. Favell (Preface to the volume published in 1796).—ED.

IV.*

PALE Roamer through the night! thou poor
   Forlorn!
Remorse that man on his death-bed possess,
Who in the credulous hour of tenderness
Betray'd, then cast thee forth to want and scorn!
The world is pitiless: the chaste one's pride
Mimic of Virtue scowls on thy distress:
Thy Loves and they that envied thee deride :†
And Vice alone will shelter wretchedness!
O! I could weep to think that there should be
Cold-bosom'd lewd ones, who ‡ endure to place
Foul offerings on the shrine of misery,
And force from famine the caress of Love;
May He shed healing on the sore disgrace,
He, the great Comforter that rules above!§

V.

TO THE AUTHOR OF *THE ROBBERS*.

[One night in winter, on leaving a College-friend's room, with whom I had supped, I carelessly took away with me "The Robbers," a drama, the very name of

---

* In the Preface to the volume of 1796 Coleridge stated that the "first half" of this poem was written by Southey.—ED.

† Thy kindred, when they see thee, turn aside.—1803.

‡ Men, born of woman, who endure, &c.—*Ib.*

§ In the edition of 1803 the two last lines stand thus :—
   " Man has no feeling for thy sore disgrace :
     Keen blows the blast upon the moulting dove!"

which I had never before heard of:—A winter midnight—the wind high—and "The Robbers" for the first time!—The readers of Schiller will conceive what I felt. Schiller introduces no supernatural beings; yet his human beings agitate and astonish more than all the *goblin* rout—even of Shakespeare.]

SCHILLER! that hour I would have wish'd to die,
  If thro' the shuddering midnight I had sent
  From the dark Dungeon of the Tower time-rent
That fearful voice, a famish'd Father's* cry—
That in no after moment aught less vast
  Might stamp me mortal! A triumphant shout
  Black Horror scream'd, aud all her *goblin* rout
From the more withering scene diminish'd past.
Ah! Bard tremendous in sublimity!
  Could I behold thee in thy loftier mood,
Wandering at eve with finely-frenzied eye
  Beneath some vast old tempest-swinging wood!
  Awhile with mute awe gazing I would brood,
Then weep aloud in a wild ecstasy!

VI.

COMPOSED ON A JOURNEY HOMEWARD; THE AUTHOR HAVING RECEIVED INTELLIGENCE OF THE BIRTH OF A SON, SEPT. 20, 1796.

OFT o'er my brain does that strange fancy roll
  Which makes the present (while the flash doth last)

---

* The Father of Moor, in the Play of the *Robbers*.

Seem a mere semblence of some unknown past,
Mix'd with such feelings, as perplex the soul
Self-question'd in her sleep; and some have said*
We lived, ere yet this robe of flesh we wore.
O my sweet baby! when I reach my door,
If heavy looks should tell me thou art dead,
(As sometimes, through excess of hope, I fear)
I think that I should struggle to believe
Thou wert a spirit, to this nether sphere
Sentenced for some more venial crime to grieve;
Didst scream, then spring to meet Heaven's quick reprieve,
While we wept idly o'er thy little bier!

VII.

TO A FRIEND WHO ASKED HOW I FELT WHEN THE NURSE FIRST PRESENTED MY INFANT TO ME.

CHARLES! my slow heart was only sad, when first
I scann'd that face of feeble infancy:
For dimly on my thoughtful spirit burst
All I had been, and all my child might be!
But when I saw it on it's mother's arm,
And hanging at her bosom (she the while
Bent o'er its features with a tearful smile)

---

* Ἦν που ἡμῶν ἡ ψύχη πρὶν ἐν τῷδε τῷ ἀνθρωπίνῳ εἴδει γενέσθαι.—*Plat. in Phædon.*

Then I was thrill'd and melted, and most warm
Impress'd a father's kiss : and all beguiled
Of dark remembrance and presageful fear,
I seem'd to see an angel-form appear—
'Twas even thine, beloved woman mild !
So for the mother's sake the child was dear,
And dearer was the mother for the child.

VIII.

ON A DISCOVERY MADE TOO LATE.

THOU bleedest, my poor heart ! and thy distress
    Reasoning I ponder with a scornful smile
And probe thy sore wound sternly, tho' the while
Swoln be mine eye and dim with heaviness.
Why didst thou listen to Hope's whisper bland?
Or, listening, why forget the healing tale,
When Jealousy with feverish fancies pale
Jarr'd thy fine fibres with a maniac's hand ?
Faint was that hope, and rayless !—Yet 'twas fair
And sooth'd with many a dream the hour of rest :
Thou should'st have loved it most, when most
    opprest,
And nursed it with an agony of care,
Even as a mother her sweet infant heir
That wan and sickly droops upon her breast !

TO AN UNFORTUNATE WOMAN

WHOM THE AUTHOR HAD KNOWN IN THE DAYS OF HER INNOCENCE.

MYRTLE leaf, that ill besped
    Pinest in the gladsome ray,
Soil'd beneath the common tread
    Far from thy protecting spray !

When the partridge o'er the sheaf
    Whirr'd along the yellow vale,*
Sad, I saw thee, heedless leaf !
    Love the dalliance of the gale.

Lightly didst thou, foolish thing !
    Heave and flutter to his sighs,
While the flatterer on his wing
    Woo'd and whisper'd thee to rise.

Gaily from thy mother stalk
    Wert thou danced and wafted high ;
Soon on this unshelter'd walk
    Flung to fade, to rot and die !

---

* When the rustic o'er his sheaf
    Caroll'd in the yellow vale—1797.

TO A YOUNG FRIEND,*

ON HIS PROPOSING TO DOMESTICATE WITH THE AUTHOR.

COMPOSED IN 1796.

A MOUNT, not wearisome and bare and steep,
But a green Mountain variously up-piled,
Where o'er the jutting rocks soft mosses creep
Or colour'd lichens with slow oozing weep;
Where cypress and the darker yew start wild;
And mid the summer torrent's gentle dash
Dance brighten'd the red clusters of the ash;
Beneath whose boughs, by those still sounds beguiled,
Calm Pensiveness might muse herself to sleep;
Till haply startled by some fleecy dam,
That rustling on the bushy cliff above
With melancholy bleat of anxious love
Made meek inquiry for her wandering lamb:
Such a green Mountain 'twere most sweet to climb
E'en while the bosom ached with loneliness—
How heavenly sweet, if some dear Friend should bless
Th' adventurous toil, and up the path sublime
Now lead, now follow; the glad landscape round,
Wide and more wide, increasing without bound!

* To C. Lloyd.—1797.

O then 'twere loveliest sympathy, to mark
The berries of the half-uprooted ash
Dripping and bright; and list the torrent's dash,—
Beneath the cypress, or the yew more dark,
Seated at ease, on some smooth mossy rock;
In social silence now, and now to unlock
The treasured heart; arm link'd in friendly arm,
Save if the one, his Muse's witching charm
Muttering brow-bent, at unwatch'd distance lag;
Till high o'er head his beckoning friend appears,
And from the forehead of the topmost crag
Shouts eagerly: for haply there uprears
That shadowing pine its old romantic limbs,
Which latest shall detain the enamour'd sight
Seen from below, when eve the valley dims,
Tinged yellow with the rich departing light;
And haply, basin'd in some unsunn'd cleft,
A beauteous spring, the rock's collected tears,
Sleeps shelter'd there, scarce wrinkled by the gale!
Together thus, the world's vain turmoil left,
Stretch'd on the crag, and shadow'd by the pine,
And bending o'er the clear delicious fount,
Ah! dearest Lloyd! it were a lot divine
To cheat our noons in moralizing mood,
While west-winds fann'd our temples toil-bedew'd:
Then downwards slope, oft pausing, from the
      mount,
To some lone mansion, in some woody dale,
Where smiling with blue eye, Domestic Bliss
Gives this the husband's, that the brother's kiss!

Thus rudely versed in allegoric lore,
The Hill of Knowledge I essay'd to trace ;
That verdurous hill with many a resting-place,
And many a stream, whose warbling waters pour
To glad and fertilize the subject plains ;
That hill with secret springs, and nooks untrod,
And many a fancy-blest and holy sod
Where Inspiration, his diviner strains
Low-murmuring, lay ; and starting from the rocks
Stiff evergreens, whose spreading foliage mocks
Want's barren soil, and the bleak frosts of age,
And Bigotry's mad fire-invoking rage !*
O meek retiring spirit ! we will climb,
Cheering and cheer'd, this lovely hill sublime ;
And from the stirring world up-lifted high,
(Whose noises, faintly wafted on the wind,
To quiet musings shall attune the mind,
And oft the melancholy theme supply)
There, while the prospect through the gazing eye
Pours all its healthful greenness on the soul,
We'll smile† at wealth, and learn to smile† at fame,
Our hopes, our knowledge, and our joys the same,
As neighbouring fountains image each the whole :
Then when the mind hath drunk its fill of truth
We'll discipline the heart to pure delight,
Rekindling sober joy's domestic flame.
They whom I love shall love thee, honour'd youth!
Now may Heaven realize this vision bright !

* And mad Oppression's thunder-clasping rage.—1797.
† Laugh.—*Ib.*

ON OBSERVING A BLOSSOM ON THE FIRST OF FEBRUARY, 1796.

WRITTEN NEAR SHEFFIELD.*

SWEET flower! that peeping from thy russet stem
Unfoldest timidly, (for in strange sort
This dark, frieze-coated, hoarse, teeth-chattering month
Hath borrow'd Zephyr's voice, and gazed upon thee
With blue voluptuous eye), alas, poor Flower!
These are but flatteries of the faithless year.
Perchance, escaped its unknown polar cave,
Even now the keen North-East is on its way.
Flower that must perish! shall I liken thee
To some sweet girl of too too rapid growth
Nipp'd by consumption mid untimely charms?
Or to Bristowa's bard,† the wondrous boy!
An amaranth, which earth scarce seem'd to own,
[Blooming mid poverty's drear wintry waste,]
Till disappointment came, and pelting wrong
Beat it to earth? or with indignant grief
Shall I compare thee to poor Poland's hope,
Bright flower of hope kill'd in the opening bud?
Farewell, sweet blossom! better fate be thine

* These lines first appeared in the Author's paper, *The Watchman*, April 11th, 1796.
† Chatterton.

And mock my boding ! Dim similitudes
Weaving in moral strains, I've stolen one hour
From anxious self, Life's cruel task-master !*
And the warm wooings of this sunny day
Tremble along my frame, and harmonize
The attemper'd organ, that even saddest thoughts
Mix with some sweet sensations, like harsh tunes
Play'd deftly on a soft-toned instrument.

THE EOLIAN HARP.

COMPOSED AT CLEVEDON, SOMERSETSHIRE.

MY pensive Sara ! thy soft cheek reclined
 Thus on mine arm, most soothing sweet it is
To sit beside our cot, our cot o'ergrown
With white-flower'd jasmine, and the broad-leaved
 myrtle,
(Meet emblems they of Innocence and Love !)
And watch the clouds, that late were rich with light,
Slow saddening round, and mark the star of eve
Serenely brilliant (such should wisdom be)
Shine opposite ! How exquisite the scents
Snatch'd from yon bean-field ! and the world so
 hush'd !
The stilly murmur of the distant sea
Tells us of silence.

* I've stolen one hour,
From black anxiety that gnaws my heart
For her who droops far off on a sick bed.
1796-1803.

                        And that simplest lute,*
Placed length-ways in the clasping casement, hark!
How by the desultory breeze caress'd,
Like some coy maid half yielding to her lover,
It pours such sweet upbraiding, as must needs
Tempt to repeat the wrong! And now, its strings
Boldlier swept, the long sequacious notes
Over delicious surges sink and rise,
Such a soft floating witchery of sound
As twilight Elfins make, when they at eve
Voyage on gentle gales from Fairy-Land,
Where Melodies round honey-dropping flowers,
Footless and wild, like birds of Paradise,
Nor pause, nor perch, hovering on untamed wing!†
O the one life within us and abroad,
Which meets all motion and becomes its soul,
A light in sound, a sound-like power in light
Rhythm in all thought, and joyance every where—‡
Methinks, it should have been impossible
Not to love all things in a world so fill'd;
Where the breeze warbles, and the mute still air
Is Music slumbering on her instrument.§

> * Hark! the still murmur of the distant sea
>   Tells us of Silence! And th' Eolian Lute.—1803.

† The above five lines were omitted in the edition of 1803, but were afterwards restored by the author.

‡ The four preceding lines were added in 1817, when the poem was reprinted in the collection of *Sibylline Leaves*.

> § Methinks it should have been impossible
>   Not to love all things in a world like this
>   Where e'en the breezes of the simple air
>   Possess the power and Spirit of melody!—1803.

And thus, my love! as on the midway slope
Of yonder hill I stretch my limbs at noon,
Whilst through my half-closed eye-lids I behold
The sunbeams dance, like diamonds, on the main,
And tranquil muse upon tranquillity;
Full many a thought uncall'd and undetain'd,
And many idle flitting phantasies,
Traverse my indolent and passive brain,
As wild and various as the random gales
That swell and flutter on this subject lute!

And what if all of animated Nature
Be but organic harps diversely framed,
That tremble into thought, as o'er them sweeps
Plastic and vast, one intellectual breeze,
At once the Soul of each, and God of all?

But thy more serious eye a mild reproof
Darts, O beloved woman! nor such thoughts
Dim and unhallow'd dost thou not reject,
And biddest me walk humbly with my God.
Meek daughter in the family of Christ!
Well hast thou said and holily dispraised
These shapings of the unregenerate mind;
Bubbles that glitter as they rise and break
On vain Philosophy's aye-babbling spring.
For never guiltless may I speak of him,
The Incomprehensible! save when with awe
I praise him, and with Faith that inly feels;
Who with his saving mercies healed me,
A sinful and most miserable man,

Wilder'd and dark, and gave me to possess
Peace, and this cot, and thee, heart-honour'd
    Maid!*

REFLECTIONS ON HAVING LEFT A PLACE OF RETIREMENT.†

‡ *Sermoni propriora.*—Hor.

LOW was our pretty Cot: our tallest rose
    Peep'd at the chamber-window. We could hear
At silent noon, and eve, and early morn,
The sea's faint murmur. In the open air
Our myrtles blossom'd; and across the porch
Thick jasmines twined: the little landscape round
Was green and woody, and refresh'd the eye.
It was a spot which you might aptly call
The Valley of Seclusion! Once I saw
(Hallowing his Sabbath-day by quietness)
A wealthy son of commerce saunter by,
Bristowa's citizen: methought, it calm'd
His thirst of idle gold, and made him muse
With wiser feelings: for he paused, and look'd
With a pleased sadness, and gazed all around,
Then eyed our Cottage, and gazed round again.

---

* "This I think the most perfect poem I ever wrote. Bad may be the best, perhaps." M.S. note by S. T. C. in a copy of the second Edition of his Poems, 1797.

† The original title was "Reflections on Entering into Active Life, a Poem which affects not to be Poetry." The lines were first printed in the *Monthly Magazine* of October, 1796.—Ed.

‡ Charles Lamb translated this motto—"properer for a Sermon." (*Table-talk of S. T. C.*, ii. 77).

And sigh'd, and said, it was a Blessed Place.
And we were blessed. Oft with patient ear
Long-listening to the viewless sky-lark's note
(Viewless, or haply for a moment seen
Gleaming on sunny wings) in whisper'd tones
I've said to my beloved, " Such, sweet girl !
The inobtrusive song of happiness,
Unearthly minstrelsy ! then only heard
When the soul seeks to hear; when all is hush'd,
And the heart listens !"

                           But the time, when first
From that low dell, steep up the stony mount
I climb'd with perilous toil and reach'd the top,
Oh ! what a goodly scene ! Here the bleak mount,
The bare bleak mountain speckled thin with sheep ;
Gray clouds, that shadowing spot the sunny fields ;
And river, now with bushy rocks o'erbrow'd,
Now winding bright and full, with naked banks ;
And seats, and lawns, the Abbey and the wood,
And cots, and hamlets, and faint city-spire ;
The Channel there, the Islands and white sails,
Dim coasts, and cloud-like hills, and shoreless
    Ocean—
It seem'd like Omnipresence ! God, methought,
Had built him there a temple : the whole World
Seem'd imaged in its vast circumference,
No wish profaned my overwhelmed heart.
Blest hour ! It was a luxury,—to be !

Ah! quiet dell! dear cot, and mount sublime!
I was constrain'd to quit you. Was it right,
While my unnumber'd brethren toil'd and bled,
That I should dream away the entrusted hours
On rose-leaf beds, pampering the coward heart
With feelings all too delicate for use?
Sweet is the tear that from some Howard's eye
Drops on the cheek of one he lifts from earth:
And he that works me good with unmoved face,
Does it but half: he chills me while he aids,
My benefactor, not my brother man!
Yet even this, this cold beneficence
Praise, praise it, O my Soul! oft as thou scann'st
The sluggard Pity's vision-weaving tribe!
Who sigh for wretchedness, yet shun the wretched,
Nursing in some delicious solitude
Their slothful loves and dainty sympathies!
I therefore go, and join head, heart, and hand,
Active and firm, to fight the bloodless fight
Of science, freedom, and the truth in Christ.

Yet oft when after honourable toil
Rests the tired mind, and waking loves to dream,
My spirit shall revisit thee, dear Cot!
Thy jasmine and thy window-peeping rose,
And myrtles fearless of the mild sea-air.
And I shall sigh fond wishes—sweet abode!
Ah!—had none greater! And that all had such!
It might be so—but the time is not yet.
Speed it, O Father! Let thy kingdom come!

TO THE REV. GEORGE COLERIDGE

OF OTTERY ST. MARY, DEVON.*

Notus in fratres animi paterni.
HOR. Carm. lib. 1, 2.

A BLESSED lot hath he, who having pass'd
His youth and early manhood in the stir
And turmoil of the world, retreats at length,
With cares that move, not agitate the heart,
To the same dwelling where his father dwelt;
And haply views his tottering little ones
Embrace those aged knees and climb that lap,
On which first kneeling his own infancy
Lisp'd its brief prayer. Such, O my earliest friend !
Thy lot, and such thy brothers too enjoy.
At distance did ye climb life's upland road,
Yet cheer'd and cheering : now fraternal love
Hath drawn you to one centre. Be your days
Holy, and blest and blessing may ye live !

To me the Eternal Wisdom hath dispensed
A different fortune and more different mind—
Me from the spot where first I sprang to light
Too soon transplanted, ere my soul had fix'd

---

* Prefixed to the edition of 1797. In a copy of that edition now in the possession of Mr. Frederick Locker, Coleridge has written underneath this Dedication as follows :—"N.B. If this Volume should ever be delivered according to its direction, *i.e.* to Posterity, let it be known that the Reverend George Coleridge was displeased and thought his character endangered by this Dedication !—S. T. COLERIDGE."

Its first domestic loves; and hence through life
Chasing chance-started friendships. A brief while
Some have preserved me from life's pelting ills;
But, like a tree with leaves of feeble stem,
If the clouds lasted, and a sudden breeze
Ruffled the boughs, they on my head at once
Dropp'd the collected shower; and some most false,
False and fair-foliaged as the Manchineel,
Have tempted me to slumber in their shade
E'en mid the storm; then breathing subtlest damps,
Mix'd their own venom with the rain from Heaven,
That I woke poison'd! But, all praise to him
Who gives us all things, more have yielded me
Permanent shelter; and beside one friend,*
Beneath the impervious covert of one oak,
I've raised a lowly shed, and know the names
Of husband and of father; not unhearing
Of that divine and nightly-whispering voice,
Which from my childhood to maturer years
Spake to me of predestinated wreaths,
Bright with no fading colours!
                                    Yet at times
My soul is sad, that I have roam'd through life
Still most a stranger, most with naked heart
At mine own home and birth-place; chiefly then,
When I remember thee, my earliest friend!
Thee, who didst watch my boyhood and my youth;
Didst trace my wanderings with a father's eye;
And boding evil yet still hoping good,

* Mr. T. Poole, of Nether Stowey, near Bridgewater, Somerset. (M.S. Note by S. T. C., *uti suprà*.)

Rebuked each fault, and over all my woes
Sorrow'd in silence ! He who counts alone
The beatings of the solitary heart,*
That Being knows, how I have loved thee ever,
Loved as a brother, as a son revered thee !
Oh ! 'tis to me an ever new delight,
[My eager eye glistening with memory's tear,]
To talk of thee and thine : or when the blast
Of the shrill winter, rattling our rude sash,
Endears the cleanly hearth and social bowl ;
Or when as now, on some delicious eve,
We in our sweet sequester'd orchard-plot
Sit on the tree crook'd earth-ward ; whose old boughs,
That hang above us in an arborous roof,
Stirr'd by the faint gale of departing May,
Send their loose blossoms slanting o'er our heads !

Nor dost not thou sometimes recal those hours,
When with the joy of hope thou gavest thine ear
To my wild firstling-lays. Since then my song
Hath sounded deeper notes, such as beseem
Or that sad wisdom folly leaves behind,
Or such as, tuned to these tumultuous times,
Cope with the tempest's swell !

      These various strains,
Which I have framed in many a various mood,
Accept, my brother ! and (for some perchance

---

* Rebuked each fault and wept o'er all my woes.
 Who counts the beatings of the lonely heart.—1797.

Will strike discordant on thy milder mind)
If aught of error or intemperate truth
Should meet thine ear, think thou that riper age
Will calm it down, and let thy love forgive it !

Nether-Stowey, Somerset, May 26, 1797.

ODE TO THE DEPARTING YEAR.*

Ἰοὺ ἰοὺ, ὢ ὢ κακά.
Ὑπ' αὖ με δεινὸς ὀρθομαντείας πόνος
Στροβεῖ, ταράσσων φροιμίοις ἐφημίοις.
*   *   *   *   *
Τὸ μέλλον ἥξει. Καὶ σύ μ' ἐν τάχει παρὼν
Ἄγαν ἀληθόμαντιν οἰκτείρας ἐρεῖς.
             Æschyl. Agam. 1215-18; 1240-41.

To Thomas Poole, of Stowey.†

My Dear Friend,
   Soon after the commencement of this month, the editor of the *Cambridge Intelligencer* (a newspaper conducted with so much ability, and such unmixed and fearless zeal for the interests of piety and freedom, that I cannot but think my poetry honoured by being permitted to appear in it), requested me, by letter, to furnish him with some lines for the last day of this year. I promised him that I would make the attempt; but

---

* This Ode was composed on the 24th, 25th, and 26th days of December, 1796: and was published on the last day of that year.

† This Dedication is reprinted for the first time from the original quarto edition.—Ed.

almost immediately after, a rheumatic complaint seized on my head, and continued to prevent the possibility of poetic composition till within the last three days. So in the course of the last three days the following Ode was produced. In general, when an author informs the public that his production was struck off in a great hurry, he offers an insult, not an excuse. But I trust that the present case is an exception, and that the peculiar circumstances which obliged me to write with such unusual rapidity give a propriety to my professions of it : *nec nunc eam apud te jacto, sed et ceteris indico; ne quis asperiore limâ carmen examinet, et a confuso scriptum et quod frigidum erat ni statim traderem.* (I avail myself of the words of Statius, and hope that I shall likewise be able to say of any weightier publication, what *he* has declared of his Thebaid, that it had been tortured * with a laborious polish)

For me to discuss the *literary* merits of this hasty composition were idle and presumptuous. If it be found to possess that impetuosity of transition, and that precipitation of fancy and feeling, which are the *essential* excellencies of the sublimer Ode, its deficiency in less important respects will be easily pardoned by those from whom alone praise could give me pleasure : and whose minuter criticisms will be disarmed by the reflection, that these lines were conceived " not in the soft obscurities of retirement, or under the shelter of Academic Groves, but amidst inconvenience and distraction, in sickness and in sorrow." I am more anxious lest the *moral* spirit of the Ode should be mistaken. You, I am sure, will not fail to recollect that among the ancients, the Bard and the Prophet were

* *Multa cruciatâ limâ.*
[Silv. lib. iv. 7, 26.]

one and the same character; and you *know* that although I prophesy curses, I pray fervently for blessings. Farewell, Brother of my Soul!

>   —— O ever found the same,
>   And trusted and beloved!

Never without an emotion of honest pride do I subscribe myself
>   Your grateful and affectionate friend,
>   S. T. COLERIDGE.

Bristol, December 26, 1796.

ARGUMENT.

THE Ode commences with an address to the Great Being or Divine Providence, who regulates into one vast harmony all the events of time, however calamitous some of them may appear to mortals. The second Strophe calls on men to suspend their private joys and sorrows, and to devote their passions for awhile to the cause of human nature in general. The first Epode refers to the late Empress of Russia, who died of an apoplexy on the 17th of November, 1796; having just concluded a subsidiary treaty with the Kings combined against France. The first Antistrophe describes the Image of the Departing Year, &c., as in a vision, and concludes with introducing the planetary Angel of the Earth preparing to address the Supreme Being. The second Epode prophesies, in anguish of spirit, the downfall of this country.

STROPHE I.

SPIRIT who sweepest the wild harp of Time!
    It is most hard with an untroubled ear
  Thy dark inwoven harmonies to hear!

Yet, mine eye fix'd on Heaven's unchanging clime,
Long had I listen'd, free from mortal fear,
  With inward stillness, and a bowed mind ;
  When lo ! its folds far waving* on the wind,
I saw the train† of the departing Year !
  Starting from my silent sadness
  Then with no unholy madness
Ere yet the enter'd cloud foreclosed‡ my sight,
I raised the impetuous song, and solemnized his
    flight.

STROPHE II.

  Hither, from the recent tomb,
  From the prison's direr gloom,
  From distemper's midnight anguish ;
And thence, where poverty doth waste and languish !
  Or where, his two bright torches blending,
    Love illumines manhood's maze ;
  Or where o'er cradled infants bending
  Hope has fix'd her wishful gaze ;
    Hither, in perplexed dance,
  Ye Woes ! ye young-eyed Joys ! advance !

  By Time's wild harp, and by the hand
    Whose indefatigable sweep
    Raises its fateful strings from sleep,§
  I bid you haste, a mix'd tumultuous band !

---

* When lo ! far onwards waving.—1796.
† The skirts.—*Ib.*   ‡ Forbade.—*Ib.*
§ Forbids its fateful strings to sleep.—1796.

ODE TO THE

    From every private bower,
      And each domestic hearth,
    Haste for one solemn hour ;
    And with a loud and yet a louder voice,
O'er Nature struggling in portentous birth,
      Weep and rejoice !
Still echoes the dread name that o'er the earth
Let slip the storm, and woke the brood of Hell :
    And now advance in saintly jubilee
Justice and Truth ! They too have heard thy spell,
  They too obey thy name, divinest Liberty ! *

EPODE.

I mark'd Ambition in his war-array !
    I heard the mailed Monarch's troublous cry—
" Ah ! wherefore does the Northern Conqueress †
    stay !

---

* In the original version the second strophe terminates as follows :—

  " And with a loud, and yet a louder voice
    O'er the sore travail of the common earth
      Weep and rejoice !
  Seized in sore travail and portentous birth
  (Her eye-balls flashing a pernicious glare),
  Sick Nature struggles ! Hark ! her pangs increase !
  Her groans are horrible ! But O ! most fair
    The promised Twins she bears—Equality and Peace !

† A subsidiary Treaty had been just concluded ; and Russia was to have furnished more effectual aid than that of pious manifestoes to the Powers combined against France. I rejoice —not over the deceased Woman (I never dared figure the Russian Sovereign to my imagination under the dear and

Groans not her chariot on its onward way?"
Fly, mailed Monarch, fly!
Stunn'd by Death's twice mortal mace,
No more on Murder's lurid face
The insatiate hag shall gloat with drunken eye!
Manes of the unnumber'd slain!
Ye that gasp'd on Warsaw's plain!
Ye that erst at Ismail's tower,
When human ruin choked the streams,
Fell in Conquest's glutted hour,
Mid women's shrieks and infants' screams!
Spirits of the uncoffin'd slain,
Sudden blasts of triumph swelling,
Oft, at night, in misty train,
Rush around her narrow dwelling!
The exterminating fiend is fled—
(Foul her life and dark her doom)
Mighty armies of the dead

venerable character of WOMAN—WOMAN, that complex term for Mother, Sister, Wife!). I rejoice, as at the disenshrining of a Dæmon! I rejoice, as at the extinction of the evil Principle impersonated! This very day, six years ago, the massacre of Ismail was perpetrated. THIRTY THOUSAND HUMAN BEINGS, MEN, WOMEN, AND CHILDREN, murdered in cold blood, for no other crime than that their garrison had defended the place with perseverance and bravery! Why should I recal the poisoning of her husband, her iniquities in Poland, or her late unmotived attack on Persia, the desolating ambition of her public life, or the libidinous excesses of her private hours! I have no wish to qualify myself for the office of Historiographer to the King of Hell ——!

December 23, 1796.

Dance, like death-fires, round her tomb!
Then with prophetic song relate,
Each some tyrant-murderer's fate!*
[When shall sceptred Slaughter cease?
   Awhile he crouch'd, O Victor France!
   Beneath the lightning of thy lance,
With treacherous dalliance wooing Peace.†
   But soon up-springing from his dastard trance

---

* Sceptred Murderer's fate.—1796.

† To juggle this easily-juggled people into better humour with the supplies (and themselves, perhaps, affrighted by the successes of the French) our ministry sent an ambassador to Paris to sue for Peace. The supplies are granted: and in the meantime the Archduke Charles turns the scale of victory on the Rhine, and Buonaparte is checked before Mantua. Straightways our courtly Messenger is commanded to *uncurl* his lips, and propose to the lofty Republic to *restore* all *its* conquests, and to suffer England to *retain* all *hers* (at least all her *important* ones), as the only terms of Peace, and the ultimatum of the negotiation!

> Θρασύνει γὰρ αἰσχρόμητις
> Τάλαινα ΠΑΡΑΚΟΠΑ πρωτοπήμων.
>
> Æschyl. Ag. 222-4.

The friends of Freedom in this country are idle. Some are timid; some are selfish; and many the torpedo touch of hopelessness has numbed into inactivity. We would fain hope that (if the above account be accurate—it is only the French account) this dreadful instance of infatuation in our ministry will rouse them to one effort more; and that at one and the same time in our different great towns the people will be called on to think solemnly, and declare their thoughts fearlessly by every method which the *remnant* of the constitution allows.

The boastful, bloody Son of Pride betray'd
His hatred of the blest and blessing Maid.
One cloud, O Freedom ! cross'd thy orb of Light,
And sure, he deem'd, that orb was quench'd in night:
For still does Madness roam on Guilt's bleak dizzy
    height !]

ANTISTROPHE I.

Departing Year ! 'twas on no earthly shore
My soul beheld thy vision !* Where alone,
  Voiceless and stern, before the cloudy throne,
Aye Memory sits : thy robe inscribed with gore,
With many an unimaginable groan
    Thou storied'st thy sad hours ! Silence ensued,
    Deep silence o'er the ethereal multitude,
Whose locks with wreaths, whose wreaths with
        glories shone.†
    Then, his eye wild ardours glancing,
    From the choired gods advancing,
The Spirit of the Earth made reverence meet,
And stood up, beautiful, before the cloudy seat.

ANTISTROPHE II.

    Throughout the blissful throng,
    Hush'd were harp and song :
Till wheeling round the throne the Lampads seven,
    (The mystic Words of Heaven)

---

* *i.e.*, thy image in a Vision.
† Whose purple locks with snow-white glories shone.

1796.

  Permissive signal make :   [spake !*
The fervent Spirit bow'd, then spread his wings and
  " Thou in stormy blackness throning
   Love and uncreated Light,
  By the Earth's unsolaced groaning,
   Seize thy terrors, Arm of might !
[By Belgium's corse-impeded flood ! †
  By Vendee steaming brother's blood !]
  By Peace with proffer'd insult scared,
   Masked hate and envying scorn !
   By years of havoc yet unborn !
And Hunger's bosom to the frost-winds bared !
   But chief by Afric's wrongs,
    Strange, horrible, and foul !
   By what deep guilt belongs
  To the deaf Synod, ' full of gifts and lies !'
By Wealth's insensate laugh ! by Torture's howl !
    Avenger, rise !
  For ever shall the thankless Island scowl,
  Her quiver full, and with unbroken bow ?
Speak ! from thy storm-black Heaven, O speak aloud !
   And on the darkling foe
Open thine eye of fire from some uncertain cloud !
  O dart the flash ! O rise and deal the blow !
The Past to thee, to thee the Future cries !

   * On every Harp, on every Tongue
    While the mute Enchantment hung ;
    Like Midnight from a thundercloud
    Spake the sudden Spirit loud ——1796.
† The Rhine.

Hark! how wide Nature joins her groans below!
Rise, God of Nature! rise."*

EPODE II.

The voice had ceased, the vision† fled;
Yet still I gasp'd and reel'd with dread.
And ever, when the dream of night
Renews the phantom‡ to my sight,
Cold sweat-drops ‖ gather on my limbs;
   My ears throb hot; my eye-balls start;
My brain with horrid tumult swims;
Wild is the tempest of my heart;
And my thick and struggling breath
Imitates the toil of death!
No stranger agony§ confounds
   The soldier on the war-field spread,
When all foredone with toil and wounds,
   Death-like he dozes among heaps of dead!
(The strife is o'er, the day-light fled,
   And the night-wind clamours hoarse!
See! the starting wretch's head
   Lies pillow'd on a brother's corse!)

---

* For ever shall the bloody Island scowl?
  For aye unbroken shall her cruel bow
  Shoot Famine's arrows o'er thy ravaged World?
  Hark! how wide Nature joins her groans below—
Rise, God of Nature, rise! Why sleep thy bolts unhurl'd?
                                      1796.

† The Phantoms.—1796.   ‡ The vision.—*Ib.*
§ Sweat-damps.—*Ib.*   ‖ No uglier agony.—*Ib.*

Not yet enslaved, not wholly vile,*
O Albion! O my mother Isle!
Thy valleys, fair as Eden's bowers,
Glitter green with sunny showers;
Thy grassy uplands' gentle swells
   Echo to the bleat of flocks;
(Those grassy hills, those glittering dells
   Proudly ramparted with rocks)
And Ocean mid his uproar wild
Speaks safety to his island-child.
   Hence for many a fearless age
   Has social Quiet loved thy shore;
Nor ever proud invader's rage †
Or sack'd thy towers, or stain'd thy fields with gore.

‡Abandon'd of Heaven! mad Avarice thy guide,
At cowardly distance, yet kindling with pride—

---

  * O doom'd to fall, enslaved and vile.—1796.
  † Nor ever sworded Foeman's rage.—*Ib.*
  ‡ The Poet, from having considered the peculiar advantages which this country has enjoyed, passes in rapid transition to the uses which we have made of these advantages. We have been preserved by our insular situation, from suffering the actual horrors of War ourselves, and we have shown our gratitude to Providence for this immunity by our eagerness to spread those horrors over nations less happily situated. In the midst of plenty and safety we have raised or joined the yell for famine and blood. Of the one hundred and seven last years fifty have been years of war.—Such wickedness cannot pass unpunished. We have been proud and confident in our alliances and our fleets—but God has prepared the cankerworm, and will smite the *gourds* of our pride.

Mid thy herds and thy corn-fields secure thou hast
    stood,
And join'd the wild yelling of famine and blood!
The nations curse thee! They with eager wondering
    Shall hear Destruction, like a vulture, scream!
    Strange-eyed Destruction! who with many a
        dream
Of central fires through nether seas upthundering
    Soothes her fierce solitude; yet as she lies
By living fount, or red volcanic stream,*
    If ever to her lidless dragon-eyes,
    O Albion! thy predestined ruins rise,
The fiend-hag on her perilous couch doth leap,
Muttering distemper'd triumph in her charmed
        sleep.

   Away, my soul, away!
  In vain, in vain the birds of warning sing—
And hark! I hear the famish'd brood of prey
Flap their lank pennons on the groaning wind!
   Away, my soul, away!
  I unpartaking of the evil thing,
    With daily prayer and daily toil
    Soliciting for food my scanty soil,†
    Have wail'd my country with a loud Lament.
Now I recentre my immortal mind

---

   * yet (as she lies
 Stretch'd on the marge of some fire-flashing fount
 In the black chamber of a sulphur'd mount).—1796.
† Soliciting my scant and blameless soil.—*Ib.*

In the deep sabbath of meek self-content;*
Cleansed from the vaporous passions† that bedim
God's Image, sister of the Seraphim.‡

> * In the long sabbath of high self-content.—1796.
> In the deep sabbath of blest self-content.—1797.
> In the blest sabbath of high self-content.—1803.
>
> † The fleshly passions.—1796.
> The fears and anguish.—1797.

‡ Cleansed from bedimming Fear, and Anguish weak and blind.—1803.

MISCELLANEOUS POEMS
(1794-1797).

MELANCHOLY.*

A FRAGMENT.

STRETCH'D on a moulder'd Abbey's broadest
    wall,
Where ruining ivies propt the ruins steep—
Her folded arms wrapping her tatter'd pall,
    Had Melancholy mused herself to sleep.
        The fern was press'd beneath her hair,
        The dark green Adder's Tongue † was there;
And still as past the flagging sea-gale weak,
The long lank leaf bow'd fluttering o'er her cheek.

That pallid cheek was flush'd : her eager look
    Beam'd eloquent in slumber! Inly wrought,
Imperfect sounds her moving lips forsook,
    And her bent forehead work'd with troubled
        thought.
    Strange was the dream that fill'd her soul,
    Nor did not whispering spirits roll
A mystic tumult, and a fateful rhyme
Mixt with wild shapings of the unborn time.

* First published in the *Morning Chronicle*, in the year 1794. [Note by S. T. C., 1817.]

† A botanical mistake. The plant I meant is called the Hart's Tongue; but this would unluckily spoil the poetical effect. *Cedat ergo Botanice.*

PARLIAMENTARY OSCILLATORS.

ALMOST awake? Why, what is this, and whence,
　　O ye right loyal men, all undefiled?
Sure, 'tis not possible that Common Sense
　　Has hitch'd her pulleys to each heavy eye-lid?

Yet wherefore else that start, which discomposes
　　The drowsy waters lingering in your eye?
　　And are you *really* able to descry
That precipice three yards beyond your noses?

Yet flatter you I cannot, that your wit
　　Is much improved by this long loyal dosing;
And I admire, no more than Mr. Pitt,
　　Your jumps and starts of patriotic prosing—

Now cluttering to the Treasury Cluck, like chicken,
　　Now with small beaks the ravenous *Bill* opposing;
With serpent-tongue now stinging, and now licking,
　　Now semi-sibilant, now smoothly glozing—

Now having faith implicit that he can't err,
　　Hoping his hopes, alarm'd with his alarms;
And now believing him a sly enchanter,
　　Yet still afraid to break his brittle charms,

Lest some mad devil suddenly unhampering,
　　Slap-dash! the imp should fly off with the steeple,
On revolutionary broom-stick scampering.—
　　O ye soft-headed and soft-hearted people,

If you can stay so long from slumber free,
My muse shall make an effort to salute ye:
 For lo! a very dainty simile
Flash'd sudden through my brain, and 'twill just suit ye!

You know that water-fowl that cries, Quack! quack!?
 Full often have I seen a waggish crew
Fasten the Bird of Wisdom on its back,
 The ivy-haunting bird, that cries, Tu-whoo!

Both plunged together in the deep mill-stream,
 (Mill-stream, or farm-yard pond, or mountain-lake,)
Shrill, as a *Church and Constitution* scream,
 Tu-whoo! quoth Broad-face, and down dives the Drake!

The green-neck'd Drake once more pops up to view,
 Stares round, cries *Quack!* and makes an angry pother;
Then shriller screams the bird with eye-lids blue,
 The broad-faced bird! and deeper dives the other.
Ye *quacking* Statesmen! 'tis even so with you—
 One peasecod is not liker to another.

Even so on Loyalty's Decoy-pond, each
 Pops up his head, as fired with British blood,
Hears once again the Ministerial screech,
 And once more seeks the bottom's blackest mud!

1794.

AD LYRAM.

IMITATION OF CASIMIR.*

* Printed in *The Watchman*, March 9, 1796. This is the only extant specimen of a work designed by Coleridge in 1794. At the end of *The Fall of Robespierre* he issued the following

"Proposals for publishing by subscription Imitations from the Modern Latin Poets, with a Critical and Biographical Essay on the Restoration of Literature. By S. T. Coleridge, of Jesus College, Cambridge.

"The work will consist of two volumes, large octavo, elegantly printed on superfine paper: Price to Subscribers, 14s. in boards; to be paid on delivery.

" DESIGN.

"At the Restoration of Literature the barbarous state of modern Languages, and the imperfect diffusion of knowledge, determined the most celebrated writers of that Era to compose principally in the Latin Language; and in later times many of our greatest Poets have made it the vehicle of their earliest Effusions. It is the design of the proposed publication to collect the most elegant of these Compositions, to exhibit them in a neat and correct form, and to render them interesting to the English reader by annexed Imitations. Of the Poems selected many have been long known and admired by the classical Reader; many of them, however, of equal merit, scattered among the heavy Collections of Gruter and others, seem to have escaped the notice even of the learned.

"In the course of the Work will be introduced a copious Selection from the Lyrics of Casimir, and a new Translation of the Basia of Secundus.

"The Volumes will be ready for delivery shortly after next Christmas. S. T. C.

Cambridge, Sept. 22, 1794."

[The design was apparently abandoned for want of encouragement, and the Ode which follows, if not all that was accomplished, is all that remains of it.] ·

[If we except Lucretius and Statius, I know not of any Latin poet, ancient or modern, who has equalled Casimir in boldness of conception, opulence of fancy, or beauty of versification. The Odes of this illustrious Jesuit were translated into English about one hundred and fifty years ago by a Thomas Hill, I think.* I never saw the translation. A few of the Odes have been translated in a very animated manner by Watts. I have subjoined the third Ode of the second book, which, with the exception of the first line, is an effusion of exquisite elegance. In the imitation attempted I am sensible that I have destroyed *the effect of suddenness*, by translating into two stanzas what is one in the original.]

THE solemn-breathing air is ended—
   Cease, O lyre! thy kindred lay!
From the poplar-branch suspended
   Glitter to the eye of Day!

On thy wires hovering, dying,
   Softly sighs the summer wind:
I will slumber, careless lying,
   By yon waterfall reclined.

In the forest hollow-roaring
   Hark! I hear a deepening sound—
Clouds rise thick with heavy louring!
   See! the horizon blackens round!

Parent of the soothing measure,
   Let me seize thy wetted string!
Swiftly flies the flatterer Pleasure,
   Headlong, ever on the wing.

* *The Odes of Casimere translated by G. Hils.* Lond. 1646.

FRAGMENT
FROM AN UNPUBLISHED POEM.*

THE early year's fast-flying vapours stray
   In shadowing trains across the orb of day:
And we, poor insects of a few short hours,
   Deem it a world of gloom.
Were it not better hope a nobler doom,
Proud to believe that with more active powers
     On rapid many-colour'd wing
     We thro' one bright perpetual Spring
Shall hover round the fruits and flowers,
Screen'd by those clouds and cherish'd by those
       showers!

COUNT RUMFORD.†

THESE, Virtue, are thy triumphs, that adorn
   Fitliest our nature, and bespeak us born
For loftiest action; not to gaze and run
From clime to clime; or batten in the sun,
Dragging a drony flight from flower to flower,
Like summer insects in a gaudy hour;
Nor yet o'er love-sick tales with fancy range
And cry, "*'Tis pitiful, 'tis passing strange!*"
But on life's varied views to look around
And raise expiring sorrow from the ground:—
And he, who thus hath borne his part assign'd
In the sad fellowship of human kind,
Or for a moment soothed the bitter pain
Of a poor brother—has not lived in vain!

   * Printed in *The Watchman*, March 25, 1796.

   † Printed in *The Watchman*, April 2, 1796, before a Review of Count Rumford's Essays.

ON A LATE CONNUBIAL RUPTURE IN HIGH LIFE.*

I SIGH, fair injured stranger ! for thy fate ;
   But what shall sighs avail thee ? thy poor heart
'Mid all the " pomp and circumstance " of state
   Shivers in nakedness. Unbidden, start

Sad recollections of Hope's garish dream,
   That shaped a seraph form, and named it Love,
Its hues gay-varying, as the orient beam
   Varies the neck of Cytherea's dove.

To one soft accent of domestic joy
   Poor are the shouts that shake the high-arch'd dome ;
Those plaudits that thy *public* path annoy,
   Alas ! they tell thee—Thou'rt a wretch *at home !*

O then retire, and weep ! *Their very woes
Solace the guiltless.* Drop the pearly flood
On thy sweet infant, as the FULL-BLOWN rose,
   Surcharged with dew, bends o'er its neighbouring BUD.

And ah ! that Truth some holy spell might lend
   To lure thy wanderer from the siren's power ;
Then bid your souls inseparably blend
   Like two bright dew-drops meeting in a flower.

* *Monthly Magazine*, September, 1796.

THE DESTINY OF NATIONS.

A VISION.*

AUSPICIOUS Reverence! Hush all meaner song,
Ere we the deep preluding strain have pour'd
To the Great Father, only Rightful King,
Eternal Father! King Omnipotent!
To the Will Absolute, the One, the Good!
The I AM, the Word, the Life, the Living God! †

Such symphony requires best instrument.
Seize, then, my soul! from Freedom's trophied dome
The harp which hangeth high between the shields
Of Brutus and Leonidas! With that
Strong music, that soliciting spell, force back
Man's free and stirring spirit that lies entranced. ‡

---

* The substance of this Vision was incorporated by Southey as part of the second book of his *Joan of Arc, an Epic Poem*, in the original quarto edition published at Bristol in 1796. It was omitted from the later editions of that work, and was reprinted by Coleridge, with its present title, in his *Sibylline Leaves*, 1817. ED.

† In the original version, instead of the two preceding lines, are the two following:—
  "Beneath whose shadowy banners wide unfurl'd
   Justice leads forth her tyrant-quelling Hosts."

‡ The harp which hanging high between the shields
  Of Brutus and Leonidas, oft gives
  A fitful music to the breezy touch
  Of patriot Spirits that demand their fame.—1796.

THE DESTINY OF NATIONS.   189

For what is freedom, but the unfetter'd use
Of all the powers which God for use had given?
But chiefly this, [with holiest habitude
Of constant Faith] him first, him last to view
Through meaner powers and secondary things
Effulgent, as through clouds that veil his blaze.
For all that meets the bodily sense I deem
Symbolical, one mighty alphabet
For infant minds ; and we in this low world
Placed with our backs to bright reality,
That we may learn with young unwounded ken
The substance from its shadow. Infinite Love,
Whose latence is the plenitude of all,
Thou with retracted beams, and self-eclipse
Veiling, revealest thine eternal Sun.*

But some there are who deem themselves most free
When they within this gross and visible sphere
Chain down the winged thought, scoffing ascent,
Proud in their meanness: and themselves they cheat
With noisy emptiness of learned phrase,
Their subtle fluids, impacts, essences,†

---

* Things from their shadows. Know thyself, my soul !
Confirm'd thy strength, thy pinions fledged for flight
Bursting this shell and leaving next thy nest
Soon upward soaring shalt thou fix intense
Thine eaglet eye on Heaven's eternal Sun !—1796.
The substance from its shadow—Earth's broad shade
Revealing by eclipse the Eternal Sun !—1817.

† Sir Isaac Newton at the end of the last edition of his Optics, supposes that a very subtle and elastic fluid, which he calls æther, is diffused through the pores of gross bodies, as

Self-working tools, uncaused effects, and all
Those blind omniscients, those almighty slaves,
Untenanting creation of its God.

well as through the open spaces that are void of gross matter; he supposes it to pierce all bodies, and to touch their least particles, acting on them with a force proportional to their number or to the matter of the body on which it acts. He supposes likewise that it is rarer in the pores of bodies than in open spaces, and even rarer in small pores and dense bodies, than in large pores and rare bodies; and also that its density increases in receding from gross matter; so for instance as to be greater at the 1-100th of an inch from the surface of any body, than at its surface; and so on. To the action of this æther he ascribes the attractions of gravitation and cohesion, the attraction and repulsion of electrical bodies, the mutual influences of bodies and light upon each other, the effects and communication of heat, and the performance of animal sensation and motion. David Hartley, from whom this account of æther is chiefly borrowed, makes it the instrument of propagating those vibrations or configurative motions which are ideas. It appears to me no hypothesis ever involved so many contradictions; for how can the same fluid be both dense and rare in the same body at one time? Yet in the Earth as gravitating to the Moon it must be very rare, and in the Earth as gravitating to the Sun it must be very dense. For, as Andrew Baxter well observes, "it doth not appear sufficient to account how this fluid may act with a force proportional to the body to which another is impelled, to assert that it is rarer in great bodies than in small ones: it must be farther asserted that this fluid is rarer or denser in the same body, whether small or great, according as the body to which that is impelled is itself small or great." But whatever may be the solidity of this objection, the following seems unanswerable:—If every particle through the whole solidity of a heavy body receive its impulse from the particles of this fluid, it should seem that the fluid

But properties are God : the naked mass
(If mass there bè, fantastic guess or ghost)
Acts only by its inactivity.
Here we pause humbly. Others boldlier think
That as one body seems the aggregate

itself must be as dense as the very densest heavy body, gold
for instance ; there being as many impinging particles in the
one as there are gravitating particles in the other which
receive their gravitation by being impinged upon ; so that,
throwing gold or any heavy body upward, against the impulse
of this fluid, would be like throwing gold through gold ; and
as this æther must be equally diffused over the whole sphere
of its activity, it must be as dense when it impels cork as when
it impels gold ; so that to throw a piece of cork upward, would
be as if we endeavoured to make cork penetrate a medium as
dense as gold ; and though we were to adopt the extravagant
opinions which have been advanced concerning the progression
of pores, yet however porous we suppose a body, if it be not
all pore, the argument holds equally ; the fluid must be as
dense as the body in order to give every particle its impulse.
It has been asserted that Sir Isaac Newton's philosophy leads
in its consequences to Atheism ; perhaps not without reason.
For if matter, by any powers or properties *given* to it, can produce the order of the visible world, and even generate thought;
why may it not have possessed such properties by *inherent*
right ? and where is the necessity of a God ? Matter is,
according to the mechanic philosophy, capable of acting most
wisely and most beneficently without Wisdom or Benevolence.
And what more does the Atheist assert ? If matter possess
those properties, why might it not have possessed them from
all eternity ? Sir Isaac Newton's Deity seems to be alternately
operose and indolent ; to have delegated so much power as to
make it inconceivable what he can have reserved. He is
dethroned by Vice-regent Second Causes. We seem placed
here to acquire a knowledge of *effects.* Whenever we would

Of atoms numberless, each organized;
So by a strange and dim similitude
Infinite myriads of self-conscious minds
Are one all-conscious Spirit, which informs *
With absolute ubiquity of thought
(His one eternal self-affirming act !)
All his involved Monads,† that yet seem
With various province and apt agency
Each to pursue its own self-centering end.
Some nurse the infant diamond in the mine ;
Some roll the genial juices through the oak ;
Some drive the mutinous clouds to clash in air,
And rushing on the storm with whirlwind speed,
Yoke the red lightnings to their volleying car.
Thus these pursue their never-varying course,
No eddy in their stream. *Others, more wild,
With complex interests weaving human fates,
Duteous or proud, alike obedient all,
Evolve the process of eternal good.

And what if some rebellious o'er dark realms
Arrogate power? yet these train up to God,

pierce into the *Adyta* of Causation we bewilder ourselves, and all that laborious conjecture can do is to fill up the gaps of imagination. We are restless, because *invisible* things are not the objects of vision—and philosophical systems, for the most part, are received not for their Truth, but in proportion as they attribute to Causes a susceptibility of being *seen*, whenever our visual organs shall have become sufficiently powerful.

* Form one all-conscious Spirit, who directs.—1796.

† All his component monads.—*Ib*.

And on the rude eye, unconfirm'd for day,
Flash meteor-lights better than total gloom.
As ere from Lieule-Oaive's vapoury head
The Laplander beholds the far-off Sun
Dart his slant beam on unobeying snows,
While yet the stern and solitary Night
Brooks no alternate sway, the Boreal Morn
With mimic lustre substitutes its gleam,
Guiding his course or by Niemi lake
Or Balda Zhiok,* or the mossy stone
Of Solfar-Kapper,† while the snowy blast
Drifts arrowy by, or eddies round his sledge,
Making the poor babe at its mother's back ‡
Scream in its scanty cradle : he the while
Wins gentle solace as with upward eye
He marks the streamy banners of the North,
Thinking himself those happy spirits shall join

* Balda Zhiok—*i.e.*, mons altitudinis, the highest mountain in Lapland.

† "Solfar Kapper; capitium Solfar, hic locus omnium quotquot veterum Lapponum superstitio sacrificiis religiosoque cultui dedicavit, celebratissimus erat, in parte sinus australis situs, semimilliaris spatio a mari distans. Ipse locus, quem curiositatis gratia aliquando me invisisse memini, duabus prealtis lapidibus, sibi invicem oppositis, quorum alter musco circumdatus erat, constabat."—*Leemius de Lapponibus.*

‡ The Lapland women carry their infants at their back in a piece of excavated wood, which serves them for a cradle. Opposite to the infant's mouth there is a hole for it to breathe through.—" Mirandum prorsus est et vix credibile nisi cui vidisse contigit. Lappones hyeme iter facientes per vastos montes, perque horrida et invia tesqua, eo presertim tempore

Who there in floating robes of rosy light
Dance sportively. For Fancy is the power
That first unsensualizes the dark mind,
Giving it new delights; and bids it swell
With wild activity; and peopling air,
By obscure fears of beings invisible,
Emancipates it from the grosser thrall
Of the present impulse, teaching self-control,
Till Superstition with unconscious hand
Seat Reason on her throne. Wherefore not vain,
Nor yet without permitted power impress'd,
I deem those legends terrible, with which
The polar ancient thrills his uncouth throng:
Whether of pitying Spirits that make their moan
O'er slaughter'd infants, or that giant bird
Vuokho, of whose rushing wings the noise
Is tempest, when the unutterable* shape
Speeds from the mother of Death, and utters once
That shriek, which never murderer heard, and
    lived.†

Or if the Greenland Wizard in strange trance
Pierces the untravell'd realms of Ocean's bed

quo omnia perpetuis nivibus obtecta sunt et nives ventis agi-
tantur et in gyros aguntur, viam ad destinata loca absque
errore invenire posse, lactantem autem infantem si quem
habeat, ipsa mater in dorso bajulat, in excavato ligno
(*Gieed'k* ipsi vocant) quod pro cunis utuntur: in hoc infans
pannis et pellibus convolutus colligatus jacet."—*Leemius de
Lapponibus.*

  * Jaibme Aibmo.
  † Speeds from the Mother of Death his destined way,
    To snatch the murderer from his secret cell!   1796.

Over the abysm, even to that uttermost cave
By mis-shaped prodigies beleaguer'd, such
As earth ne'er bred, nor air, nor the upper sea :
Where dwells the Fury Form, whose unheard name
With eager eye, pale cheek, suspended breath,
And lips half-opening with the dread of sound,
Unsleeping Silence guards, worn out with fear
Lest haply 'scaping on some treacherous blast
The fateful word let slip the elements
And frenzy Nature. Yet the wizard her,
Arm'd with Torngarsuck's* power, the Spirit of
    Good,
Forces to unchain the foodful progeny
Of the Ocean stream ;—— thence thro' the realm
    of Souls,
Where live the Innocent, as far from cares
As from the storms and overwhelming waves
That tumble on the surface of the Deep,
Returns with far-heard pant, hotly pursued
By the fierce Warders of the Sea, once more,
Ere by the frost foreclosed, to repossess

---

* They call the Good Spirit Torngarsuck. The other great but malignant spirit is a nameless female ; she dwells under the sea in a great house, where she can detain in captivity all the animals of the ocean by her magic power. When a dearth befalls the Greenlanders an Angekok or magician must undertake a journey thither. He passes through the kingdom of souls, over a horrible abyss into the palace of this phantom, and by his enchantments causes the captive creatures to ascend directly to the surface of the ocean.—See *Crantz's History of Greenland*, vol. i. 206.

His fleshly mansion, that had stay'd the while
In the dark tent within a cowering group
Untenanted.—Wild phantasies! yet wise,
On the victorious goodness of high God
Teaching reliance, and medicinal hope,
Till from Bethabara northward, heavenly Truth
With gradual steps, winning her difficult way,
Transfer their rude Faith perfected and pure.

If there be beings of higher class than Man,
I deem no nobler province they possess,
Than by disposal of apt circumstance
To rear * up kingdoms: and the deeds they prompt,
Distinguishing from mortal agency,
They choose their human ministers from such states
As still the Epic song half fears to name,
Repell'd from all the minstrelsies that strike
The palace-roof and soothe the monarch's pride.
† And such, perhaps, the Spirit, who (if words
Witness'd by answering deeds may claim our faith)

> * To rear some realm with patient discipline
> Aye bidding Pain, dark Error's uncouth child,
> Blameless Parenticide! his snaky scourge
> Lift fierce against his Mother! Thus they make
> Of transient Evil ever-during Good
> Themselves probationary, and denied
> Confess'd to view by preternatural deed
> To o'erwhelm the will, save on some fated day
> Headstrong, or with petition'd might from God.
> 1796.
>
> † And such perhaps the guardian Power whose ken
> Still dwelt on France. He from the Invisible World

Held commune with that warrior-maid of France
Who scourged the Invader. From her infant days,
With Wisdom, mother of retired thoughts,
Her soul had dwelt; and she was quick to mark
The good and evil thing, in human lore
Undisciplined. For lowly was her birth,
And Heaven had doom'd her early years to toil
That pure from tyranny's least deed, herself
Unfear'd by fellow-natures, she might wait
On the poor labouring man with kindly looks,
And minister refreshment to the tired
Way-wanderer, when along the rough-hewn bench
The sweltry man had stretch'd him, and aloft
Vacantly watch'd the rudely-pictured board
Which on the mulberry-bough with welcome creak
Swung to the pleasant breeze. Here, too, the Maid
Learnt more than schools could teach: Man's
    shifting mind,
His vices and his sorrows! And full oft
At tales of cruel wrong and strange distress
Had wept and shiver'd. To the tottering eld
Still as a daughter would she run: she placed
His cold limbs at the sunny door, and loved
To hear him story, in his garrulous sort,
Of his eventful years, all come and gone.

So twenty seasons past. The Virgin's form,
Active and tall, nor sloth nor luxury

> Burst on the Maiden's eye, impregning air
> With voices and strange shapes, illusions apt,
> Shadowy of Truth, &c. 1796.

Had shrunk or paled. Her front sublime and broad,
Her flexile eye-brows wildly hair'd and low,
And her full eye, now bright, now unillumed,
Spake more than Woman's thought; and all her
    face
Was moulded to such features as declared
That pity there had oft and strongly work'd,
And sometimes indignation. Bold her mien,
And like a haughty huntress of the woods
She moved: yet sure she was a gentle maid!
And in each motion her most innocent soul
Beam'd forth so brightly, that who saw would say
Guilt was a thing impossible in her!
Nor idly would have said—for she had lived
In this bad World, as in a place of tombs,
And touch'd not the pollutions of the dead.

    'Twas the cold season when the rustic's eye
From the drear desolate whiteness of his fields
Rolls for relief to watch the skiey tints
And clouds slow-varying their huge imagery;
When now, as she was wont, the healthful Maid
Had left her pallet ere one beam of day
Slanted the fog-smoke. She went forth alone
Urged by the indwelling angel-guide, that oft,
With dim inexplicable sympathies
Disquieting the heart, shapes out Man's course
To the predoom'd adventure. Now the ascent
She climbs of that steep upland, on whose top
The Pilgrim-man, who long since eve had watch'd
The alien shine of unconcerning stars,

Shouts to himself, there first the Abbey-lights
Seen in Neufchatel's vale; now slopes adown
The winding sheep-track vale-ward : when, behold
In the first entrance of the level road
An unattended team ! The foremost horse
Lay with stretch'd limbs; the others, yet alive
But stiff and cold, stood motionless, their manes
Hoar with the frozen night-dews. Dismally
The dark-red dawn new glimmer'd; but its gleams
Disclosed no face of man. The maiden paused,
Then hail'd who might be near. No voice replied.
From the thwart wain at length there reach'd her
    ear
A sound so feeble that it almost seem'd
Distant : and feebly, with slow effort push'd,
A miserable man crept forth : his limbs
The silent frost had eat, scathing like fire.
Faint on the shafts he rested. She, meantime,
Saw crowded close beneath the coverture
A mother and her children—lifeless all,
Yet lovely ! not a lineament was marr'd—
Death had put on so slumber-like a form !
It was a piteous sight; and one, a babe,
The crisp milk frozen on its innocent lips,
Lay on the woman's arm, its little hand
Stretch'd on her bosom.

                      Mutely questioning,
The Maid gazed wildly at the living wretch.
He, his head feebly turning, on the group
Look'd with a vacant stare, and his eye spoke

The drowsy calm that steals on worn-out anguish.
She shudder'd ; but, each vainer pang subdued,
Quick disentangling from the foremost horse
The rustic bands, with difficulty and toil   [rived,
The stiff cramp'd team forced homeward. There ar-
Anxiously tends him she with healing herbs,
And weeps and prays—but the numb power of
     Death
Spreads o'er his limbs ; and ere the noontide hour,
The hovering spirits of his wife and babes
Hail him immortal ! Yet amid his pangs,
With interruptions long from ghastly throes,
His voice had falter'd out this simple tale.

   The village, where he dwelt a husbandman,
By sudden inroad had been seized and fired
Late on the yester-evening.   With his wife
And little ones he hurried his escape.   [heard
They saw the neighbouring hamlets flame, they
Uproar and shrieks ! and terror-struck drove on
Through unfrequented roads, a weary way !
But saw nor house nor cottage.   All had quench'd
Their evening hearth-fire : for the alarm had spread.
The air clipp'd keen, the night was fang'd with frost,
And they provisionless !   The weeping wife
Ill hush'd her children's moans ; and still they
     moan'd,
Till fright and cold and hunger drank their life.
They closed their eyes in sleep, nor knew 'twas
     death.
He only, lashing his o'er-wearied team,

Gain'd a sad respite, till beside the base
Of the high hill his foremost horse dropp'd dead.
Then hopeless, strengthless, sick for lack of food,
He crept beneath the coverture, entranced, .
Till waken'd by the maiden.—Such his tale.

Ah! suffering to the height of what was suffer'd,
Stung with too keen a sympathy, the Maid
Brooded with moving lips, mute, startful, dark!
And now her flush'd tumultuous features shot
Such strange vivacity, as fires the eye
Of misery fancy-crazed! and now once more
Naked, and void, and fix'd, and all within
The unquiet silence of confused thought
And shapeless feelings. For a mighty hand
Was strong upon her, till in the heat of soul
To the high hill-top tracing back her steps,
Aside the beacon, up whose smoulder'd stones
The tender ivy-trails crept thinly, there,
Unconscious of the driving element,
Yea, swallow'd up in the ominous dream, she sate
Ghastly as broad-eyed Slumber! a dim anguish
Breathed from her look! and still with pant and sob,
Inly she toil'd to flee, and still subdued,
Felt an inevitable Presence near.

Thus as she toil'd in troublous ecstasy,
A horror of great darkness wrapt her round,
And a voice utter'd forth unearthly tones,
Calming her soul,—" O Thou of the Most High
Chosen, whom all the perfected in Heaven
Behold expectant——

[The following fragments were intended to form part of the poem when finished.]

"Maid beloved of Heaven!
(To her the tutelary Power exclaim'd)
Of Chaos the adventurous progeny
Thou seest; foul missionaries of foul sire,
Fierce to regain the losses of that hour
When Love rose glittering, and his gorgeous wings
Over the abyss flutter'd with such glad noise,
As what time after long and pestful calms,
With slimy shapes and miscreated life
Poisoning the vast Pacific, the fresh breeze
Wakens the merchant-sail uprising.   Night
A heavy unimaginable moan
Sent forth, when she the Protoplast beheld
Stand beauteous on Confusion's charmed wave.
Moaning she fled, and enter'd the Profound
That leads with downward windings to the cave
Of Darkness palpable, desert of Death
Sunk deep beneath Gehenna's massy roots.
There many a dateless age the beldam lurk'd
And trembled; till engender'd by fierce Hate,
Fierce Hate and gloomy Hope, a Dream arose,
Shaped like a black cloud mark'd with streaks of
         fire.
It roused the Hell-Hag: she the dew-damp wiped
From off her brow, and through the uncouth maze
Retraced her steps; but ere she reach'd the mouth
Of that drear labyrinth, shuddering she paused,
Nor dared re-enter the diminish'd Gulf.
As through the dark vaults of some moulder'd tower

(Which, fearful to approach, the evening hind
Circles at distance in his homeward way)
The winds breathe hollow, deem'd the plaining groan
Of prison'd spirits; with such fearful voice
Night murmur'd, and the sound thro' Chaos went.
Leap'd at her call her hideous-fronted brood!
A dark behest they heard, and rush'd on earth;
Since that sad hour, in camps and courts adored,
Rebels from God, and tyrants o'er Mankind!"*

      From his obscure haunt
Shriek'd Fear, of Cruelty the Ghastly dam,
Feverous yet freezing, eager-paced yet slow,
As she that creeps from forth her swampy reeds,
Ague, the biform hag! when early Spring
Beams on the marsh-bred vapours.

   "Even so (the exulting Maiden said)
The sainted heralds of good tidings fell,
And thus they witness'd God! but now the clouds
Treading, and storms beneath their feet, they soar
Higher, and higher soar, and soaring sing
Loud songs of triumph! O ye spirits of God,
Hover around my mortal agonies!"
She spake, and instantly faint melody
Melts on her ear, soothing and sad, and slow,
Such measures, as at calmest midnight heard
By aged hermit in his holy dream,
Foretell and solace death; and now they rise

  * Monarchs o'er mankind!—1796.

Louder, as when with harp and mingled voice
The white-robed* multitude of slaughter'd saints
At Heaven's wide-open'd portals gratulant
Receive some martyr'd patriot. The harmony
Entranced the Maid, till each suspended sense
Brief slumber seized, and confused ecstasy.

At length awakening slow, she gazed around :
† And through a mist, the relict of that trance
Still thinning as she gazed, an Isle appear'd,
Its high, o'er-hanging, white, broad-breasted cliffs,
Glass'd on the subject ocean. A vast plain
Stretch'd opposite, where ever and anon
The ploughman following sad his meagre team
Turn'd up fresh sculls unstartled, and the bones
Of fierce hate-breathing combatants, who there
All mingled lay beneath the common earth,
Death's gloomy reconcilement! O'er the fields
Stept a fair Form, repairing all she might,
Her temples olive-wreathed; and where she trod,
Fresh flowerets rose, and many a foodful herb.

---

* *Revelation*, vi. 9, 11. "And when he had opened the fifth seal I saw under the altar the souls of them that were slain for the word of God, and for the testimony which they held. And white robes were given unto every one of them, and it was said unto them that they should rest yet for a little season, until their fellow-servants also and their brethren, that should be killed as they were, should be fulfilled."

† But lo! no more was seen the ice-piled mount
   And meteor-lighted dome. An Isle appear'd, &c.

1796.

But wan her cheek, her footsteps insecure,
And anxious pleasure beam'd in her faint eye,
As she had newly left a couch of pain, .
Pale convalescent! (yet some time to rule
With power exclusive o'er the willing world,
That blest prophetic mandate then fulfill'd—
Peace be on Earth!) A happy while, but brief,
She seem'd to wander with assiduous feet,
And heal'd the recent harm of chill and blight,
And nursed each plant that fair and virtuous grew.

But soon a deep precursive sound moan'd hollow:
Black rose the clouds, and now, (as in a dream)
Their reddening shapes, transform'd to warrior-
    hosts,
Coursed o'er the sky, and battled in mid-air.
[The Sea meantime his billows darkest roll'd,
And each stain'd wave dash'd on the shore a corse.]
Nor did not the large blood-drops fall from heaven
Portentous! while aloft were seen to float,
Like hideous features looming on the mist,
Wan stains of ominous light! Resign'd, yet sad,
The fair Form bow'd her olive-crowned brow,
Then o'er the plain* with oft-reverted eye
Fled till a place of tombs she reach'd, and there
Within a ruin'd sepulchre obscure
Found hiding-place.

* His hideous features blended with the mist,
   The long black locks of Slaughter. Peace beheld,
   And o'er the plain, &c.   1796.

                                    The delegated Maid
Gazed through her tears, then in sad tones ex-
    claim'd;—
"Thou mild-eyed Form! wherefore, ah! where-
    fore fled?
The power of Justice like a name all light,
Shone from thy brow;* but all they, who unblamed
Dwelt in thy dwellings, call thee Happiness.
Ah! why, uninjured and unprofited,
Should multitudes against their brethren rush?
Why sow they guilt, still reaping misery?
Lenient of care, thy songs, O Peace! are sweet,
As after showers the perfumed gale of eve,
That flings the cool drops on a feverous cheek;†
And gay thy grassy altar piled with fruits.
But boasts the shrine of demon War one charm,
Save that with many an orgie strange and foul,
Dancing around with interwoven arms,
The maniac Suicide and giant Murder
Exult in their fierce union! I am sad,
And know not why the simple peasants crowd
Beneath the Chieftains' standard!" Thus the Maid.

  To her the tutelary Spirit said:
"When Luxury and Lust's exhausted stores
No more can rouse the appetites of kings;
When the low flattery of their reptile lords

---

   * The name of Justice written on thy brow
      Resplendent shone, &c.   1796.
 † That plays around the sick man's throbbing temples.—*Ib.*

Falls flat and heavy on the accustom'd ear;
When eunuchs sing, and fools buffoonery make,
And dancers writhe their harlot limbs in vain;
Then War and all its dread vicissitudes
Pleasingly agitate their stagnant hearts;
Its hopes, its fears, its victories, its defeats,
Insipid Royalty's keen condiment!
Therefore uninjured and unprofited,
(Victims at once and executioners)
The congregated husbandmen lay waste
The vineyard and the harvest. As along
The Bothnic coast, or southward of the Line,
Though hush'd the winds and cloudless the high
    noon,
Yet if Leviathan, weary of ease,
In sports unwieldy toss his island-bulk,
Ocean behind him billows, and before
A storm of waves breaks foamy on the strand.
And hence, for times and seasons bloody and dark,
Short Peace shall skin the wounds of causeless War,
And War, his strained sinews knit anew,
Still violate the unfinish'd works of Peace.
But yonder look! for more demands thy view!"
He said: and straightway from the opposite Isle
A vapour sail'd, as when a cloud, exhaled
From Egypt's fields that steam hot pestilence,
Travels the sky for many a trackless league,
Till o'er some death-doom'd land, distant in vain,
It broods incumbent. Forthwith from the plain,
Facing the Isle, a brighter cloud arose,
And steer'd its course which way the vapour went.

The Maiden paused, musing what this might
   mean.
But long time pass'd not, ere that brighter cloud
Return'd more bright; along the plain it swept;
And soon from forth its bursting sides emerged
A dazzling form, broad-bosom'd, bold of eye,
And wild her hair, save where with laurels bound.
Not more majestic stood the healing God,
When from his bow the arrow sped that slew*
Huge Python. Shriek'd Ambition's giant throng,
And with them hissed the locust-fiends that crawl'd
And glitter'd in Corruption's slimy track.
Great was their wrath, for short they knew their
   reign;
And such commotion made they, and uproar,
As when the mad tornado bellows through
The guilty islands of the western main,
What time departing for their native shores,
Eboe, or *Koromantyn's plain of palms,
The infuriate spirits of the murder'd make
Fierce merriment, and vengeance ask of Heaven.
Warm'd with new influence, the unwholesome plain
Sent up its foulest fogs to meet the morn:
The Sun that rose on Freedom, rose in blood!

" Maiden beloved, and Delegate of Heaven!
(To her the tutelary Spirit said)
Soon shall the morning struggle into day,

---

* The slaves in the West India islands consider death as a passport to their native country.

The stormy morning into cloudless noon.
Much hast thou seen, nor all canst understand—
But this be thy best omen—Save thy Country!"
Thus saying, from the answering Maid he pass'd,
And with him disappear'd the heavenly Vision.

" Glory to Thee, Father of Earth and Heaven!
All-conscious Presence of the Universe!
Nature's vast ever-acting energy!
In will, in deed, impulse of All to All!
Whether thy Love* with unrefracted ray
Beam on the Prophet's purged eye, or if
Diseasing realms the enthusiast, wild of thought,
Scatter new frenzies on the infected throng,
Thou both inspiring and predooming both,
Fit instruments and best, of perfect end:
Glory to Thee, Father of Earth and Heaven!"

      And first a landscape rose
More wild and waste and desolate than where
The white bear, drifting on a field of ice,
Howls to her sunder'd cubs with piteous rage
And savage agony.

* Law—1796.

LINES ADDRESSED TO A YOUNG MAN OF FORTUNE

WHO ABANDONED HIMSELF TO AN INDOLENT AND CAUSELESS MELANCHOLY.*

HENCE that fantastic wantonness of woe,
   O Youth to partial Fortune vainly dear!
To plunder'd Want's half-shelter'd hovel go,
   Go, and some hunger-bitten infant hear
   Moan haply in a dying mother's ear:
Or when the cold and dismal fog-damps brood
O'er the rank church-yard with sere elm-leaves
      strew'd,
Pace round some widow's grave, whose dearer part
   Was slaughter'd where o'er his uncoffin'd limbs
The flocking flesh-birds scream'd! Then, while
      thy heart
   Groans, and thine eyes a fiercer sorrow dims,
Know (and the truth shall kindle thy young mind)
   What Nature makes thee mourn, she bids thee
      heal!
O abject! if, to sickly dreams resign'd,
All effortless thou leave life's common-weal
   A prey to tyrants, murderers of mankind.†

---

   * Printed at the end of the original quarto edition of the *Ode on the Departing Year*, 1796.
   † All effortless thou leave Earth's commonweal
      A prey to the throned murderers of mankind!—1796.

SONNETS ATTEMPTED IN THE MANNER OF CONTEMPORARY WRITERS.*

I.

PENSIVE at eve on the hard world I mused,
   And my poor heart was sad: so at the moon
I gazed—and sigh'd, and sigh'd!—for, ah! how soon
Eve darkens into night. Mine eye perused
With tearful vacancy the dampy grass
Which wept and glitter'd in the paly ray;
And I did pause me on my lonely way,
And mused me on those wretched ones who pass
O'er the black heath of Sorrow. But, alas!
Most of myself I thought: when it befell
That the sooth Spirit of the breezy wood
Breathed in mine ear—" All this is very well;
But much of one thing is for no thing good."
Ah! my poor heart's inexplicable swell!

               NEHEMIAH HIGGINBOTTOM.

* *Monthly Magazine*, November, 1797.
   Coleridge acknowledged the authorship of these three sonnets, and reprinted them in his *Biographia Literaria*, London, 1817, vol. i. pp. 26-28, prefaced by the following remarks:—" Under the name of Nehemiah Higginbottom I contributed three sonnets, the first of which had for its object to excite a good-natured laugh at the spirit of doleful egotism and at the recurrence of favourite phrases, with the double defect of being at once trite and licentious. The second on low creeping language and thoughts under the pretence of *simplicity*. And the third, the phrases of which

II.

TO SIMPLICITY.

O! I do love thee, meek Simplicity!
   For of thy lays the lulling simpleness
Goes to my heart and soothes each small distress,
Distress though small, yet haply great to me!
'Tis true on Lady Fortune's gentlest pad
I amble on; yet, though I know not why,
So sad I am!—but should a friend and I
Grow cool and miff, O! I am very sad!
And then with Sonnets and with sympathy
My dreamy bosom's mystic woes I pall;
Now of my false friend plaining plaintively,
Now raving at mankind in general;
But, whether sad or fierce, 'tis simple all,
All very simple, meek Simplicity!

                    NEHEMIAH HIGGINBOTTOM.

were borrowed entirely from my own poems, on the indiscriminate use of elaborate and swelling language and imagery. So general at that time and so decided was the opinion concerning the characteristic vices of my style that a celebrated physician, speaking of me in other respects with his usual kindness to a gentleman who was about to meet me at a dinner-party, could not, however, resist giving him a hint not to mention *The House that Jack built* in my presence, for that I was as sore as a boil about that sonnet, he not knowing that I was myself the author of it."

III.

ON A RUINED HOUSE IN A ROMANTIC COUNTRY.

AND this reft house is that the which he built,
    Lamented Jack! And here his malt he piled,
Cautious in vain! These rats that squeak so wild
Squeak not unconscious of their father's guilt.
Did ye not see her gleaming thro' the glade?
Belike 'twas she, the maiden all forlorn.
What though she milk no cow with crumpled horn,
Yet aye she haunts the dale where erst she stray'd;
And aye beside her stalks her amorous knight!
Still on his thighs their wonted brogues are worn,
And thro' those brogues, still tatter'd and betorn,
His hindward charms gleam an unearthly white;
As when thro' broken clouds at night's high noon
Peeps in fair fragments forth the full-orb'd harvest-
    moon!
        NEHEMIAH HIGGINBOTTOM.

ON THE CHRISTENING OF A FRIEND'S CHILD.*

THIS day among the faithful placed
    And fed with fontal manna,
O with maternal title graced,
    Dear Anna's dearest Anna!

While others wish thee wise and fair,
    A maid of spotless fame,
I'll breathe this more compendious prayer—
    Mayst thou deserve thy name!

Thy mother's name, a potent spell,
    That bids the Virtues hie
From mystic grove and living cell,
    Confess'd to Fancy's eye;

Meek Quietness without offence;
    Content in homespun kirtle;
True Love; and True Love's Innocence,
    White Blossom of the Myrtle!

Associates of thy name, sweet Child!
    These Virtues mayst thou win;
With face as eloquently mild
    To say, they lodge within.

* Printed in the Supplement to the Second Edition of Coleridge's Early Poems, published in 1797.

So, when her tale of days all flown,
　　Thy mother shall be miss'd here;
When Heaven at length shall claim its own
　　And Angels snatch their Sister;

Some hoary-headed friend, perchance,
　　May gaze with stifled breath;
And oft in momentary trance,
　　Forget the waste of death.

Even thus a lovely rose I've view'd
　　In summer-swelling pride;
Nor mark'd the bud, that green and rude
　　Peep'd at the rose's side.

It chanced I pass'd again that way
　　In Autumn's latest hour,
And wondering saw the selfsame spray
　　Rich with the selfsame flower.

Ah fond deceit! the rude green bud
　　Alike in shape, place, name,
Had bloom'd where bloom'd its parent stud,
　　Another and the same!

TO A PRIMROSE

THE FIRST SEEN IN THE SEASON.*

*Nitens et roboris expers
Turget et insolida est: et spe delectat.*
                                OVID. METAM.

THY smiles I note, sweet early flower,
　　That peeping from thy rustic bower
The festive news to earth dost bring,
A fragrant messenger of spring.

But, tender blossom, why so pale?
Dost hear stern winter in the gale?
And didst thou tempt the ungentle sky
To catch one vernal glance and die?

Such the wan lustre sickness wears
When health's first feeble beam appears;
So languid are the smiles that seek
To settle on the care-worn cheek

When timorous hope the head uprears,
Still drooping and still moist with tears,
If, through dispersing grief, be seen
Of bliss the heavenly spark serene.

And sweeter far the early blow,
Fast following after storms of woe,
Than (comfort's riper season come)
Are full-blown joys and pleasure's gaudy bloom.

---

* Printed in *The Watchman*, April 27, 1796.

SONNET.*

THE piteous sobs that choke the virgin's breath
    For him, the fair betrothed youth, who lies
Cold in the narrow dwelling, or the cries
With which a mother wails her darling's death,
These from our nature's common impulse spring,
Unblamed, unpraised; but o'er the piled earth
Which hides the sheeted corse of grey-hair'd
    worth,
If droops the soaring youth with slacken'd wing;
If he recall in saddest minstrelsy
Each tenderness bestow'd, each truth imprest,
Such grief is Reason, Virtue, Piety!
And from the Almighty Father shall descend
Comforts on his late evening, whose young breast
Mourns with no transient love the aged friend.

  * Prefixed to " Poems on the death of Priscilla Farmer by her Grandson Charles Lloyd." (Printed in the second edition of Coleridge's Poems, 1797.)

APPENDIX.

APPENDIX.

Page 26. *Introduction to a Greek Ode.*

The following is a translation by Robert Southey of a Greek Ode on Astronomy by S. T. Coleridge, written for the prize at Cambridge, 1793.* (The Ode was unsuccessful, and the original is not now known to be extant.)

I.

HAIL, venerable Night!
    O first-created, hail!
Thou who art doom'd in thy dark breast to veil
    The dying beam of light,
    The eldest and the latest thou,
    Hail, venerable Night!
    Around thine ebon brow
    Glittering plays with lightning rays
    A wreath of flowers of fire.
    The varying clouds with many a hue attire
    Thy many-tinted veil.
Holy are the blue graces of thy zone!
    But who is he whose tongue can tell
The dewy lustres which thine eyes adorn?
Lovely to some the blushes of the Morn;
    To some the glory of the Day,
    When blazing with meridian ray
The gorgeous Sun ascends his highest throne;
    But I with solemn and severe delight
Still watch thy constant car, immortal NIGHT!

II.

For then to the celestial Palaces
    Urania leads, Urania, she

---

* *Poems by Robert Southey*, London, 1806. Third edition, vol. ii., pp. 1-9.

The Goddess who alone
   　　Stands by the blazing throne,
Effulgent with the light of Deity.
Whom Wisdom, the Creatrix, by her side
   　　Placed on the heights of yonder sky,
And smiling with ambrosial love, unlock'd
The depths of Nature to her piercing eye.
Angelic myriads struck their harps around,
   　　And with triumphant song
The host of Stars, a beauteous throng,
   　　Around the ever-living Mind
In jubilee their mystic dance begun;
   　　When at thy leaping forth, O Sun!
   　　The Morning started in affright,
Astonish'd at thy birth, her Child of Light!

III.

   　　Hail, O Urania, hail!
Queen of the Muses! Mistress of the Song!
For thou didst deign to leave the heavenly throng.
   　　As earthward thou thy steps wert bending
A ray went forth and harbinger'd thy way;
   　　All Ether laugh'd with thy descending.
Thou hadst wreathed thy hair with roses,
The flower that in the immortal bower
   　　Its deathless bloom discloses.
Before thine awful mien, compell'd to shrink,
Fled Ignorance abash'd and all her brood;
   　　Dragons and Hags of baleful breath,
   　　Fierce Dreams that wont to drink
   　　The Sepulchre's black blood;
   　　　　Or on the wings of storms
   　　　　Riding in fury forms
Shriek'd to the mariner the shriek of Death.

IV.

I boast, O Goddess, to thy name
That I have raised the pile of fame!
   Therefore to me be given
To roam the starry path of Heaven,
To charioteer with wings on high,
And to rein in the tempests of the sky.

V.

Chariots of happy Gods! Fountains of Light!
   Ye Angel-Temples bright!
May I unblamed your flamy threshold tread?
   I leave Earth's lowly scene;
   I leave the Moon serene,
   The lovely Queen of Night;
   I leave the wide domains
Beyond where Mars his fiercer light can fling,
   And Jupiter's vast plains,
      (The many-belted King;)
Even to the solitude where Saturn reigns,
Like some stern tyrant to just exile driven;
   Dim-seen the sullen power appears
   In that cold solitude of Heaven,
      And slow he drags along
The mighty circle of long-lingering years.

VI.

Nor shalt thou escape my sight,
Who at the threshold of the sun-trod domes
Art trembling, youngest Daughter of the Night!
   And you, ye fiery-tressed strangers! you,
      Comets who wander wide,
   Will I along your pathless way pursue,
   Whence bending I may view
The Worlds whom elder Suns have vivified.

VII.

For Hope with loveliest visions soothes my mind,
That even in Man, Life's winged power,
  When comes again the natal hour,
  Shall on heaven-wandering feet
    In undecaying youth,
  Spring to the blessed seat;
Where round the fields of Truth
The fiery Essences for ever feed;
And o'er the ambrosial mead,
    The breezes of serenity
Silent and soothing glide for ever by.

VIII.

There, Priest of Nature! dost thou shine,
Newton! a King among the Kings divine.
  Whether with harmony's mild force
  He guides along its course
The axle of some beauteous star on high;
  Or gazing in the spring
  Ebullient with creative energy,
Feels his pure breast with rapturous joy possest,
  Inebriate in the holy ecstasy!

IX.

I may not call thee mortal then, my soul!
Immortal longings lift thee to the skies:
Love of thy native home inflames thee now
    With pious madness wise.
Know then thyself! expand thy wings divine!
Soon mingled with thy fathers thou shalt shine
  A star amid the starry throng,
  A God the Gods among.
1801.

Page 55. *Monody on the Death of Chatterton.*

The following letter appeared in the *Monthly Magazine* of January, 1798 :—

To the Editor of *The Monthly Magazine.*

Sir,—I hope that this letter may arrive time enough to answer its purpose. I cannot help considering myself as having been placed in a very ridiculous light by the gentlemen who have remarked, answered, and rejoined concerning my Monody on Chatterton. I have not seen the compositions of my competitors (unless indeed the exquisite poem of Warton's, entitled *The Suicide*, refer to this subject), but this I know, that my own is a very poor one. It was a school exercise, somewhat altered; and it would have been omitted in the last edition of my poems but for the request of my friend Mr. Cottle, whose property those poems are. If it be not in your intention to exhibit my name on any future month, you will accept my best thanks, and not publish this letter. But if Crito and the Alphabet-men should continue to communicate on this subject, and you should think it proper for reasons best known to yourself to publish their communications, then I depend on your kindness for the insertion of my letter; by which it is possible those your correspondents may be induced to expend their remarks, whether panegyrical or vituperative, on nobler game than on a poem which was, in truth, the first effort of a young man, all whose poems a candid critic will only consider as first efforts.

Yours, with due respect,
Shrewsbury.   S. T. COLERIDGE.

Page 65. *Lines on an Autumnal Evening.*
[*O (have I sigh'd) were mine the Wizard's rod!*

Here in the first edition (1796) is appended the following note :—

"I entreat the public's pardon for having carelessly suffered to be printed such intolerable stuff as this and the thirteen following lines. They have not the merit even of originality; as every thought is to be found in the Greek Epigrams. The lines in this poem from the 27th to the 36th I have been told are a palpable imitation of the passage from the 355th to the 370th line of the *Pleasures of Memory*, part 3. I do not perceive so striking a similarity between the two passages; at all events I had written the Effusion several years before I had seen Mr. Rogers's poem."

Page 123. *The Silver Thimble.*

"A poetical Epistle which he called ' Sara's,' but of which my mother told me she wrote but little. Indeed it is not very like some simple affecting verses, which were wholly by herself, on the death of her beautiful infant Berkeley in 1799."—Biographical Supplemen (by Sara Coleridge) to *Biographia Literaria*, London 1847, ii. 411.

END OF VOL. I.

ROBERT ROBERTS, PRINTER, BOSTON.

www.ingramcontent.com/pod-product-compliance
Lightning Source LLC
Chambersburg PA
CBHW030001240426
43672CB00007B/781